BY APPOINTMENT TO
H.R.H. THE PRINCE OF WALES
SUPPLIERS OF FISHING TACKLE AND
WATERPROOF CLOTHING
C. FARLOW & CO. LTD. LONDON

Farlow's

FISHING
SHOOTING

COUNTRY
CLOTHING

A TRADITION FOR OVER 150 YEARS

5 PALL MALL, LONDON, S.W.1.
Telephone: 071-839 2423

Open till 6 p.m. weekdays and 4 p.m. Saturdays

Only 3 minutes walk from Piccadilly Circus & Trafalgar Square

Until you can visit us, our full colour catalogue will give you a glimpse of what is in store
Free on request

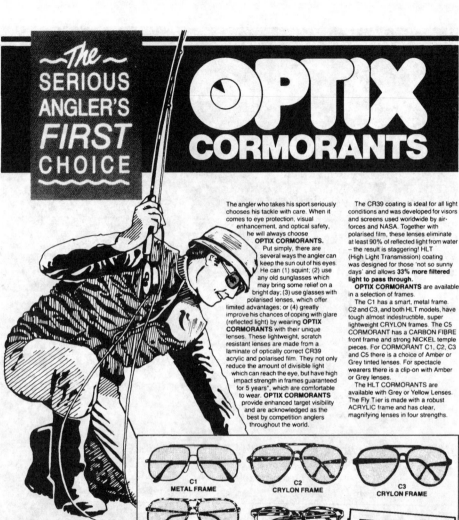

**Trout - Loch Fishing in the Highlands
By Leslie Crawford. See Page 33**

CONTENTS

RIVERS, LOCHS AND SEA ANGLING

Cover Design by Jennifer Thomson, Edinburgh

Pastime Publications Ltd gratefully acknowledge the assistance of The Scottish Tourist Board, Area Tourist Boards and others in compiling this guide.

First published by The Scottish Tourist Board 1970
U.K. distribution by A.A. Developments Ltd.
Typesetting by Typewise.
Printed and Bound in the U.K.

AA

**Worldwide distribution by
The British Tourist**

ADVERTISERS' INDEX

ALSO SEE COLOUR ADVERTS

USEFUL ADDRESSES IN SCOTTISH SPORT FISHERIES

Scottish Tourist Board,
23 Ravelston Terrace,
Edinburgh EH4 3EU.
Tel: 031-332 2433.

Department of Agriculture & Fisheries for Scotland,
Pentland House,
47 Robb's Loan,
Edinburgh EH14 1YQ.
Tel: 031-244 6015.

Inspector of Salmon Fisheries,
Pentland House (Room 227),
47 Robb's Loan,
Edinburgh EH14 1YQ.
Tel: 031-244 6227.

S.O.A.F.D.,
Officer in Charge,
Freshwater Fisheries
Laboratory, Faskally, Pitlochry
PH16 5LB.
Tel: (0796) 472060.

S.O.A.F.D. Marine Laboratory,
P.O. Box 101, Victoria Road,
Aberdeen AB9 8DB.
Tel: (0224) 876544.

Secretary, Scottish River Purification Boards Association,
1 South Street,
Perth PH2 8NJ.
Tel: (0738) 27989.

Scottish Sports Council,
Caledonia House, South Gyle,
Edinburgh EH12 9DQ.
Tel: 031-317 7200.

Scottish Natural Heritage Nature Conservancy Council,
12 Hope Terrace,
Edinburgh EH9 2AS.
Tel: 031-447 4784.

Forestry Commission,
Dawn McNiven,
Information Officer,
231 Corstorphine Road,
Edinburgh EH12 7AT.
Tel: 031-334 0303.

Scottish Hydro-Electric plc,
16 Rothesay Terrace,
Edinburgh EH3 7SE.
Tel: 031-225 1361.

Institute of Fisheries Management,
Secretary (Scottish branch),
Gordon Struthers, "Torshavn",
Lettoch Road, Pitlochry
PH16 5AZ.
Tel: (home) (0796) 472846.
Tel: (work) (0796) 472060.

Anglers' Cooperative Association,
Secretary, Iain Mackenzie,
46 Ormidale Terrace,
Edinburgh EH12 6EF.
Tel: 031-337 7587.

Scottish Anglers' National Association,
Secretary, Mr. A.D. Jamieson,
5 Cramond Glebe Road,
Edinburgh
EH4 6ND.
Tel: 031-445 5969.

Central Scotland Anglers' Association,
Secretary, Kevin Burns,
53 Fernieside Crescent,
Edinburgh.
Tel: 031-664 4685.

Federation of Highland Angling Clubs,
Secretary, W. Brown, Coruisk,
Strathpeffer,
Ross-shire
IV14 9BD.
Tel: (0997) 421446.

Department of Forestry and Natural Resources,
University of Edinburgh,
Kings Buildings,
Mayfield Road,
Edinburgh
EH9 3JU.
Tel: 031-650 1000.

Institute of Aquaculture,
University of Stirling,
Stirling
FK9 4LA.
Tel: (0786) 73171.

The Effects of POLLUTION may take years to disappear from a river
REPORT ALL CASES IMMEDIATELY
Keep samples of dead fish
Please telephone
Forth River Purification Board
031-441 1674 (24 hours) or 0786 51741
or **Forth District Salmon Fishery Board 0836 722 647**
or your local **Police Office**

GAME ANGLING CLUBS

CLUB	SECRETARY
Aberfeldy Angling Club	G. MacDougall, 60 Moness Crescent, Aberfeldy, Perthshire PH15. Tel: (0887) 20653
Airdrie Angling Club	Roy Burgess, 21 Elswick Drive, Caldercruix, Lanarkshire.
Annan & District Angling Club	J. Glen, 110 High Street, Annan, Dumfriesshire.
Badenoch Angling Association	J. Dallas, The Mills, Kingussie, Inverness-shire.
Berwick & District Angling Association	D. Cowan, 3 Church Street, Berwick TD15 1EE. Tel: (0289) 330145
Blairgowrie, Rattray & District Angling Association	W. Matthew, 4 Mitchell Square, Blairgowrie, Perthshire. Tel: (0250) 3679
Brechin Angling Club	D.E. Smith, 3 Friendly Park, Brechin, Angus.
Castle Douglas & District Angling Association	Ian Bandall, Tommy's Sports Shop, Castle Douglas, Kirkcudbrightshire. Tel: (0556) 2851
Chatton Angling Association	A. Jarvis, 7 New Road, Chatton, Alnwick, Northumberland NE66 5PU.
Coldstream & District Angling Association	Brian Turnbull, Binning Cottage, Duns Road, Coldstream, Berwickshire TD12 4DR. Tel: (0890) 2941.
Cramond Angling Club	E. McCrindle, 36 John Humble Street, Mayfield, Dalkeith, Midlothian EH22 5QZ. Tel: (0875) 22506

CLUB	SECRETARY
Dalbeattie Angling Association	G.W. Garroch, 15 Church Crescent, Dalbeattie DG5 4BA. Tel: (0556) 611373
Devon Angling Association	R. Breingan, 33 Redwell Place, Alloa, Clackmannanshire FK10 2BT. Tel: (0259) 215185
Dreghorn Angling Club	Mr. S. Wallace, 14 Lismore Way, Dreghorn. Tel: (0294) 218475.
Dumfries & Galloway Angling Association	D. Byers, 4 Bloomfield, Edinburgh Road, Dumfries DG1 1SG. Tel: (0387) 53850
Dunkeld & Birnam Angling Association	Mr. K.L. Scott, "Mandaya", Highfield Place, Bankfoot, Perthshire PH1 4AX. Tel: (0738) 87448.
Dunoon & District Angling Club	A.H. Young, "Ashgrove", 28 Royal Crescent, Dunoon PA23 7AH. Tel: (0369) 5732
Earlston Angling Association	P. Hessett, 2 Arnot Place, Earlston, Berwickshire TD4 6DP. Tel: (089 684) 577
Eckford Angling Association	R.B. Anderson, W.S., Royal Bank Buildings, Jedburgh, Roxburghshire. Tel: (0835) 3202
Elgin & District Angling Association	W. Mulholland, 9 Conon Crescent, Elgin, Moray.
Esk & Liddle Fisheries Association	R.J.B. Hill, Solicitor, Bank of Scotland Buildings, Langholm, Dumfriesshire DG13 0AD.
Esk Valley Angling Improvement Association	K. Burns, 53 Fernieside Crescent, Edinburgh.
Eye Water Angling Club	W.S. Gillie, 2 Tod's Court, Eyemouth, Berwickshire.

Ford & Etal Estates Fishing Club	W.M. Bell, Heatherslaw, Cornhill on Tweed. Tel: Crookham (089 082) 221	**Lairg Angling Club**	J.M. Ross, St. Murie, Church Hill Road, Lairg, Sutherland IV27 4BL. Tel: (0549) 2010
Fyvie Angling Association	J.D. Pirie, Prenton, South Road, Oldmeldrum, Aberdeenshire AB51 0AB.	**Larbert & Stenhousemuir Angling Club**	A. Paterson, 6 Wheatlands Avenue, Bonnybridge, Stirlingshire.
Gordon Fishing Club	Mrs. M. Forsyth, 47 Main Street, Gordon, Berwickshire. Tel: (057 381) 359	**Lauderdale Angling Association**	D.M. Milligan, Gifford Cottage, Main Street, Gifford, East Lothian EH41 4QH.
Greenlaw Angling Club	J. Purves, 9 Wester Row, Greenlaw, Berwickshire TD10 6XE.	**Lochgilphead & District Angling Club**	Inter Sport, Lochnell Street, Lochgilphead, Argyll.
Hawick Angling Club	R. Sutherland, 20 Longhope Drive, Hawick. Tel: (0450) 75150	**Loch Keose & Associated Waters**	M. Morrison, Handa, 18 Keose Glebe, Lochs, Isle of Lewis Tel: (085 183) 334
Inverness Angling Club	G.M. Smith, 50 Nevis Park, Inverness.	**Loch Lomond Angling Improvement Association**	R.A. Clements, C.A., 224 Ingram Street, Glasgow.
Irvine & District Angling Club	A. Sim, 51 Rubie Crescent, Irvine.	**Loch Rannoch Conservation Association**	Mrs. Steffen, Coilmore Cottage, Kinloch Rannoch, Perthshire.
Jedforest Angling Club	J.T. Renilson, 4 Canongate, Jedburgh, Roxburghshire.	**Melrose & District Angling Association**	T. McLeish, Planetree Cottage, Newstead, Melrose. Tel: (089 682) 2232
Kelso Angling Association	R. Yule, 6 High Croft, Kelso, Roxburghshire. Tel: (0573) 23907	**Morebattle Angling Club**	H. Fox, Orchard Cottage, Morebattle.
Killin, Breadalbane Angling Club	D. Allan, 12 Ballechroisk, Killin. Tel: (05672) 362	**Murthly & Glendelvine Trout Angling Club**	Chairman, A.M. Allan, Drummond Hall, Murthly, Perthshire.
Kilmaurs Angling Club	J. Watson, 7 Four Acres Drive, Kilmaurs, Ayrshire.	**New Galloway Angling Association**	J. McCubbing, Carsons Knowe, New Galloway. Tel: (064 42) 448
Kintyre Fish Protection & Angling Club	F.W. Neate, Kilmoray Place, High Street, Campbeltown, Argyll.	**North Uist Angling Club**	J. Cheyne, 6 Clachan, Locheport, North Uist PA82 5EU. Tel: (08764) 322
Kyles of Bute Angling Club	R. Newton, Viewfield Cottage, Tighnabruaich, Argyll.	**Peeblesshire Trout Fishing Association**	D.G. Fyfe, 39 High Street, Peebles. Tel: (0721) 20131
Ladykirk & Norham Angling Association	R.G. Wharton, 8 St. Cuthbert's Square, Norham. Tel: (0289) 82467	**Perth & District Anglers' Association**	G. Nichols, 30 Wallace Crescent, Perth PH1 2RF.

Pitlochry Angling Club	R. Harriman, Sunnyknowe, Nursing Home Brae, Pitlochry, Perthshire. Tel: (0796) 2484	**Stormont Angling Club**	The Factor, Scone Estates Office, Scone Palace, Perth.
Rannoch & District Angling Club	J. Brown, The Square, Kinloch Rannoch, Perthshire. Tel: (0882) 632268	**Stranraer & District Angling Association**	J. Nimmo, Inchparks Schoolhouse, Stranraer. Tel: (0776) 4568
River Almond Angling Association	H. Meikle, 23 Glen Terrace, Deans, Livingston, West Lothian.	**Strathmore Angling Improvement Association**	Mrs. A. Henderson, 364 Blackness Road, Dundee DD2 1SF. Tel: (0382) 68062
St. Andrews Angling Club	Secretary, 54 St. Nicholas Street, St. Andrews, Fife. Tel: (0334) 76347	**Turriff Angling Association**	I. Masson, 6 Castle Street, Turriff AB53 7BJ.
St. Marys Loch Angling Club	J. Miller, 25 Abbotsford Court, Colinton Road, Edinburgh EH10 5EH. Tel: 031-447 4187.	**Upper Annandale Angling Association**	A. Dickson, 1 Police Houses, High Street, Moffat, Dumfriesshire DG10 9HF. Tel: (0683) 21054
Selkirk & District Angling Association	A. Murray, 40 Raeburn Meadows, Selkirk. Tel: (0750) 21534	**Upper Nithsdale Angling Club**	K. Mclean, Pollock & McLean, Solicitors, 61 High Street, Sanquhar DG4 6DT. Tel: (0659) 50241
Stanley & District Angling Club	Stewart Grant, 12a Perth Road, Stanley, Perth PH1 4NQ. Tel: (0738) 828179.	**Whiteadder Angling Association**	R. Baker, Milburn House, Duns, Berwickshire. Tel: (0361) 83086

TO ASSIST WITH HOLIDAY ENQUIRIES SEE OUR BOOKING FORMS ON PAGES 85 & 105

Suggested General Dry Fly Patterns for Scottish Trouting

By Alan Spence

Pattern	March Brown
Hook	Partridge Captain Hamilton down eyed code L4A
Size	10, 12 and 14
Tail	Strands partridge hackle
Silk	Yellow or orange
Body	Reddish hares fur dubbed on yellow or orange silk
Rib	Gold wire or yellow floss
Hackles	Partridge backed with ginger cock
Wing	Hen pheasant tail or wing feather.

Pattern	Dry Greenwell
Hook	Partridge Captain Hamilton L4A 12, 14 and 16 or K3A Swedish dry fly Hook size 18
Tail	Fibres 'Greenwell Hackle'
Body	Waxed yellow or primrose silk
Rib	Fine gold wire
Hackle	From Greenwell Cock
Wing	Dark starling wing, blue dun or goose neck hackle point or bunch of blue grey Antron body yarn.

By varying the body shade, hackle colour and size this basic pattern can be used to represent many olives throughout the season.

Pattern	Gold ribbed hares ear
Hooks	As for dry Greenwell
Tail	Red game hackle fibres
Silk	Yellow or primrose April to June; orange June to August
Body	Dubbed fur from hares ear
Rib	Gold wire
Hackle	Red game, light to dark
Wing	As for dry Greenwell

A handy general pattern when olives are hatching, leave the body straggly with dubbing picked out and only lightly hackled. This works well as a parachute fly tied on Partridge K3A Swedish hook.

Pattern	Iron Blue Dun
Hook	Partridge Captain Hamilton L4A 16 or 18
Silk	Crimson
Tail	Dyed iron blue hackle fibres
Body	Lightly dubbed mole's fur, silk is left exposed at tail
Hackle	Dyed iron blue dun.

Spinner Patterns

Pattern	Pheasant tail spinner
Hook	Partridge Captain Hamilton L4A 14, 16 and 18
Silk	Orange
Tail	Light honey dun hackle fibres
Body	Three fibres from cock pheasant tail ribbed gold wire
Hackle	Pale honey dun
Wing	Blue dun hackle points, or Antron body floss tied spent.

Use the bottom dressing on the previous page with the following bodies for:

Red Spinner, red floss with gold wire rib
Sherry Spinner, bright orange floss with gold wire rib
Hackle shade and colour can also be adjusted to suit, ranging from dark red game to blue dun and grizzle.

Pattern	Sedge
Hook	Partridge L4A 10, 12 and 14
Silk	Green or red
Tail	None
Body	Red, green or brown seals fur
Hackle	From dark to light red game or brown palmered down body secured with gold wire.

These are some general patterns for Scottish rivers. Dressings for smaller flies were given in the 1990 edition for 'Scotland for Fishing'. For flies such as the badger series, try bodies of yellow. Red or green floss are useful general patterns as is Whickhams Fancy with either the traditional dark starling wing or a white slip from the underwing of a mallard.

For the amateur fly dresser experimentation is the fun of the game. Standard patterns as listed in fly tying manuals, are there because they are well proven, yet they do not always suit feeding trout. Subtle changes in materials can bring success on local rivers. Perhaps of more importance than exact imitation is size. Trout which ignore or merely swirl at a size 14 artificial may well succumb to one tied on 16 or 18 hooks on a fine well degreased leader.

MINIMUM QUALIFYING SIZES OF FISH PRESENTED FOR WEIGH-IN FROM 1 JANUARY 1992.

1. Bass (Dicentrarchus labrax) — 36 cm. (14.2 in.)
   Brill (Scophthalmus rhombus) — 30 cm. (11.8 in.)
   Coalfish (Pollachius virens) — 35 cm. (13.8 in.)
   Cod (Gadus morhua) — 35 cm. (13.8 in.)
   n.b. In U.K. Fishery area V11a from 1st October to 31 December the minimum size for Cod will be — 45 cm. (17.7 in.)
   Dab (Limanda limanda) — 23 cm. (9.06 in.)
   Dogfish – all species (Scyliorhinus, Squalius sp) — 35 cm. (13.8 in.)
   Eel Common (Anguilla anguilla) — 35 cm. (13.8 in.)**
   Eel Conger (Conger conger) — 58 cm. (22.8 in.)
   Flounder (Platichthys flesus) — 25 cm. (9.8 in.)
   Haddock (Melanogrammus aeglefinus) — 30 cm. (11.8 in.)
   Hake (Merluccius merluccius) — 30 cm. (11.8 in.)
   Halibut (Hippoglossus hippoglossus) — 35 cm. (13.8 in.)
   Ling (Molva molva) — 58 cm. (22.8 in.)**
   Mackerel (Scomber scombrus) — 30 cm. (11.8 in.) (North Sea only)
   Megrim (Lepidorhombus wiffiagonis) — 25 cm. (9.8 in.)
   Pollack (Pollachius pollachius) — 35 cm. (13.8 in.)
   Plaice (Pleuronectes platessa) — 27 cm. (10.6 in.)
   Rays (Raja sp) — 35 cm. (13.8 in.)
   Seabream, Red (Pagellus bogaraveo) — 25 cm. (9.8 in.)
   Seabream, Black (Spondyliosoma cantharus) — 23 cm. (9.05 in.)
   Skates (Raja batis, alba, oxyrinchus sp) — 11.35 kg. (25 lbs.)
   Sole Lemon (Microstomus kitt) — 25 cm. (9.8 in.)
   Sole (Solea solea) — 24 cm. (9.4 in.)
   Tope (Galeorhinus galeus) — 9.10 kg. (20 lbs.)
   Turbot (Scophthalmus maximus) — 30 cm. (11.8 in.)
   Wrasse Ballan — 25 cm. (9.8 in.)
   Whiting (Merlangius merlangus) — 27 cm. (10.6 in.)
   Witches (Glyptocephalus gynoglossus) — 28 cm. (11.0 in.)
   All other species — 20 cm. (7.9 in.)

   **These sizes may be altered when the European Community determine the new limit for the species.

2. A maximum of three mackerel may be presented for weigh-in.

3. TOPE AND SKATE: Common (R. batis); long-nosed (R. oxyrhinchus) or white (R. alba) are not to be brought ashore during events designated as TOPE or SKATE competitions. They are to be weighed immediately after capture and returned to the sea. (This rule does not apply to potential national record fish which must be brought ashore for weighing.) In designated TOPE competitions no minimum size for weighing will be applied as long as fish are weighed on board and returned alive.

4. Any obviously undersized fish presented for weigh-in will result in the entrant being disqualified.

   Note: Twaite Shad (Alosa Fallax) and Allis Shad (Alosa Alosa) cannot be legally landed.

SCOTTISH FEDERATION OF SEA ANGLERS OFFICIALS

President/Chairman
David Neil,
30 Woodfield Road, Ayr KA8 8LZ.
Tel: (0292) 266549.

Vice-President
Mrs. Libby Walker,
Springvale Cottage, Halket Road, Lugton,
Ayrshire KA3 4EE. Tel: 050-585 593.

Hon. Treasurer
Robert Keltie,
76 Stewart Avenue, Bo'ness,
West Lothian EH51 9NW. Tel: (0506) 826274

Secretary/Administrator
Mrs. Helen S.C. Murray,
Caledonia House, South Gyle,
Edinburgh EH12 9DQ. Tel: 031-317 7192

Hon. Fish Recorder
Gordon Morris,
8 Burt Avenue, Kinghorn, Fife KY3 9XB.
Tel: (0592) 890055

Coaching Co-ordinator
Henry Hamilton-Willows,
15 Carrick Drive, North Mount Vernon,
Glasgow G32 0RW. Tel: 041-778 4454.

Public Relations Officer
Brian Burn,
Flat 2, 16 Bellevue Road, Ayr KA7 2SA.
Tel: (0292) 264735.

REGIONAL SECRETARIES

Clyde
A.P. Brown,
32 Swisscot Walk, Fairhill,
Hamilton ML3 8DX. Tel: (0698) 427085

Central
Mrs. Margaret McCallum,
58 Pottery Street, Kirkcaldy KY1 3EU.
Tel: (0592) 51710

West
I.B. McClymont,
41 Corrie Crescent, Saltcoats,
Ayrshire KA21 6JL. Tel: (0294) 61830.

North East
Norman Pickard,
3 Grant Street, Whitehills, Banff.
Tel: (0309) 690926.

Eastern
Steve Souter,
14/8 Figgate Street, Portobello,
Edinburgh EH15 1HL.

Highlands & Islands
W. Mackintosh,
'Schiehallion', 16 Glengarry Road,
Inverness IV3 6NJ. Tel: (0463) 235850.

Western Isles
F.G. Jefferson,
No. 1 Sheshader, Point, Isle of Lewis
PA86 0EW. Tel: (0851) 870214.

A SCOTTISH ANGLING TRIP

by Jim McLanaghan

"I'm coming to Scotland for some sea angling. Where do I start?" - a common enough question but for a stranger a very daunting problem when you look at our long and very deeply indented coastline. It always helps to narrow the search down a bit and when faced with this query my first response is - "Are you fishing from a boat or shore? What are you looking for?" One could also ask "What time of year do you plan to go?" All very relevant and necessary questions if any angler is to maximise his trip to Scotland as some areas can entail a long journey before you even start fishing.

To do full justice to such a subject would take a whole book but since space is limited I can but highlight some of the more known productive areas. I underline this word since there is undoubtedly many many marks as yet unfished which must hold enormous potential.

Coming north into Scotland up the A1, the visiting angler has a multitude of ports including Berwick, Eyemouth and Dunbar which are all served with charter boats but also have facilities for launching. The fishing here is remarkably consistent, summer and winter with good catches of cod and ling being the mainstay. This is an area where pirks can be used to good effect and a lot of fish are taken on the drop, so it pays to wind up occasionally then drop back. This area has also some good potential for large fish as my son's friend found out one day. Hoping to latch into a better than average cod during a competition, he stuck on a whole herring to a 70 lbs trace, only to have the rod almost wrenched from his hands a few minutes later as something took herring, trace and all!!! Almost certainly it was a porbeagle, so it may be worth a few days trial sharking.

The shoreline along this stretch of coast has in the past few summers produced lovely bags of cod to lug and rag baits with some nice pollack thrown in for some superb sport, these to rags and Mister Twisters. Between the Tay and Forth estuaries lies some of the most picturesque harbours one could imagine and the summer coding from the boat can be superb, right to a few yards from the shore - but the bottom!! It can be horrific in places - plenty of weights. Once again the shore angler has a lot of choice with some nice cod to double figures from between Crail and St. Andrews. There is even one mark south of Kirkcaldy which is reputed to hold turbot - from the shore! One spot which warrants a good looking at is May Island, off Anstruther. It has all the hall marks of a superb pollack mark.

Further up the east coast are the ports of Arbroath and Stonehaven, both well catered for with regard to charter boats and equally well catered for in fishing potential with lovely codling, ling and plaice. Haddock too, that fish so beloved in Scotland for its eating properties, is beginning to make a showing once more at Stonehaven. It should also be borne in mind that the former British Record ling of 57 lbs was taken at Stonehaven.

The Moray Firth has its share of good fishing too plus some secrets and surprises. Once again, the whole coastline is studded with little harbours, some of which offer nice plaice from the harbour walls and surprise, surprise, a run of smoothhounds in the summer. These same species plus cod are obviously available to the boat angler with the bonus of good pollack close to the cliffs. Pointing the car in the general direction of John O'Groats takes the visiting angler through some lovely villages such as Brora and Helmsdale and with boats available all along the coast the potential here must be quite enormous.

We are now entering the big fish country of the shark, skate, halibut and anyone who wets a line from a boat in this area runs the risk of an encounter with one of these giants. Unless he goes "tooled up" as it were, the encounter is liable to be shortlived and very onesided.

The jewel of the north in angling terms must be Scrabster. This village has seen fish of all sizes, shapes, species and quantities come to the scales in such profusion as to beggar belief. More and more anglers are turning north to Scrabster in the winter months and for the most surprising of reasons - sharks! It has long been renowned for a winter cod area and a few years back it was noted that fish were being snatched off lines with monotonous regularity. The culprits were huge porbeagle sharks. Interest in these giant predators is so high that getting a boat booked between January and April can be quite a chore. The sharking potential here is enormous with a world record a very definite possibility. Indeed, a claim is now in for a new Scottish Record with a fish of 414 lbs. This same fish is hoped to qualify for a World Record on 50 lbs class line. Halibut are an ever present prospect also in these tide swept waters and although no-one has seriously fished for common skate recently, this area has produced good specimens in the past and could do so again.

Where access to water level in this northern corner is possible, the prospects are superb for cod, good pollack and wrasse but tackle losses could be quite high over some of the rougher ground.

Heading west through Bettyhill, charter boats become fewer but the potential for launching your own is still good. Remember though, although the fishing is superb all along this coast, the tide is one of the strongest in the world and should be treated with enormous respect.

The Hebrides are justly renowned for the quality of their sea angling and by comparison to most of the country the bags at recent competitions have been huge. One aspect of angling in the north of Scotland which is raising a few eyebrows is the huge success of artificial eels, especially Mister Twister style. So good are these lures that Gordon Morris, fish recorder for the Sea Angling Federation, commented "If you haven't got eels, you may as well stay at home". Beats digging bait too!

Ullapool is another renowned huge skate area of years gone by and one which I feel is due for a resurgence since there are a host of untapped marks and I feel some of them could produce shark or halibut. The pollack fishing around the Summer Isles and down past Gruinard can be positively arm aching as I experienced some years ago on a surveying trip and I'm sure, if anything, it has probably never been touched since. The beaches around Achiltibuie have also had their share of glory - producing common skate of 150 lbs on a beach rod.

So wild and inaccessible is this north west part of Scotland that much - nay - most of its coastline has never seen rod and line and has some of the greatest potential in Europe.

Nowhere is this more true probably than the Isle of Skye. If this area could not produce sharks, then I'll eat my bunnet. It has its share of skate and pollack to 20 lbs - yes 20 lbs - have been taken from the shore and the same anglers were broken by larger fish. Whiting and haddock along with some fine plaice are all available in the sea lochs such as Loch Brittle, even from the shore.

Mull has its own magic and its own piece of angling history since Brian Swinbank has made it justly famous for its huge "barndoor" skate. There is no shortage of other species in and around this island but since most anglers come here for the big ones, they tend to take second place. Across the waters at Loch Aline you can even put your beachcaster through its paces as from this pier several large skate have been landed to over 100 lbs. It is a reasonable assumption that most areas along this west coast to as far south as the Mull of Kintyre are capable of producing huge skate for the angler with the time and the patience. One problem which the skate angler could encounter would be tope which can swarm in large concentrations at times, particularly around Islay and Gigha to the south that would be a delightful hardship in my book.

Rounding the most southerly tip of the Mull of Kintyre, there are enough wrecks in this area to keep the most ardent angler happy for a good long while and tope and shark have both been hooked in the tide races which scour the headland. The one drawback to this area is the huge land trip required to reach it but with its virtually virgin sea angling, it should be well worth while.

The Clyde - probably no stretch of water in Britain has had so much written about it, has seen so much trawling, has produced such huge bags of giant cod and seen such shortages of fish that in angling terms it was nearly written off. All of this is true and yet year after year anglers return to the Clyde for one reason and one reason only - they catch fish.

A few years ago the cod vanished and calls of pollution, nuclear waste, over fishing etc. echoed in political halls. The anglers, being more philosophical, went out and found new marks, tried new techniques and, as always, caught fish. The cod have returned to the Clyde but now the anglers have itchy feet. They travel for the weekend to Pladda at the south end of Arran for the good hardfighting pollack, the tope and, hopefully, a haddock or two.

Tony Wass is now operating a fine boat out of Girvan, one of the most underfished ports in the area, and one with great potential. Not for Tony the one mile from harbour and drift. He is seeking wrecks and giant pollack and wrasse close into the spectacular Ailsa Craig - the trip alone is worth it. There are also some fine tope in the area which very few people fish for.

The top end up at Fairlie has proved to be a mecca for the small boat angler which gives ready access to the ore terminal at Hunterston. This huge pier complex is an absolute paradise for pollack anglers. Indeed, sport can become so steady and hectic it can be rather tiring. Well, that's the time to put down the conger baits.

Shore anglers have unlimited choice from pollack on Holy Isle to sea trout or dogfish at Largs or mullet and flats from any of the many harbours. As I write, there is a claim for a new Scottish mullet record of 6.5 lbs from Ayr Harbour. A plea - if you catch any mullet below this weight and do not intend to eat it, please return it alive or any other fish for that matter.

Finally, we arrive in the south west, one of our richest angling areas in all senses, plenty of species, good shore marks, hosts of harbours and charter boats all year through and good bait availability.

Boats are available at Portpatrick, Drummore, Port William, Isle

Whithorn, Garlieston, Kirkcudbright. Bill Carter also runs a small boat hire business at the top of Luce Bay at Auchenmalg. The only major species which I have not known to be caught from this area is the halibut but that may be a matter of time. That apart, the list is endless and all techniques will produce fish on the day.

The shore angler is spoiled for choice, almost any point on the Mull of Galloway will give access to deep water on the west with dogs, tope, pollack, wrasse and even shark for anyone who can devise some rigs to compensate for the tides. Inside Luce Bay flatties, skate and bass with the ever present dogs. Burrow Head at the Isle of Whithorn has some superb rock stances giving access to deep water but be very careful anywhere in this area. Tides are fierce and swells can be large and sudden. Last but by no means least is Balcary Point, certainly Britain's most productive shore mark for large - 20 lbs plus - cod. This area can get very crowded at times so be prepared to be patient and if your access is via farmland, please be tidy.

Scotland is fortunate in having such a wealth of good angling freely available to all and good manners when launching, bait digging or gaining access to a shore mark will ensure that it will remain accessible. Weather, tides and seasons all have enormous effect on our angling and where possible local advice should be sought beforehand.

A little forward planning can help turn your Scottish angling trip into the holiday of a lifetime.

Porbeagle shark – they abound in Scotland.

Nice cod from Stonehaven.

Ling such as this abound in Scottish waters.

An 11lb Spring salmon, Dee.

ONE MAN'S YEAR
(of Scottish Game Fishing)
by Bill Currie

Like every other angler, whether a resident or a visitor to Scotland, I plan my season's fishing carefully. Where will the best places be for salmon, sea trout and brown trout? Will I make an effort to plan at least one trip in 1993 which will take me to new lochs or rivers, and perhaps open up new vistas on my own doorstep? To make what I hope are helpful suggestions to readers of Scotland for Fishing, I am going to work through some of my own fishing plans for 1993 and in this way share some of the recent tic-tac on where good fishing is to be found.

I am certain I will feel the urge to fish early for salmon and for the past two years I have been lucky enough to get a day or two on the Tay in the first few days of its season in mid-January. I have also, recently, been able to fish the opening day on the Dee (1st February). Let me put these early days into perspective. I have thoroughly enjoyed them, even if the weather was cold. There were kelts in plenty coming to fly and in the case of the Tay, some big kelts and one baggot pulled well. I did not get a fresh fish around the opening last year, on Tay, Dee or Tweed, but fresh fish were caught on the beats I was on. Yet I revelled in these days. I suppose I am being a little philosophical in saying that, although our earliest runs of salmon on the big-name rivers of our east coast have been poor for the past three seasons or so, I will enthusiastically fish them all again, partly because, even if the winter-spring runs have been thin, hope rises each time that the next pull to the fly will be a fresh fish.

I have my 1993 eye on the smaller northern salmon rivers in Scotland. In 1992 they far outshone the great waters further south. They come into their own from late February onwards, and quite a number of estates and local hotels and a few select angling clubs listed in this booklet can offer fishing on Thurso, Helmsdale, Brora, Cassley, Oykel and other waters of the north east. It is well worth a few telephone calls to local hotels and estate offices to find if there are vacancies. These northern rivers have a great charm. They are set in magnificent landscape and in spring they have usually excellent flow. They are fly fishing waters and for the keen salmon fisher they represent as high a chance of opening the 1993 salmon catches as you would be able to find anywhere in Scotland.

Where shall we fish for sea trout in 1993? I am happy to say that a number of rivers reported good returns of sea trout in 1992, where 1991 had seemed to pose problems. I saw decent stocks of fish in the Annan in early July where the previous two seasons had yielded little or nothing. There was every evidence that the Solway was again producing reasonable (not huge) numbers of fish in the two pound class and they were reported on the Annan (July), the Border Esk (in June - mid-July), the Nith and tributaries. The east coast rivers showed some really nice runs in June and July. I had some good fish off the South Esk, for example, had reports of good numbers and sizes in June on the Spey, had excellent reports of good bags of sea trout on the Dee in late May and June and in general had an optimistic feeling about runs after the troubles. I was particularly glad to hear of better runs into Loch Maree in June and July and to have better reports from the west coast generally, because it was the west which suffered in the late eighties.

I had some very nice May fly fishing on the Dee, but the total numbers of fish there in 1992 were low compared with the great runs of the mid and late eighties. Fishing the Dee is, for many of us, as much a spiritual matter as a question of bags, however. I could not think of a year without the lovely floating line fly fishing of the late spring and early summer. Two or three fish for a rod/week seems reasonable and I am sure 1993 will produce that on many of the beats from Banchory to Ballater with the best water in the middle sections of that area. Use the hotel guide in the booklet to help you to find fishing and act early to book it. Write to local estate offices and contact local tourist information centres. Good Dee fishing is hard to come by, but I suspect some of the beats may have vacancies in 1993, especially in June. My plan would be to do a bit of research, or have a local sporting agency do it for you, and give the middle Dee a try in May-June 1993.

I always try to make myself a summer sandwich of fishing around the end of June. If I can line up a couple of nights of sea trout fishing somewhere in the West Highlands, I try to add on a couple of days of loch trout fishing and with a bit of luck this blend of sport can be delightful. Try the same mix in the Hebrides around the middle of July. The trout in the West Highlands and in the Hebrides come on in late May and June, but the sea trout runs in the smaller rivers of the Hebrides seem to appear a fortnight or so later than on the mainland. In many ways this kind of fishing is the jewel of the Scottish scene. It takes you to little frequented areas,

makes you walk a mile or so over the moor to the lochs, and for me, that brings you into contact with the real experience of the Highlands. A June holiday brings you north when there are plenty of vacancies in the local hotels and bed and breakfast houses. Indeed, your hotel may have trout lochs at their disposal. I strongly recommended this formula for an early summer break.

As the summer goes on a number of smaller waters on the west coast begin to show their quality as salmon rivers. I have in mind, particularly, the rivers of the south west, Galloway and Ayrshire. These rivers have a great deal to offer. Waters like the Cree at and above Newton Stewart, and its curious neighbour the Bladenoch can be excellent after rain. The Stinchar in southern Ayrshire is a glorious river with what can sometimes be memorable runs of summer salmon and sea trout. It is a water which gives sport right into the autumn and even has an extension to its season in early November. Twenty miles or so to the north of that, is the Doon, running from the Southern Uplands into the lowland plains of Ayrshire. It is fed by the large Loch Doon and benefits from compensation flow in dry weather. It is not widely known that this river can yield, in a good year, 1800-2000 salmon to its anglers. These fish come mostly in August, September and October. The Doon can produce in three months more fish than some of the exclusive northern Scottish rivers can in a season running from early spring to the end of September. Access to the Doon is by way of local clubs, local hotels and rentals and - a new approach - local time-share fisheries such as the excellent Smithston water downstream from Patna.

I finish my season on Tweed and its tributaries. There the renowned autumn fisheries provide sport until the end of November. In 1992 the lower and middle rivers had splendid fishing, but the more accessible middle and upper waters had to wait until November for their sport. It is not always like that. I have known years when the river from Galashiels to Peebles and above outshone the fatter beats lower down. It all depends on weather and water. I am lucky in that I live near Tweed and Teviot, and in 1991 and 1992 I was impressed by the Teviot as a good salmon water, given the right levels, from late September right to the end of the season in November. It is fly-only in the autumn, as is the Tweed. For me a fish or two (often returned if they are coloured) from Teviot or Tweed is a splendid rounding off of the fishing year.

In my recommendation, I am revealing my own hopes and plans for the year. Fishing is not, for me, about headcounts. It is about my own homeland, its beauty, its wildness and the quality of its sport. A year can be more or less productive, but the variety of landscape, waters and sport is the memorable thing. This is where Scotland scores.

Bill Currie's latest book was produced in the autumn of 1992. It is THE RIVER WITHIN - A Life of Fly-Fishing (Lochar Publishing, £14.99). In this book he writes about his wide experience of Scottish fishing and the special pleasure it brings. The book also draws on some of Currie's travels, giving fascinating accounts of his fishing in northern Europe and America, including Alaska. This is a mature collection of writings from a long and varied fishing life and it gives the reader a thoughtful, passionate and personal sense of the delight experienced by the game fisher. The book is well illustrated by colour shots taken by the author.

Tweed, Autumn.

River Helmsdale, February.

TROUT ANGLING IN BERWICKSHIRE

by Alan Spence

Trout anglers resident in or visiting the part of the Border country formerly the county of Berwickshire have the choice of a wide variety of waters for their sport. Trout angling is available here to suit most tastes, while there are few pockets which cannot afford the modest fee for a season ticket whose cost seldom exceeds £20. The Tweed of course forms the southern boundary of the old county, and the Scottish English Border. Rightly famed as one of, if not the best of Scotland's salmon rivers, Tweed is also a notable trout river in its own right.

It is undeniable that Tweed trouting can be difficult, during low water levels in summer 'many anglers myself included, find themselves changing to ever smaller flies and thinner nylon points in an effort to put something in the bag. Often it is to no avail then along comes a freshet, a two or three feet rise in the river level when for a brief period trout feed avidly and will take any reasonably presented artificial fly.

The first Protection Order in Scotland for trout fisheries, 1980 if memory serves correct, was granted to the Tweed, opening up a great deal of more water to the public and giving protection to clubs who leased water for trout angling purposes making it an offence to fish for brown trout without written permission.

Where the Tweed winds through Berwickshire two clubs control the majority of the trout angling. 'The Coldstream and District Angling Association' and 'The Ladykirk and Norham Angling Association'. With some exceptions where small stretches of the river have been reserved for private use, virtually both banks from above the village of Birgham to the tidal water below Norham Castle are available for trout angling.

Coldstream run one of the tightest clubs in the Borders, a strict artificial fly only rule is applied with a six trout per angler daily limit. The end result of this policy is that the water controlled by the Coldstream Association now ranks as one of the best on the Tweed, with a head of larger fish which have not succumbed to the charms of low water worm or minnow fishing.

Tweed is of course, a vastly different river here in the Merse than in its upper reaches within Tweedale, the rush and dash of its infant waters replaced by the long deep pools, or as they are called dubs. Up to a mile in length, the dubs are fed by gravel or stone bedded streams while the pools themselves are often formed upon the naked bedrock.

Dry fly fishing on these dubs has been dealt with fully in an earlier edition of Scotland for Fishing, but to re-cap briefly, sport is at its best in May, June and July which can be stretched to include August if the river has been refreshed with spate water. What of the remainder of the trout season you may ask? Once neither wild horses, nor threats and intimidation would have kept me from the waterside on the first Saturday of the season. Now it is usually April before the first outing is contemplated, as the weather improves, which is not always the case unfortunately the early days of April '92 saw snow, sleet and rain over the Borders with Tweed rising to one of its highest levels for many years.

Most years in April the trout angler can expect some sport on the wet fly, although personally speaking I find it increasingly difficult to take trout by this method on the Tweed today. Some more skilled in this branch of the art can winkle a pounder or two from the water over the gravel streams in the opening weeks of the season.

By far the most dominant fly in April is the dark olive, local anglers refer to this simply as the Greenwell, the artificial fly devised by James Wright of Sprouston on behalf of Canon Greenwell to imitate this early season natural fly. For some years I had written off the March Brown as having vanished from the Tweed in any numbers, happily two years ago there were again heavy hatches with the trout apparently quite willing to partake of this large delicacy.

For a wet fly cast the Greenwells Glory, March Brown and a Gold Ribbed Hares Ear would be my favourite choice in April. Size 14 would be ideal for most work but move up a size to 12s in heavy streams or coloured water, down to 16s when the opposite conditions prevail. Wet fly fishing for trout on the broad reaches of the lower river means across and downstream, the exponents of the short line up and across now but a memory.

Rises to the surface fly in the early part of the season tend to be spasmodic, the trout making a brief foray to the surface before returning to sub-surface activity. Adult flies may still sail downstream with pert drying wings, yet to all intents and purposes there are no trout in the river. Suddenly the quieter waters are again ringed by rising fish, almost as if they had received some prearranged signal to co-ordinate their movements. Dry Greenwells or March Browns can prove the downfall of many an April trout, watch out however for the less obvious Iron Blue Dun which despite its smaller size can be taken in preference to larger meatier mouthfuls.

One of Tweed's principal tributaries, the Whiteadder cuts its way across the Berwickshire countryside, like its own main tributary the Blackadder, the names mean simply water, that is the white water and the black water. Both streams are born in upland situations but end their course through the rich farmland of the Merse, their character completely changed.

Control of the complete length of the Whiteadder was once in the hands of the Whiteadder Angling Association and the Berwick and District Angling Association. This has been slightly eroded in recent years due to a change in ownership of riverside farms and estates holding the fishing rights, yet a considerable mileage remains with those clubs. Where the Blackadder is concerned fishing in the upper part around Greenlaw is administered by, who else but the Greenlaw Angling Club, there is some lower private water where the cost of a ticket appears to have remained static for the last thirty years at least.

Perhaps the term white water comes from the rocky course of the river where it dashes between steep rocky gullies before plunging into another pool of unfathomable depths. At Abbey St. Bathans and again at Cumledge Mill this is certainly the case, but the latter is really the last fling for the river as a hill stream. Lower down, the Whiteadder has many characteristics of Tweed, albeit on a smaller scale.

Smaller pools eliminate the problems often found on the main river, mainly in the shape of the monster trout feeding just beyond casting range. The monster trout of the smaller river may instead be rising below an overhanging tree, or in a place where a backcast with a fly rod is impossible. Also to be considered is the shyness of trout in a small stream, fish which in my mind seem always ever more alert to the fisher's shadow or heavy tread than their river dwelling brethren.

Not that these rivers lie totally encased in a Borders jungle, there are many places where close cropped pasture reaches right to the riverside. For the others where woodlands encroach, bait fishing is allowed where some of the techniques discussed in the 1992 Scotland for Fishing can be employed.

Although falling under the same Protection Order as the Tweed, the Eye Water is a totally independent stream. On the lower part of this stream the Eyemouth Angling Association administer almost three miles of the river, while upstream several private beats can be fished at a moderate cost. The same selection of wet flies will serve well in the tributaries, and the Eye Water as in Tweed, perhaps there is a case for a smaller size of hook, but again this depends upon the prevailing water conditions.

Both the Whiteadder and Blackadder are hill burns in their upper parts, a definite case here for the traditional spider dressings, Snipe and Purple, Waterhen Bloa or that great and deadly favourite - Partridge and Orange. Where the river can be easily covered from either bank casting upstream is the best bet, in fact whatever the method used the cast from below the fish is essential. These trout are wary to the extreme, swift to panic and scuttle to safety below the nearest stone or rock, losing temporarily the desire to seize any fly be it natural or artificial.

Quicksilver in their reaction to any offering, tributary trout require a much faster response from the angler on the strike than the slow rolling pounder of Tweed's dubs. A threequarter pound trout is about an average fish for the Whiteadder, a half pounder for the Blackadder and Eye Water, there are always surprises, three pounders being not uncommon on the first mentioned river.

Not all trout angling in Berwickshire is restricted to Tweed and its tributaries, sport is also to be had on what people like to term stillwaters, the 'replacement' collective term for lochs and reservoirs. Berwickshire can boast but one natural stillwater, Coldingham Loch, sited above and half mile distant from the North Sea, the loch's outlet stream plunges hundreds of feet over the cliffs to the sea.

Despite its situation on the edge of Coldingham Moors this loch with its sandstone bed is highly fertile, producing a wide range of aquatic life on which the trout thrive fat. Overwintered rainbows here bear the same streamlined shape as seatrout, their flesh equally pink, their fighting capabilities equal to the freshest run salmon trout.

Fed exclusively by springs, Coldingham Loch is totally dependant upon artificial stocking for the brown and rainbow trout which make it a byword in angling circles. Stocking first began at the turn of the century, originally with the Loch Leven strain of trout, making Coldingham one of, if not the earliest put and take trout fisheries in Scotland. Prior to this the perch which share the water, are said to be a legacy of nearby Coldingham Priory harvested to provide the essential fish for Friday meals.

Fishing on Coldingham Loch has improved considerably since the present owner Dr. Ted Wise took over its running in the 1970's rearing more of the stock fish in house. An aeration plant, known to regulars as the jacuzzi, prevents stagnation in summer and may have been responsible for an increase in the number of lake olives and caneis.

Advance booking is advised for both bank and boat fishing at this popular venue, this is especially applicable at weekends and peak holiday periods. The season here runs from 15th March to 5th October for brown trout, and until 31st October for rainbows, unlike the rivers in the Merse, Sunday fishing is allowed. With a mixed stocking of brown and rainbow trout it follows that a diversity of fly angling techniques can be used with an equally diverse degree of success or failure. As in any stocked fishery, some Coldingham anglers feel they have not had their money's worth unless they have flung the latest fashionable lure towards the horizon then retrieved their deep sinking line as fast as possible to repeat the operation over and over again.

Certainly there are days, notably during times when the tiny crustacea Daphnia blooms that only something big, fast and flashy will divert the rainbows from this fixation. In early season a black lure fished deep and slow makes a reasonable imitation of the leech which forms part of the aquatic diet in March.

Soon however the first of the natural flies are hatching, small black duck flies which get larger as the season progresses, including some whopper buzzers in June and July. Pupae patterns, from 12s down to 20s may prove tempting in calm conditions, while with a bit of a ripple the blae and blacks and black pennel type patterns come into their own. Or again when fish are obviously taking surface flies a small dry spider may do the trick.

Sedges appear by June when either direct imitations or suggestive patterns, the Invicta which seems to suggest the final pupae stage of several caddis flies, in size 12 and 14 is a good general pattern. June can also bring the first evening hatches of the dreaded green midge, the d.g.m. is small, in fact minuscule and the trout love them. Many anglers are convinced that as these hatch the trout simply swim around in circles with open mouths scooping up a natural bounty, what chance has even the most craftily tied artificial among millions of natural insects.

Anglers who take a limit bag during an evening hatch of the d.g.m. can well afford to award themselves a gentle pat on the back. Some of the most exciting fishing at Coldingham takes place not when insects are hatching from the loch but when terrestrials are blown upon it. First in the season in any quantity is the hawthorn fly, usually in late May or early June. One of the straggly legged direct copy artificials fished semi bouyant in the surface film seems to do the trick, other anglers are content with traditional patterns, again the blae and black or similar seems equally appealing to the trout.

Throughout the season occasional cow dung flies are blown on the water, these very often receive the attention of the trout, especially on a bright windy day when few aquatic flies are hatching. Authentic dry flies tied as copies of the cow dung fly can be tried but sometimes the soberer Gold Ribbed Hares Ear, or Woodcock and Hare Lug is the most effective.

September sees trout turning to the most important terrestrial of the year the crane fly or in common parlance the daddy long legs. While throughout the summer many of these long gangling creatures skim and skip across the surface it is only in September that they become prolific enough to interest the trout, which at first treat these meaty mouthfuls with a degree of caution then later fall upon them with avarice. Most artificial crane fly patterns will suffice, or anything straggly such as a static muddler minnow.

Lying in the Lammermuirs near the village of Longformacus the Watch

Water, Berwickshire's major reservoir serves a dual purpose as water supply and trout fishery. Since this was taken over by Berwick on Tweed business man Bill Renton in 1988 the fishing and facilities have been greatly enhanced. The two boats available in 1992 to complement the bank fishing, should if the proprietor's plans bear fruit, be increased to at least four by the time you read this.

Being stream fed the Watch Water has contained brown trout since the waters were first impounded back in the early 1950's, these being supplemented by stockings of brown and a few rainbow trout introduced by the angling club which controlled the Watch until recently. Since the present proprietor has taken charge the fishing has developed more of a put and take style, with regular stockings predominantly of rainbow trout.

Despite being an acidic loch the feeding is plentiful enough for rainbows to thrive and grow fairly rapidly, four inch escapees from a holding cage for instance grew to over a pound in just two seasons. Some remarkable hatches of caneis occur on the Watch Water,

literally in clouds, the newly hatched mini olives casting their shucks to become spinners by the thousand on bankside anglers' clothing.

Most of the natural flies are however, black, in this Watch differs none from many upland waters. Bill Renton recommends, Bibio, Kate Maclaren and Black Pennel as among the most reliable traditional flies in 12s and 14s. Suspender buzzers 14s and 16s are useful in calm conditions while for lure fishing Ace of Spades and Montana Nymphs in size 10 and 12 are advised. A small number of lake olives occur at infrequent intervals, which like the caneis can be imitated with a small Grey Hen and Yellow, or Grey Hen and Red when the spinner of the former species is on the water.

Sunday fishing is allowed on the Watch, the brown trout season running from 15th March to 5th October, rainbow trout can be fished for all year round.

This then has been a brief flirtation with some of the trout fishing in the Eastern Borders, sometimes difficult, always enjoyable with a new challenge around each river bend for those who care to see it out.

TROUT LOCH FISHING IN THE HIGHLANDS

by Lesley Crawford

The Northern Highlands of Scotland represent to many anglers one of the last remaining areas where 'true' wild brown trout fishing may be experienced. By this I mean the visitor can enjoy wild scenery, an abundance of hard fighting fish, solitude and grandeur and be unencumbered by traffic jams, full car parks, rows of anglers strung along shorelines and the threat of making a 'bag limit' before the allotted hour runs out. The plethora of lochs which exists in, for example, the County of Sutherland, would take almost a lifetime to fish so little wonder the touring angler can quite literally be spoilt for choice. However, despite tales of thousands of waters brimming with fish, a visiting angler may well find he does not always meet with the success he would like when fishing on our trout lochs. Just why this should be, can often be put down to a general lack of understanding of the often complex art of fishing for the wild brown trout.

I am frequently amazed by the number of visiting anglers who come to the Highlands expecting our trout to fling themselves obligingly at their flies and who think that only the minimum of effort is reqired to achieve double figure catches. If they are experienced fishers more often than not they have fished almost exclusively for the rainbow trout, a very different fish from our own brown trout, and have grown accustomed to some very different techniques from the kind used in the north. They may think that their reservoir skills are instantly transferable from a 'stew pond' species to a trout born and bred in a moorland stream when in fact what they have already learned can be largely ineffective in the far north. Without some necessary adaptations they then go home swearing that angling instructors like me are telling lies and that all those wild brown trout are nowhere to be seen! Then again they might be complete novices who come to the Highlands anticipating that a full knowledge of the brown trout, his environment AND how to fish for him can be learned in a afternoon, when in fact it has taken their teacher well over 20 years and she is still learning!

So let's look at some simple steps to follow which, while not guaranteeing instant success, will at least point the way to making your trout fishing more enjoyable with hopefully one or two fish at the end of the day. First of all it is vitally important to be willing to adapt, refine and change your techniques according to the type of fish, the time of year, the time of day and the constantly changing weather conditions. Never assume anything about our brown trout fishing for it is quite likely that in a day's outing you can experience triumph, disaster, frustration, failure and success and that may be in the space of five minutes! Some will say that this is because trout fishing is governed by the laws of Lady Luck and little else but in fact it is simply because the trout we fish for react in far more sensitive and subtle ways to their constantly changing environment than perhaps we fishers

Lesley Crawford with a beautifully marked Loch Calder trout of 1lb 4oz

want to admit. To an angler a change of wind direction, a change of light and shadow, an increase in air or water temperature, a rise in water levels, a shower of rain or a hatch of a particular insect may be so subtle as to be hardly noticeable yet to a trout these factors govern everything in his life. They will put him off or on the feed, make him lethargic or lively, frighten him or make him bold and aggressive. Trout act out of deeply ingrained instincts and we must fit in with their world and try and understand why a particular response is given or received for they certainly will not fit in to ours!

To illustrate this let's look at a typical day out on one of our freer rising and reasonably well fished lochs. Before we even start to fish an assessment of the water will bring rich reward. Resist the temptation to charge headlong to the nearest bank or boat for it pays dividends to first take a simple walk down to the water's edge. Is the water peat stained or clear; does it shelve gently out or is it a straight drop into the deeps; does the water feel warm or icy cold to the touch; are there any prominent feeding areas for the fish like weed beds, skerries, boulders, islands; is the surrounding land fertile and green or barren peat and hard rock; are there obvious signs of feeding fish? Assessing these factors take only minutes yet it is surprising how many anglers take the trouble to do so. Which way is the wind blowing, is there a wave or just a ripple and where is the sun in relation to the wind? You should consider all these conditions BEFORE putting up the rod or opening any fly box.

Let's say that we have chosen to fish on this typical Highland loch on a 'typical' summer's day. Overhead are reasonable conditions of some warmth, sun and cloud. (Perfect conditions of slate grey skies and occasional smirls of rain are actually quite infrequent). The loch itself is slightly peaty, it has a shingle and stone shoreline, is reasonably shallow with a few attractive promontories runnning out from the shore and a weed bed at one end. The surrounding country is heather, grass, marl and peat with a reasonable buzz of insect life. The water feels cool to the touch despite the fact it is July indicating that the trout will still be feeding quite close in, it is only when the water is overly warm that you will expect to find them in the cooler middle. All these environmental factors give a fair indication of the loch's fertility, for example if it were deep black water with little weed growth and surrounded by acidic peat bog it may not be nearly so productive. Here and there you can hear a few encouraging plops of feeding trout. These noises of bloops, splutters or swirls are important for at least you will then know that some fish are feeding and your next job will be to find out on what. However do not be put off if you can hear nothing for there are a number of lochs in the Highlands where it is rare to see a rise at all though when the trout take sub surface they can almost wrench the rod from your hands!

Now you can kit up with your light carbon based rod (anything in the 9-10 feet range will suffice), lightweight reel, floating line, 4-6 lbs nylon and an appropriate first fly. Bear in mind the axioms 'dark day dark fly', and also 'dark water dark fly' and their opposites for they do help and if you have never fished the particular water before I would always plump for something black and red like a Zulu or Bibio as these general representations and colours are often the most favoured in the North. 'Big wave, big fly, small wave, smaller fly' can also apply and in most cases I would use a size 20 or 12 as I like to give the trout something to aim at.

The wind is blowing into the shore on which we are standing so let's move round to get a better fly presentation with the wind coming over one shoulder or the other rather than directly from behind. As the trout are all facing into the wind we should aim to draw the fly over the noses of the trout showing its whole outline to them rather than just a hook end. I would not start where the water plummets into the deepest part of the loch for few fish lie in icy depths instead head for likely looking bays annd promontories where shallow water meets deep. Concentrate your efforts about likely looking feeding areas bearing in mind the trout requires three things, food, shelter and somewhere to reproduce. He will obtain good sources of food from weed beds and other aquatic plants, islands and boulders near the shore, inflowing burns, submerged grass and clay or marl type mud providing it is not a thick deoxygenated silt. He will find shelter to hide from danger at the edges of weed beds and behind submerged rocks or rocky shelves and when it is the beginning or end of his spawning time (September and March respectively) he will be in the vicinity of his spawning streams. It's interesting to note that other than at the beginning or end of spawning the brown trout will select his own 'lies' and rarely move away from them. The biggest trout have the best territories, that is how they have grown big and it is up to you to find these by constantly covering new water. I always recommend fishing down a bank about as fast as you would be drifting in a boat so as to cast over as much water as possible. Standing stationary in the hope that a trout will eventually swim past will achieve little yet it is a technique that many visitors persist in using usually when they have learned their fishing on rainbow trout fisheries where, if you are prepared to wait long enough, the stocked fish will eventually swim past in a shoal. Our brown trout by comparison are very

solitary creatures though it is possible to find a number together in a particularly fertile area of a loch giving the appearance of a 'shoal'.

Try and keep your technique relaxed and fluid and remember our wild brown trout are exceptionally fast fish and you may miss as many as you catch. To assist your catch rates check your rod tip is being kept parallel to the water and the line is lying straight out across the wave to give a good striking action. Are you retrieving the fly to give it plenty of life and are you aware of exactly where it is in the water? Limp dangling flies with a rod pointing skyward and their owner gazing absent mindedly around instead of concentrating on what is in front of him rarely catch fish. Neither is it necessary to flash line back and forward in a prolonged show of 'false casting' to achieve the required length of line, in fact it can put a lot of trout down before you even begin. False casting may look pretty but save it for those casting competitions, up here the wind is likely to blow the whole thing round your neck anyway!

And if your technique seems OK but the fish suddenly appear to have gone 'off' have a look above your head for more often than not there lies the answer. It may be that the sun has moved round to align itself with the wind and when our light sensitive trout have to look into bright sunshine they quite simply turn away from it and will not see your fly however well presented. 'When sun and wind align the fishing will be far from fine' is a little saying I made up to remind beginners that while it is in their power to improve on general techniques they are powerless to change weather patterns. Other changes in the weather are less noticeable to the human eye but nevertheless have a direct bearing on how the trout are moving or not moving as the case may be. A sudden shower of rain or a change in air temperature can bring on a hatch of insects and a loch which previously appeared fishless can for a time positively heave with rising trout. At certain times of the year the trout become obsessed with feeding on a specific food be it snails, water shrimps, minnows or any of the huge variety of insects we have, sedge, olive or mayfly being just a few. It pays to spoon any trout you do catch to gain a rough idea of what they are feeding on, failing that look into both the water and the air for any signs of prospective food.

Finally always try to treat your Highland trout fishing with the magnaminity it deserves. All the variables I have mentioned can change incredibly, even in the short space of a single day so please accept that as part and parcel of the excitement and challenge of trout fishing in the Highlands. The more you are able to do it the better you should become but do not let the taking of large numbers of fish be the be all and end all of your enjoyment of trouting. While our wild brown trout is perhaps not yet an endangered species it is up to all anglers, experienced or beginner, visiting or local, to ensure he has a safe future.

Choosing a fly - Loch Hakel, Sutherland

CLOSE SEASON

The following are the statutory close season dates for trout and salmon fishing in Scotland.

TROUT

The close season for trout in Scotland is from 7 October to 14 March, both days inclusive, but many clubs extend this close season still further to allow the fish to reach better condition.

Fresh trout may not be sold between the end of August and the beginning of April, and not at any time if less than eight inches long.

SALMON

Net Fishing	Rod Fishing	River District
1 Sept-15 Feb	1 Nov-15 Feb	Add
27 Aug-10 Feb	1 Nov-10 Feb	Ailort
27 Aug-10 Feb	1 Nov-10 Feb	Aline
27 Aug-10 Feb	1 Nov-10 Feb	Alness
27 Aug-10 Feb	1 Nov-10 Feb	Applecross
27 Aug-10 Feb	1 Nov-10 Feb	Arnisdale (Loch Hourn)
27 Aug-10 Feb	16 Oct-10 Feb	Awe
27 Aug-10 Feb	1 Nov-10 Feb	Ayr
27 Aug-10 Feb	1 Nov-10 Feb	Baa & Goladoir
27 Aug-10 Feb	1 Nov-10 Feb	Badachro & Kerry (Gairloch)
27 Aug-10 Feb	16 Oct-10 Feb	Balgay & Shieldaig
27 Aug-10 Feb	16 Oct-10 Feb	Beauly
27 Aug-10 Feb	1 Nov-10 Feb	Berriedale
10 Sept-24 Feb	1 Nov-24 Feb	Bervie
27 Aug-10 Feb	1 Nov-10 Feb	Bladenoch
27 Aug-10 Feb	1 Nov-10 Feb	Broom
27 Aug-10 Feb	16 Oct-31 Jan	Brora
10 Sept-24 Feb	1 Nov-24 Feb	Carradale
27 Aug-10 Feb	1 Nov-10 Feb	Carron (W. Ross)
10 Sept-24 Feb	1 Nov-24 Feb	Clayburn (Isle of Harris (East))
27 Aug-10 Feb	1 Nov-10 Feb	Clyde & Leven
27 Aug-10 Feb	1 Oct-25 Jan	Conon
14 Sept-28 Feb	15 Oct-28 Feb	Cree
27 Aug-10 Feb	17 Oct-10 Feb	Creed or Stornoway and Laxay (Isle of Lewis)
27 Aug-10 Feb	1 Nov-10 Feb	Creran (Loch Creran)
27 Aug-10 Feb	1 Nov-10 Feb	Croe & Shiel
27 Aug-10 Feb	1 Oct-31 Jan	Dee (Aberdeenshire)
27 Aug-10 Feb	1 Nov-10 Feb	Dee (Kirkcudbrightshire)
27 Aug-10 Feb	1 Nov-10 Feb	Deveron
27 Aug-10 Feb	1 Nov-10 Feb	Don
27 Aug-10 Feb	1 Nov-10 Feb	Doon
1 Sept-15 Feb	16 Oct-15 Feb	Drummachloy or Glenmore (Isle of Bute)
27 Aug-10 Feb	16 Oct-10 Feb	Dunbeath
21 Aug- 4 Feb	1 Nov-31 Jan	Earn
1 Sept-15 Feb	1 Nov-15 Feb	Echaig
1 Sept-15 Feb	1 Nov-15 Feb	Esk, North
1 Sept-15 Feb	1 Nov-15 Feb	Esk, South
27 Aug-10 Feb	1 Nov-10 Feb	Ewe (Isle of Harris (West))
27 Aug-10 Feb	6 Oct-10 Feb	Findhorn
10 Sept-24 Feb	1 Nov-24 Feb	Fleet (Kirkcudbright)
10 Sept-24 Feb	1 Nov-24 Feb	Fleet (Sutherland)
27 Aug-10 Feb	1 Nov-10 Feb	Forss
27 Aug-10 Feb	1 Nov-31 Jan	Forth
1 Sept-15 Feb	1 Nov-15 Feb	Fyne, Shira & Aray (Loch Fyne)
10 Sept-24 Feb	1 Nov-24 Feb	Girvan
27 Aug-10 Feb	1 Nov-10 Feb	Glenelg
27 Aug-10 Feb	1 Nov-10 Feb	Gour
27 Aug-10 Feb	1 Nov-10 Feb	Greiss, Laxdale or Thunga
27 Aug-10 Feb	1 Nov-10 Feb	Grudie or Dionard
27 Aug-10 Feb	1 Nov-10 Feb	Gruinard and Little Gruinard
27 Aug-10 Feb	1 Oct-11 Jan	Halladale, Strathy, Naver & Borgie
27 Aug-10 Feb	1 Oct-10 Jan	Helmsdale
27 Aug-10 Feb	1 Oct-11 Jan	Hope and Polla or Strathbeg
10 Sept-24 Feb	1 Nov-24 Feb	Howmore
27 Aug-10 Feb	1 Nov-10 Feb	Inchard
10 Sept-24 Feb	1 Nov-24 Feb	Inner (on Jura)
27 Aug-10 Feb	1 Nov-10 Feb	Inver
10 Sept-24 Feb	1 Nov-24 Feb	Iora (on Arran)
10 Sept-24 Feb	1 Nov-24 Feb	Irvine & Garnock
27 Aug-10 Feb	1 Nov-10 Feb	Kannaird
27 Aug-10 Feb	1 Nov-10 Feb	Kilchoan
27 Aug-10 Feb	1 Nov-10 Feb	Kinloch (Kyle of Tongue)
27 Aug-10 Feb	1 Nov-10 Feb	Kirkaig
27 Aug-10 Feb	1 Nov-10 Feb	Kishorn
27 Aug-10 Feb	1 Oct-10 Jan	Kyle of Sutherland
10 Sept-24 Feb	1 Nov-24 Feb	Laggan & Sorn (Isle of Islay)
27 Aug-10 Feb	1 Nov-10 Feb	Laxford

Net Fishing	Rod Fishing	River District	Net Fishing	Rod Fishing	River District
27 Aug-10 Feb	1 Nov-10 Feb	Little Loch Broom	27 Aug-10 Feb	1 Nov-10 Feb	Pennygowan or
27 Aug-10 Feb	1 Nov-10 Feb	Loch Duich			Glenforsa & Aros
27 Aug-10 Feb	1 Nov-10 Feb	Loch Luing			
27 Aug-10 Feb	17 Oct-10 Feb	Loch Roag	27 Aug-10 Feb	1 Nov-10 Feb	Resort
27 Aug-10 Feb	1 Nov-10 Feb	Lochy	1 Sept-15 Feb	1 Nov-15 Feb	Ruel
27 Aug-10 Feb	16 Oct-10 Feb	Lossie			
10 Sept-24 Feb	1 Nov-24 Feb	Luce	27 Aug-10 Feb	1 Nov-10 Feb	Sanda
27 Aug-10 Feb	1 Nov-10 Feb	Lussa	27 Aug-10 Feb	1 Nov-10 Feb	Scaddle
		(Isle of Mull)	10 Sept-24 Feb	1 Nov-24 Feb	Shetland Isles
			27 Aug-10 Feb	1 Nov-10 Feb	Shiel
27 Aug-10 Feb	1 Nov-10 Feb	Moidart	27 Aug-10 Feb	1 Nov-10 Feb	Sligachan
27 Aug-10 Feb	1 Nov-10 Feb	Morar	27 Aug-10 Feb	1 Nov-10 Feb	Snizort
20 Sept-24 Feb	1 Nov-24 Feb	Mullangaren,	27 Aug-10 Feb	1 Oct-10 Feb	Spey
		Horasary and	10 Sept-24 Feb	1 Nov-24 Feb	Stinchar
		Lochnaciste	27 Aug-10 Feb	1 Nov-10 Feb	Sunart
		(Isle of North Uist)			(except Earn)
			21 Aug- 4 Feb	16 Oct-14 Jan	Tay
27 Aug-10 Feb	1 Oct-10 Feb	Nairn	27 Aug-10 Feb	6 Oct-10 Jan	Thurso
27 Aug-10 Feb	1 Nov-10 Feb	Nell, Feochan	27 Aug-10 Feb	1 Nov-10 Feb	Torridon
		and Euchar	15 Sept-14 Feb	1 Dec-31 Jan	Tweed
27 Aug-10 Feb	16 Oct-14 Jan	Ness			
10 Sept-24 Feb	1 Dec-24 Feb	Nith	10 Sept-24 Feb	1 Nov- 9 Feb	Ugie
			27 Aug-10 Feb	1 Nov-10 Feb	Ullapool
			10 Sept-24 Feb	1 Dec-24 Feb	Urr
10 Sept-24 Feb	1 Nov-24 Feb	Orkney Isles			
27 Aug-10 Feb	1 Nov-10 Feb	Ormsary (Loch	27 Aug-10 Feb	1 Nov-10 Feb	Wick
		Killisport), Loch			
		Head & Stornoway	10 Sept-24 Feb	1 Nov-10 Feb	Ythan

There is no close season for coarse fishing.

THE FORTH FISHERY CONSERVATION TRUST

The Trust was formed in August 1987, with the aim of improving all the fisheries within the Forth catchment area which extends from Fifeness to Balquidder in the north, and Loch Katrine to Torness in the south. The initial aim was to purchase a boat to assist the Forth District Salmon Fishery Board stop illegal netting of salmon on the Estuary.

Within twelve weeks two 18ft high speed launches were acquired for use by the new Superintendent Water Bailiff, Ian Baird, and the impact on the illegal netting operations has been dramatic. The River Teith and its tributaries experienced a good run of spring salmon and sea trout are running through almost unhindered.

The Trust has also stimulated discussions on salmon poaching and fish conservation at the hghest legal and government levels and will continue that dialogue.

Although a number of enthusiastic clubs have worked hard to open up fisheries, to restock and protect them, the Forth catchment area remains a virtually untapped fishery. These could be developed to provide leisure, tourism and employment for the region.

There are three major tasks the Trust wishes to undertake.

1. To increase efforts to eliminate all illegal fishing both on the estuary and throughout the whole river system.
2. To identify ownership of all stretches of water and fisheries in the area so that more effective supervision may be introduced.
3. To review the existing population and habitat of all fish species and assess the potential for increasing their numbers throughout the area.

This information will help all clubs, landowners and local inhabitants to make the best possible use of available resources and improve the quality of salmon, sea trout and coarse fishing throughout the Forth catchment area.

SCOTTISH BOAT AND SHORE (rod and line caught) MARINE FISH RECORDS

B - Boat Records   S - Shore Records   Spec. - Specimen Qualifying Weight

Species		lb.	oz.	dm.	kg.	Place of Capture	Angler	Year	Spec. lb.
ANGLERFISH	B	45	0	0	20.412	Sound of Mull	D. Hopper	1978	20
Lophius piscatorius	S	38	0	0	17.237	Blairmore Pier Loch Long	L. C. Hanley	1970	15
ARGENTINE	B		5	3	0.147	Arrochar	I. Millar	1978	4oz.
Argentina sphyraena	S	OPEN AT ANY WEIGHT							
BARRACUDINA	B	OPEN AT ANY WEIGHT							any
(Paralepis coreganoides borealis)	S	0	1	14	0.054	Newton Shore	D. Gillop	1987	1½oz.
BASS	B	8	14	3	4.025	Balcary Bay	D. Shaw	1975	6
Dicentrarchus labrax	S	13	4	0	6.010	Almorness Point	G. Stewart	1975	6
BLACKFISH	B	3	10	8	1.658	Heads of Ayr	J. Semple	1972	2½
Centrolophus niger	S	OPEN AT ANY WEIGHT							any
BLENNY, SHANNY	B	OPEN AT ANY WEIGHT							any
Blennius pholis	S	0	1	10	0.046	Carolina Port Dundee Docks	M. S. Ettle	1983	1oz.
BLENNY, TOMPOT	B	OPEN AT ANY WEIGHT							any
Blennius gattorugine	S		2	12	0.078	Portpatrick	G. Dods	1977	2oz.
BLENNY, VIVIPAROUS	B		10	0	0.283	Craigendoran	T. Lambert	1977	7oz.
Zoarces viviparus	S		11	3	0.317	Craigendoran	D. Ramsay	1975	7oz.
BLENNY, YARREL'S	B	OPEN AT ANY WEIGHT							any
Chirolophis ascanii	S		2	1	0.059	Gourock	D. McEntee	1979	1½oz.
BLUEMOUTH	B	3	2	8	1.431	Loch Shell	Mrs A. Lyngholm	1976	2½
Helicolenus dactylopterus	S	OPEN AT ANY WEIGHT							any
BREAM, BLACK	B	2	9	0	1.162	Kebock Head Lewis	T. Lumb	1974	1
Spondyllosoma cantharus	S	1	13	8	0.836	Gareloch	A. L. Harris	1973	1
BREAM, GILTHEAD	B	OPEN AT ANY WEIGHT							any
Sparus aurata	S	1	1	5	0.490	Dunnet Head	W. Thornton	1988	1
BREAM, RAYS	B	6	3	13	2.829	West of Barra Head	J. Holland	1978	4
Brama brama	S	6	6	8	2.905	Portobello	G. Taylor	1973	4
BREAM RED	B	4	10	0	2.097	Ardnamurchan	R. Steel	1969	1
Pagellus bogaraveo	S	OPEN AT ANY WEIGHT							any
BRILL	B	1	4	0	0.567	Portpatrick	J. Dickson	1984	1
Scophthalmus rhombus	S	1	2	0	0.510	Killintrinnan Lighthouse	P. Baisbrown	1971	1
BULL HUSS	B	20	3	8	9.171	Mull of Galloway	J. K. Crawford	1971	15
scyliorhinus stellaris	S	15	8	0	7.031	West Tarbet Mull of Galloway	A. K. Paterson	1976	10
BUTTERFISH	B	OPEN AT ANY WEIGHT							any
Pholis gunnellus	S		1	2	0.032	Gourock	D. McEntee	1978	1oz.
CATFISH, COMMON	B	13	12	11	6.256	Burnmouth	D. Brown	1985	7
Anachichas lupus	S	12	12	8	5.797	Stonehaven	G. M. Taylor	1978	4
COALFISH	B	28	4	0	12.814	Eyemouth	L. Gibson	1982	12
Pollachius virens	S	11	7	8	5.202	Loch Long	S. Mather	1976	7
COD	B	46	0	8	20.879	Gantocks	B. Baird	1970	25
Gadus morhua	S	40	11	8	18.470	Balcary Point	K. Robinson	1988	15
DAB	B	2	12	4	1.254	Gairloch	R. Islip	1975	1½
Limanda limanda	S	2	5	0	1.049	Cairnryan	A. Scott	1969	1½

B - Boat Records   S - Shore Records   Spec. - Specimen Qualifying Weight

Species		lb.	oz.	dm.	kg.	Place of Capture	Angler	Year	Spec. lb.
DAB LONG ROUGH	B		6	6	0.180	Helensburgh	J. Napier	1984	4oz.
Hippoglossoides platessoides	S		5	8	0.155	Coulport	I. McGrath	1975	4oz.
DOGFISH BLACK-MOUTHED	B	2	13	8	1.288	Loch Fyne	J. H. Anderson	1977	1½
Galeus melastromus	S	OPEN AT ANY WEIGHT							any
DOGFISH LESSER-SPOTTED	B	3	15	12	1.807	Portpatrick	R. I. Carruthers	1987	3
Scyliorhinus caniculus	S	4	15	3	2.246	Abbey Burnfoot	S. Ramsay	1988	3
DRAGONET COMMON	B		5	0	0.142	Gareloch	T. J. Ashwell	1985	4oz.
Callionymus lyra	S		5	0	0.143	Loch Long	J. Crawford	1985	4½
EEL, COMMON	B	1	13	7	0.834	Gareloch	P. Fleming	1976	1½
Anguilla anguilla	S	3	0	0	1.360	Ayr Harbour	R. W. Morrice	1972	2
EEL, CONGER	B	48	1		21.820	Largs	R. Bond	1985	30
Conger conger	S	63	8	0	28.803	Balcary	B. Ford	1991	25
FLOUNDER	B	2	13	11	1.295	Portnockie	K. F. Mackay	1985	2½
Platichthys flesus	S	4	11	8	2.140	Musselburgh	R. Armstrong	1970	2½
GARFISH	B	1	11	8	0.799	Brodick	R. Stockwin	1970	1
Belone belone	S	1	11	0	0.764	Bute	Miss McAlorum	1971	1
GOBY BLACK	B		1	4	0.035	Cairnryan	J. Price	1976	1oz.
Gobius niger	S		2	4	0.063	Inveraray	F. O'Brien	1980	1oz.
GURNARD, GREY	B	2	7	0	1.105	Caliach Point	D. Swinbanks	1976	1¾
Eutrigla gurnardus	S	1	5	0	0.595	Peterhead	A. Turnbull	1973	1
		1	5	0	0.595	Port William	J. W. Martin	1977	1
GURNARD, RED	B	2	8	8	1.148	Tobermory	D. V. Relton	1985	1½
Aspitrigla cuculus	S	1	2	5	0.519	Gareloch	G. Smith	1981	12oz.
GURNARD STREAKED	B		10	10	0.301	Isle of Mull	J. Duncan	1985	any
Trigloporus lastoviza	S	1	6	8	0.637	Loch Goil	H. L. Smith	1971	1
GURNARD, TUB	B	5	5	0	2.409	Luce Bay	J. S. Dickinson	1975	3½
Trigla lucerna	S	1	1	0	0.481	Carrick Bay	A. E. Maxwell	1978	12oz.
HADDOCK	B	9	14	12	4.501	Summer Isles	M. Lawton	1980	6
Melanogrammus aeglefinus	S	6	12	0	3.061	Loch Goil	G. B. Stevenson	1976	3
HAKE	B	18	5	8	8.321	Shetland	B. Sinclair	1971	10
Merluccius merluccus	S		11	7	0.324	Gourock	S. Moyes	1979	8oz.
HALIBUT	B	234	0	0	106.136	Scrabster	C. Booth	1979	50
Hippoglossus hippoglossus	S	OPEN AT ANY WEIGHT							any
HERRING	B	1	2	0	0.510	Loch Long	R. C. Scott	1974	14oz.
Culpea harengus	S		11	11	0.331	Port Logan	R. Smith	1984	10oz.
LING	B	57	8	0	26.082	Stonehaven	I. Duncan	1982	20
Molva molva	S	12	4	0	5.557	Scrabster	A. Allan	1984	6
LUMPSUCKER	B	4	11	4	2.133	Innellan	G. T. Roebuck	1976	3
Cyclopterus lumpus	S	5	12	10	2.626	Cruden Bay	M. Rennie	1987	3
MACKEREL	B	3	12	0	1.701	Ullapool	E. Scobie	1965	2
Scomber scombrus	S	2	5	9	1.063	Wick	W. Richardson	1969	2
MEGRIM	B	3	12	8	1.715	Gareloch	P. Christie	1973	2
Lepidorhombus whiffiagonis	S		11	6	0.325	Loch Ryan	C. N. Dickson	1989	any
MULLETT, GOLDEN GREY	B	OPEN AT ANY WEIGHT							any
Lisa aurata	S		11	0	0.312	Fairlie	I. McFadyen	1972	8oz.

Species		lb.	oz.	dm.	kg.	Place of Capture	Angler	Year	Spec. lb.
MULLET, THICK LIPPED GREY	B	3	6	0	1.531	Luce Bay	R. Williamson	1976	3
Crenimugil labrosus	S	6	14	14	3.143	Ayr Harbour	T. Parker	1992	4½
NORWAY HADDOCK	B	1	10	5	0.750	Eyemouth	P. Skala	1988	14oz.
Sebastes viviparus	S	OPEN AT ANY WEIGHT							any
PIPEFISH GREATER	B	OPEN AT ANY WEIGHT							any
Sygnathus acus	S		0	13	0.023	Coulport	H. Holding	1975	any
PLAICE	B	10	3	8	4.635	Longa Sound	H. Gardiner	1974	5
Pleuronectes platessa	S	5	8	0	2.494	Arrochar	A. Holt Jnr.	1971	3½
POLLACK	B	18	0	0	8.165	Scrabster	N. Carter	1971	10
Pollachius pollachius	S	13	14	0	6.293	Furnace	J. Arthur	1974	8
POOR COD	B	1	4	0	0.567	Arbroath	F. Chalmers	1969	1
Trisopterus minutus	S	1	0	0	0.453	Loch Fyne	F. Johnstone	1970	12oz.
POUTING	B	3	8	0	1.587	Gourock	J. Lewis	1977	2
Trisopterus luscus	S	3	3	7	1.458	Kirkcudbright	R. Cartwright	1984	1½
RAY BLONDE	B	26	11	0	12.105	Caliach Point	B. Swinbanks	1977	15
Raja brachyura	S	OPEN AT ANY WEIGHT							any
RAY CUCKOO	B	5	4	4	2.388	Gairloch	A. Bridges	1979	4
Raja naevus	S	4	11	0	2.126	Gourock	R. A. H. McCaw	1973	3¾
RAY SPOTTED	B	8	3	14	3.739	Isle of Whithorn	G. Brownlie	1989	4
Raja montagui	S	5	12	0	2.608	Cairnryan	G. C. Styles	1975	4
RAY THORNBACK	B	29	8	10	13.399	Luce Bay	A. McLean	1982	15
Raja clavata	S	21	12		9.866	Kirkcudbright	S. Ramsay	1985	4
ROCKLING, FIVE BEARDED	B	OPEN AT ANY WEIGHT							any
Ciliata mustela	S		7	0	0.198	Balcarry Point	K. Greason	1988	4½oz.
ROCKLING, FOUR BEARDED	B		1	7	0.040	Gourock	S. Hodgson	1981	1¼oz.
Rhinomenus cimbrius	S	OPEN AT ANY WEIGHT							any
ROCKLING SHORE	B	OPEN AT ANY WEIGHT							any
Gairdropsarus mediterraneus	S		14	8	0.411	Loch Long	A. Glen	1982	7oz.
ROCKLING, THREE BEARDED	B	1	14	4	0.857	Stonehaven	W. Murphy	1972	1¼
Gairdropsaus vulgaris	S	2	11	9	1.235	Kirkcudbright	A. Johnstone	1981	1½
SANDEEL, GREATER	B		8	0	0.227	Caliach Point	T. J. Ashwell	1984	6oz.
Hyperoplus lanceolatus	S	0	4	4	0.120	Isle of Lewis	R. McMillan	1987	3oz.
SCAD (HORSE MACKEREL)	B	1	7	0	0.652	Loch Sheil	D. MacNeil	1976	1
Trachurus trachurus	S	3	0	14	1.384	Cockenzie	R. Dillon	1981	1
SEA SCORPION, LONGSPINED	B		3	6	0.096	Rhu Narrows	C. Heath	1985	2½oz.
Taurulus bubalis	S		5	9	0.157	Aberdeen	T. J. Ashwell	1982	2½oz.
SEA SCORPION SHORTSPINED	B	2	3	0	0.992	Kepple Pier	R. Stevenson	1973	1¾
Myoxocephalus scorpius	S	2	3	0	0.992	Cloch, Gourock	W. Crawford	1979	1½
SHAD, TWAITE	B	OPEN AT ANY WEIGHT							any
Alosa fallax	S	2	12	0	1.247	Garlieston	J. W. Martin	1978	1½
SHARK, BLUE	B	85	8	0	38.781	Stornoway	J. Morrison	1972	50
Prionace glauca	S								any

B - Boat Records   S - Shore Records   Spec. - Specimen Qualifying Weight

Species		lb.	oz.	dm.	kg.	Place of Capture	Angler	Year	Spec. lb.
SHARK PORBEAGLE	B	414	0	0	188.00	Dunnet Head	R. Richardson	1992	300
Lamna nasus	B	404	0	0	183.244	Sumburgh Head	P. White	1978	300
	S	OPEN AT ANY WEIGHT							any
SKATE, COMMON	B	227	0	0	102.967	Tobermory	R. Banks	1986	100
Raja batis	S	154	0	0	69.854	Achiltibuie	M. J. Traynor	1971	50
SMELT	B	OPEN AT ANY WEIGHT							any
Osmerus Eperlanus	S		5	4	0.149	Riverside, Dundee	M. Ettle	1988	4½oz.
SMOOTHHOUND	B	OPEN AT ANY WEIGHT							any
STARRY									
Mustelus asterias	S	7	12	14	3.540	Kirkcudbright	M. Roberts	1987	5
SOLE, DOVER	B	1	12	0	0.793	Killintrinnon	W. Hannah	1974	1
Solea Solea	S	2	0	8	0.922	Balcary	W. Lees	1989	8oz.
SOLE LEMON	B	2	2	0	0.963	Lochgoilhead	J. Gordon	1976	1
Microstomus kitt	S	1	6	2	0.627	Peterhead	B. N. Davidson	1982	12oz.
SPURDOG	B	18	14	0	8.560	Tobermory	J. Bean	1988	14
Squalus acanthias	S	12	8	12	5.691	Millport	R. Paterson	1983	8
TADPOLE FISH	B		14	14	0.421	Firth of Clyde	R. Donnelly	1981	8oz.
Raniceps raninus	S	1	3	0	0.538	Dunbar	W. Dickson	1977	10oz.
TOPE	B	74	11	0	33.877	Loch Ryan	P. Marsland	1989	45
Galeorhinus galeus	S	54	4	0	24.606	Loch Ryan	D. Hastings	1975	30
TOPKNOT	B	OPEN AT ANY WEIGHT							any
Zeugopterus punctatus	S		8	8	0.241	Peterhead	G. M. Taylor	1975	6oz.
TORSK	B	15	7	2	7.006	Pentland Firth	D. J. Mackay	1982	8
Brosme brosme	S	OPEN AT ANY WEIGHT							any
TRIGGER FISH	B	OPEN AT ANY WEIGHT							any
Balistes Carolinesis	S	1	12	5	0.804	Newton Shore	J. Murphy	1989	1
TURBOT	B	25	4	0	11.453	Mull	I. Jenkins	1982	15
Scophthalmus maximus	S	2	13	12	1.300	Cairnryan	G. Calderwood	1989	1
WEAVER, GREATER	B	OPEN AT ANY WEIGHT							any
Trachinus draco	S	1	1	14	0.508	Mull of Galloway	W. Allison	1984	1
WHITING	B	6	8	0	2.948	Girvan	A. M. Devay	1969	3
Merlangius merlangus	S	3	0	0	1.360	Gourock	D. McTehee	1970	2
WHITING, BLUE (POUTASSOU)	B	1	12	0	0.793	Loch Fyne	J. H. Anderson	1977	8oz.
Micromesistius poutassou	S	OPEN AT ANY WEIGHT							any
WRASSE BALLAN	B	4	12	4	2.161	Calgary Bay, Mull	K. F. J. Hall	1983	3½
Labrus bergylta	S	5	0	0	2.268	Girvan	T. McGeehan	1971	3½
WRASSE, CORKWING	B	OPEN AT ANY WEIGHT							any
Crenilabrus melops	S		6	3	0.175	Wigton	I. Wilson	1989	4oz.
WRASSE, CUCKOO	B	3	0	0	1.361	Scrabster	Mrs H. Campbell	1969	1¼
Labrus mixtus	S	1	2	0	0.510	Neist Point, Skye	Q. A. Oliver	1972	12oz.
WRASSE	B	0	0	12	0.021	Lochaline	D. D. Morrison	1983	1oz.
GOLDSINNY	B		2	8	0.071	Lunderston Bay	J. Baillie	1990	1½oz.
Ctenolabrus rupestris	S		1	13	0.051	Loch Goil	T. Lambert	1977	1½oz.
			1	13	0.051	Mull of Galloway	G. V. R. Griffiths	1985	1½oz.
WRASSE	B	OPEN AT ANY WEIGHT							any
SMALL MOUTHED ROCK COOK									
Centrolabrus exoletus	S		2	0	0.056	Achiltibuie pier	D. F. McKendrick	1985	1½oz.
WRASSE, SCALE RAYED	B	0	10	15	0.310	Tobermory	J. T. Bishop	1986	8oz.
Acantholabrus palloni	S	OPEN AT ANY WEIGHT							any

The above records are based on information received up to 21.8.92 by the S.F.S.A. Honorary Fish Recorder, G. T. Morris, 8 Burt Avenue, Kinghorn, Fife.

SCOTTISH FRESHWATER FISH RECORDS

Bream	8lbs, 1oz (3.629kg) Castle Loch, Lochmaben D. Beattie 1990
Carp	26lbs, 2oz (11.849kg) Duddingston S. Killen 1990
Dace	1lb, 3oz, 8dr (0.553kg) River Tweed, Coldstream G. Keech 1979
Eel	5lbs, 8oz (2.495kg) Loch Ochiltree T. May 1987
Goldfish	1lb, 9oz (0.709kg) Forth & Clyde Canal B. Stevenson 1978
Grayling	2lbs, 14oz, 2dr (1.308kg) Lyne Water R. Brown 1987
Perch	4lbs, 14oz (2.210kg) Loch Ard J. Walker 1989
Pike	47lbs, 11oz (21.631kg) Loch Lomond T. Morgan 1947
Roach	2lbs, 11oz (1.219kg) Strathclyde stillwater P. Russell 1987
Tench	6lbs, 00oz, 4dr (2.729kg) Lanark Loch A. Gardner 1991

No record exists for the following species, however qualifying weights are as follows:

Barbel	1lb	**Rudd**	2 lbs
Bleak	2oz	**Ruffe**	4oz
Chub	4lbs	**S/Bream**	8oz
Gudgeon	4oz	**Zander**	1lb
Orfe	2 lbs		

How to claim a record:

1. No claims will be considered for dead fish. All fish must be returned to the water alive.
2. The claim should be made on a form available from the Development Committee who must be satisfied by the evidence that the fish was correctly identified and weighed, and was captured by fair angling.
3. New claims will be considered subject to the following minimum requirements:

   a) Photographs of the fish must be available.

   b) The scales must be certified as being accurate.

   c) Witnesses will assist the claim and if possible these should be experienced anglers.

   In the case of a fish over the British record weight please telephone either Peterborough (0733) 54084 (day) or 25248 (night) for advice.

SCOTTISH FEDERATION FOR COARSE ANGLING

The Federation was formed in 1975 to promote and encourage the sport of Coarse Angling in Scotland. It is recognised by the Scottish Sports Council as being the governing body for Coarse Angling throughout Scotland.

Objects and Functions
To obtain waters for coarse angling.
To assist with fisheries management.
To assist with stocking of waters.
To promote and develop coarse angling in Scotland.
To promote and organise competitions and league matches.
To provide team representation at the World Championships (CIPS-FIPS-ED).
To organise international events for Scottish anglers.

Members
At present, 13 clubs are affiliated to the Federation. Individual membership of the Federation is available although it is preferred that individuals join clubs affiliated to the Federation. The annual subscription for Club Membership of the SFCA is £30 with a joining fee of £15. Individual membership is offered at £3.

Coaching and Courses
Some SFCA member clubs hold 'in class' coaching sessions for novice anglers, while others operate 'on the bank' instruction thus providing knowledge under varying conditions.

Committee Structure
The affairs of the Federation are at present conducted by a Management Committee comprising the Chairman, Hon. Secretary, Hon. Treasurer and Club representatives. A development and a Match Angling Committee also exist to deal with specific projects.

Office Bearers
Chairman
Ralston McPherson,
17 Barrhill Court,
Rosebank,
Kirkintilloch G66 3PL.
Secretary
Iain Bain,
33 Gibson Street,
Edinburgh EH11 11AS.
Treasurer
Robert Crossan,
2 Quarryknowe Place,
Bellshill ML4 2AW.
National Team Manager
Alastair Keir,
'Tigh-na-Fleur',
Mill O'Gryffe Road,
Bridge of Weir.
Match Committee Secretary
Alan Pellow,
8 Brouton Gardens,
Summerston, Glasgow.

Barochan Angling Club
A.H. Keir,
'Tigh Na Fleur,
Mill O'Gryffe Road,
Bridge of Weir.

Edinburgh Coarse Anglers
Ron Woods,
23 Terregles, Penicuik.

Fife Coarse Angling Association Tony Root,
21 Winneyhill Crescent,
Inverkeithing.

Glasgow Match Angling Club Frank Revell,
93 Woodhead Crescent,
Tannochside,
Uddingston G71.

Glasgow & West of Scotland Regional Association of the Pike Anglers Club of G.B.
Ralston McPherson,
17 Barrhill Court,
Rosebank, G66 3PL.

Kirkintilloch Match Angling Club
Jim Brown,
13 Boghead Road.

Lanarkshire Colts Angling Club John Rae,
44 Ryde Road,
Wishaw ML2 7DX.

Linlithgow Coarse Angling Club
David Hood,
161 Bailielands.

Monklands Coarse Angling Club
William Sinclair,
17 Ailsa Court,
Monklands, Coatbridge.

Milton Coarse Angling Club
John Keir,
150 Ronaldsay Street,
Milton, Glasgow.

Royal Navy Coarse Angling Club

Royal Air Force (Kincaple A.C.)

Strathclyde Coarse Angling Club
J. Byers,
16 Jade Terrace, Bellshill.

Competition
Summer and Winter Club Leagues are held each year. Overall results provide the Scottish Team and Individual champions. Scottish National Junior Open Championship.

All Scotland championship - Scottish residents only.

Scottish Federation Open.

Scottish Federation Cup - Federation members only.

Home International Series.
International friendlies against other countries.

Participation in the World Championships.

Scottish Pole Angling Championship. Member clubs also arrange club match programmes throughout spring, summer and autumn.

Specimen Group
A newly formed and active element of the Federation. Objectives include: Providing an efficiently managed fishery befitting the Federation membership. Continually updating the 'Available Waters Register' for the benefits of all Scottish coarse anglers and visitors.

THE S.F.C.A. COARSE ANGLER'S COUNTRY CODE

1. Never throw away hooks, line or shot.
   Take them home and get rid of them properly.

2. Plastic bags can kill.
   Take away all rubbish from your spot,
   even if it was there before.

3. Know the fishery rules and return all coarse fish,
   including pike and eels, unharmed.

4. Help protect wildlife, plants and trees.
   Fish well away from birds' nesting places.

5. Place your keepnet to hold your fish properly.
   Stake it out if you can.

6. Use barbless hooks when you can.
   Take care when casting.

7. Park cars away from entrances.
   Keep to paths and close all gates.

8. Carbon rods conduct electricity.
   Keep well away from overhead power lines.

9. Don't light fires.
   Report any sign of pollution.

10. Keep dogs under control.
    Don't disturb the peace of the countryside.

DEFEND YOUR SPORT
JOIN THE SCOTTISH FEDERATION FOR COARSE ANGLING

A
R
G
Y
L
L

C A I T H N E S S   C L A C K M A N N A N

D U M F R I E S S H I R E

TRADES DESCRIPTION ACT

The accommodation mentioned in this holiday guide has not been inspected, and the publishers rely on information provided. The publishers have every confidence in their advertisers but cannot be held responsible for the accuracy of the descriptions published.

CRAIGDAM
Castle Douglas, Kirkcudbrightshire.

Craigdam is a family run sporting lodge with 25,000 sporting acres. All bedrooms are ensuite and there is a lovely oak panelled diningroom which offers cordon bleu cooking. Meal times are flexible and arranged around the day's sport.

The trout loch is stocked with up to 6lbs rainbows and has a wonderful view of Galloway. There is a 2 mile stretch of the River Urr and fishing can be arranged on the Nith and the Annan. A ghillie and fishing instructions are available.

Please phone Richard or Celia on 055665 233.

Galloway for your 1993 Holiday.

High-quality self-catering accommodation.
Over 190 houses throughout South West Scotland.

★ **Peaceful Country Cottages**
★ **Elegant Country Houses**
★ **Convenient Town Houses**
★ **Quiet Farm Houses**
★ **Free fishing with some houses**
SUPERB SCENERY, SANDY BEACHES,
FRIENDLY PEOPLE, FISHING AVAILABLE

For free colour brochure, contact: G.M. THOMSON & CO., 27 King Street, Castle Douglas, Kirkcudbrightshire DG7 1AB. Tel: Castle Douglas 2701/2973 (ansaphone service).

YOUR CHALET IN BONNIE GALLOWAY

Only 1 hour from the M6 at Carlisle

Luxurious self-catering log houses in outstandingly beautiful countryside. So many amenities near your holiday home. **Private fishing**, golf courses, a riding school and pony-trekking. The Granary Restaurant serves dinner in the evening, while the 2 bars serve food all day. Nearby (within walking distance) is Sandyhills beach. There are many places locally of historical interest to visit, too. Dogs welcome. Colour T.V. centrally-heated, continental quilt and all linen provided.

★ "Indoor heated swimming pool". Sauna. Sunbed.

For Details Barend Properties Ltd. Barend 25, Sandyhills, Dalbeattie, Kirkcudbrightshire. Telephone Southwick (0387 78) 663/648

TO ASSIST WITH YOUR BOOKINGS OR ENQUIRIES YOU WILL FIND IT HELPFUL TO MENTION THIS
Pastime Publications Guide

**K
I
R
K
C
U
D
B
R
I
G
H
T
S
H
I
R
E**

58

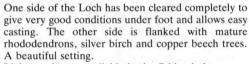
**P
E
R
T
H
S
H
I
R
E**

P E R T H S H I R E

Buccleuch Arms Hotel, St. Boswells
Tel: (0835) 22243.
Fax: (0835) 23965.

In the Heart of the Scottish Borders offering the discerning sportsman excellent shooting on many of the top local estates ranging from driven grouse to small walked up days.

Fishing available on the Tweed for salmon or trout. Golfing packages can also be arranged. The Buccleuch Arms Hotel is within 30 minutes of ten local courses, nine and eighteen holes.

All accommodation is of a high standard and all with en suite facilities.

***For further information
please contact Bill Dodds***

Tackle, Tack & Clothing

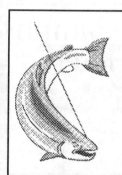

**46 Henderson St.,
Bridge of Allan FK9 4HS
Tel: 0786 834495**

Stockists of Quality Tackle & Country Clothing.

Permits available for Rivers Tay, Earn, Forth, Teith and Allan

★ OPEN 7 DAYS ★

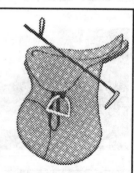

Cast a fly on Carron Reservoir

Central Regional Council's premier brown trout fishery. Free-rising wild brown trout for classic `loch-style' fly fishing.

Office hours:
Monday to Friday 9am-5pm
Bookings:
Director of Finance
Viewforth, Stirling
Tel: (0786) 442000
Central Regional Council

Central Regional Council
Serving the Heart of Scotland

DUNROAMIN HOTEL

The Dunroamin Hotel can arrange fishing packages i.e. permits for the Kyle of Sutherland.

There are 3 trout lochs nearby with boats available. Other interests include golf, superb beaches and historic places of interest to visit in the area.

Meals are available all day from a la carte to bar suppers. All rooms have H. & C., colour TV and tea/coffee making facilities.

For further details contact:
**Dunroamin Hotel,
Bonar Bridge IV24 3EA.
Tel: (08632) 236.**

**Kylesku, Sutherland.
Tel: (0971) 2231**

To the visiting angler, the Highlands offer a variety of sport almost unsurpassed elsewhere in Scotland. Sea angling off the tidal race points provides a wide variety of fish. Pollack Saithe, Mackerel, Caddies etc. For game fishing the hotel offers numerous lochs with the very best of Brown Trout fishing and Salmon and Sea Trout by arrangement. After a hard day's fishing, the hotel's bar and the restaurant have food and wine to match any in the Highlands.

SUTHERLAND

FORSINARD HOTEL

All inclusive Trout fishing package holidays:
4 nights, 3 days fishing - £208.00 per person; 7 nights, 6 days fishing - £358.00 per person.
Based on B. & B. in shared double room or single (all en suite) with packed lunch and dinner.
No hidden extras. Boats/ghillies provided. Wild brown trout fishing on hotel lochs.

Salmon Fishing on the River Halladale & Strathy - 3 beats (2 rods per beat) from 1st Feb - 30th Sept.

For brochure and details contact:
**Forsinard Hotel, Forsinard KW13 6YT.
Tel: Halladale (064 17) 221.**

S U T H E R L A N D

DRUMLAMFORD ESTATE
SOUTH AYRSHIRE-WIGTOWNSHIRE

River Cree, 1 mile, salmon and trout
Loch Drumlamford ⎫ – Stocked trout at £10 per day.
Loch Nahinie ⎭ – Fly fishing only
Loch Dornal – Stocked trout and coarse spinning allowed at £10 per day.
Loch Maberry – Coarse at £3 per day.

Boats at £5 per day. Permits apply Keeper, Barrhill (046 582) 256.

**SELF CATERING HOLIDAY COTTAGES also available
apply Mrs. Beale, Barrhill (046 582) 220**

Bait
Supply

PALAKONA
GUEST HOUSE & CRAICHLAW FISHERIES

Permits
Sold

3 Coarse waters carp, tench, roach, bream etc. River venue for pike, perch and salmon. Brown trout pool exclusive to guests. Specialists in angling accommodation.

Ring Ken or Jacqui for details:

Palakona Guest House, Queen Street, Newton Stewart DG8 6JL. Tel: (0671) 2323.

CORSEMALZIE HOUSE HOTEL
AA/RAC ★★★ S.T.B. 4 Crowns Commended

Come and relax in the beautiful Galloway countryside. We have 10 miles of salmon/trout fishing on the Rivers Bladnoch and Tarff for exclusive use by our guests. Good Spring and Autumn salmon runs. Trout and coarse fishing also available. Stay in our secluded country house and enjoy good food, wines and every comfort. Good rough shooting also available. Golfing arranged on two local courses.

Write or phone for brochure.

Port William, Newton Stewart DG8 9RL. Tel: Mochrum (098 886) 254.

Egon Ronay Recommended

Ask your bookshop
for
**Pastime Publications
other Holiday Guides
Scotland Home of Golf
Scotland for Motorist**

WIGTOWNSHIRE

TRADES DESCRIPTION ACT

The accommodation mentioned in this holiday guide has not been inspected, and the publishers rely on information provided. The publishers have every confidence in their advertisers but cannot be held responsible for the accuracy of the descriptions published.

WARNING

Carbon fibre fishing rods must be kept well clear of overhead cables.

Otherwise serious injuries may be caused

BORDERS

Area Tourist Board
Scottish Borders Tourist Board

Director of Tourism
Scottish Borders Tourist Board
Municipal Buildings
High Street
Selkirk TD7 4JX.
Tel: Selkirk (0750) 20555

RIVER PURIFICATION BOARD
TWEED RIVER PURIFICATION BOARD
Burnbrae
Mossilee Road
Galashiels.
Tel: (0896) 2425

RIVERS

Water	Location	Species	Season	Permit available from	Other Information
Blackadder	Greenlaw	Brown Trout	1 Apr. to 6 Oct.	Greenlaw Angling Club J. Purves, 9 Wester Row, Greenlaw. All hotels.	No bait fishing till 15 Apr. Sunday fishing. No spinning. No Sunday competitions.
Bowmont Water	Morebattle	Trout Grayling	15 Mar. to 6 Oct.	D.Y. Gray, 17 Mainsfield Avenue, Morebattle.	No ground baiting, No Sunday fishing from Primeside Mill up.
Eden Water	Kelso	Brown Trout	1 Apr. to 30 Sept.	Forrest & Sons, 35 The Square, Kelso. Tel: (0573) 224687. Intersport, 43 The Square, Kelso. Tel: (0573) 223381. Border Hotel, Woodmarket, Kelso TD5 7AX. Tel: (0573) 224791.	Fly only. No spinning. Restricted to 3 rods.
	Gordon	Brown Trout	15 Mar. to 6 Oct.	J.H. Fairgrieve, Burnbrae, Gordon. Tel: (057 381) 357.	No Spinning. No Sunday fishing.
Ettrick & Yarrow	Bowhill	Salmon Trout	1 Feb.-30 Nov. 15 Mar. -30 Sep.	Buccleuch Estates Ltd., Estate Office, Bowhill, Selkirk. Tel: (0750) 20753.	Fly only.
	Selkirk	Brown Trout	1 Apr. to 30 Sept.	P. & E. Scott (Newsagents), 6 High Street, Selkirk. Tel: (0750) 20749.	Night fishing 15 May-14 Sept. Week ticket only. No minnows or spinning. No Sundays.
Ettrick	Ettrick Bridge	Brown Trout Salmon	1 Apr.-30 Sep. 1 Feb.-30 Nov.	Ettrickshaws Hotel, Tel: (0750) 52229.	Packed Lunches and flask for residents. Permits also available for other waters.
Kale Water	Eckford	Trout Grayling	1 Apr. to 30 Sept.	Mr. Graham, Eckford Cottage, Eckford, Kelso. Tel: (083-55) 255.Grayling	No Sundays.
	Morebattle	Trout	15 Mar. to 6 Oct.	D.Y. Gray, 17 Mainsfield Avenue, Morebattle. Templehall Hotel, Morebattle. Tel: (05734) 249.	No ground baiting. No Sunday fishing.

Water	Location	Species	Season	Permit available from	Other Information
Leader Water	Lauderdale	Trout	15 Mar. to 6 Oct.	R. & A. Dickson Newsagent, Lauder. J.S. Main, Saddler, 87 High Street, Haddington. Tel: (062 082) 2148. Lauder Post Office. Tower Hotel, Oxton, By Lauder. Tel: (05785) 235. Anglers Choice, 23 Market Square, Melrose TD6 9PL. Tel: (089 682) 3070.	No Spinning. Sunday fishing. No Grayling fishing.
Leader Water/ Tweed	Earlston	Trout	15 Mar. to 30 Sept.	Earlston Angling Association P. Hessett, 2 Arnot Place, Earlston. Tel: 577. E. & M. Browne, Newsagent, Earlston. L. & M. Pollard Newsagents, The Square, Earlston. Tel: (0896) 84330. Anglers Choice, 23 Market Square, Melrose. Tel: (089 682) 3070. Hotels & pubs.	No Sunday fishing. Other restrictions as per permit.
Liddle Water	Newcastleton	Sea Trout	1 May to 30 Sept.	J.D. Ewart, Fishing Tackle Shop, Newcastleton. Tel: (03873) 75257.	Day & weekly tickets available.
	South Roxburgh shire	Salmon Sea Trout Herling Brown Trout	1 Feb.-31 Oct. 1 May to 30 Sept. 15 Apr. to 30 Sept.	Esk & Liddle Fisheries Assoc. per R.J.B. Hill, Secretary, Bank of Scotland Buildings, Langholm. Tel: (03873) 80428. George Graham, Hagg-on-Esk, Old School, Canonbie. Tel: (03873) 71416. Peter Lillie, 19 Rowanburn, Canonbie. Tel: (03873) 71224.	Spinning allowed until 14 Apr. and otherwise only when water is above markers at Newcastleton, Kershopefoot and Penton Bridges. No Sunday ishing.
Lyne Water	Tweed Junction to Flemington Bridge	Trout Grayling	1 Apr. to 30 Sept.	Peeblesshire Trout Fishing Association D.G. Fyfe, 39 High Street, Peebles. Tel: (0721) 720131. Tweeddale Tackle Centre, 1 Bridgegate, Peebles EH45 8RZ. Tel: (0721) 720979. Sonny's Sports Shop, Innerleithen. Tel: (0896) 830806. Tweed Valley Hotel, Walkerburn. Tel: (089 687) 636. J. Dickson & Son, 21 Frederick Street, Edinburgh. Tel: 031-225 4218. Crook Inn, Tweedsmuir. Tel: (089 97) 272.	No Sundays. No spinning. No bait fishing April & Sept. Tickets also cover Tweed.
Oxnam Water	Morebattle	Trout Grayling	15 Mar. to 6 Oct.	D.Y. Gray, 17 Mainsfield Avenue, Morebattle.	No ground baiting, no Sunday fishing from Bloodylaws up.

Water	Location	Species	Season	Permit available from	Other Information
Teviot	Kelso	Brown Trout Grayling	1 Apr. to 30 Sept.	Forrest & Sons, 35, The Square, Kelso. Tel: (0573) 224687. Intersport, 43, The Square, Kelso. Tel: (0573) 223381. Border Hotel, Woodmarket, Kelso TD5 7AX. Tel: (0573) 224791.	No Sundays. Restrictions on spinning. No maggots or ground bait. Size limit 10".
	Eckford	Salmon Sea Trout Brown Trout	1 Feb.-30 Nov. 15 Mar. to 30 Sep.	Mr. Graham Eckford Cottage, Eckford, Kelso. Tel: (083-55) 255.	No Sundays. Limited to 4 day permits. Bait and spinning 15 Feb.-15 Sept., only. Spinning for Trout and Grayling prohibited.
	Jedforest	Salmon	1 Feb. to 31 Nov.	Jedforest Angling Association J.T. Renilson, 4 Canongate, Jedburgh.	No Sundays. Salmon: 4 rods per day. Spinning 15 Feb.-14 Sept. Fly only 15 Sept.-30 Nov.
		Trout	1 Apr. to 30 Sept.	Shaws (Newsagent), 10 Canongate, Jedburgh.	No Sundays, No spinning. Fly only until 1st May.
Teviot (and Ale Slitrig Borthwick Rule)	Hawick	Brown Trout	15 Mar. to 30 Sept.	Porteous & Newcombe, Howgate, Hawick. The Pet Store, 1 Union Street, Hawick. Tel: (0450) 73543.	All rules and regulations on ticket.
		Salmon	1 Feb. to 30 Nov.	The Pet Store, Union Street, Hawick. Tel: (0450) 73543.	
		Grayling	1 Jan. to 30 Sept.	The Pet Store, 1 Union Street, Hawick. Tel: (0450) 73543.	
Teviot	Above Chesters	Salmon Sea Trout	1 Feb. to 30 Nov.	The Pet Store, Union Street, Hawick. Tel: (0450) 73543.	All rules and regulations on ticket. Limited to 9 rods on 3 beats per day. (9 day tickets Mon-Fri. 6 visitor season tickets only on application to:) Mr. R.A. Sutherland, Hawick Angling Club, 20 Longhope Drive, Hawick TD9 0DU. Tel: 0450 75150.
Tweed	Tweedsmuir	Brown Trout Grayling	1 Apr. to 30 Sept.	Crook Inn, Tweedsmuir. Tel: (08997) 272.	All rules and regulations on permits.
	Peeblesshire (substantial stretch of river)	Trout Grayling	1 Apr. to 30 Sept.	Tweed Valley Hotel, Walkerburn. Tel: (089 687) 636. F. & D. Simpson, 28/29 West Preston Street, Edinburgh EH8 9PZ. Tel: 031-667 3058. J. Dickson & Son, 21 Frederick Street, Edinburgh. Tel: 031-225 4218.	No spinning. No bait fishing, Apr. & Sept. No Sunday fishing. Tickets also cover Lyne Water. Waders desirable. Fly only on Tweed from Lynefoot upstream.

Water	Location	Species	Season	Permit available from	Other Information
Tweed cont.	Peebles (Wire Bridge Pool to Nutwood Pool - excluding Kailzie)	Salmon	21 Feb. to 30 Nov.	Peeblesshire Salmon Fishing Association Seasons: Blackwood & Smith, W.S., 39 High Street, Peebles. Tel: (0721) 720131. Day permits: Tweeddale Tackle Centre, 1 Bridgegate, Peebles EH45 8RZ. Tel: (0721) 720979.	Strictly fly fishing only. No Sunday fishing. Other regulations on tickets.
	Walkerburn	Salmon/ Sea Trout Trout	1 Feb.to 30 Nov. 1 Apr.-30 Sep.	Tweed Valley Hotel, Walkerburn. Tel: (089 687) 636.	Salmon tickets for hotel guests only after 14 Sept. Special salmon and trout weeks, tuition. Trout and grayling permits available to all.
	Peel	Salmon Sea Trout	1 Feb. to 30 Nov.	Tweed Valley Hotel, Walkerburn. Tel: (089 687) 636.	Private 2-rod salmon beat on south bank. Week or day lets Spring/Summer. Week lets only October and November. Angling Course September.
	Nest	Salmon Sea Trout Trout	1 Feb.to 30 Nov. 1 Apr.-30 Sep.	Tweed Valley Hotel, Walkerburn. Tel: (089 687) 636.	Private salmon/sea trout beat approx. $1^3/_4$ miles. 4 rods. Fly only 15 Sept. to 30 Nov. Trout and grayling permits available to all. Week or day lets Spring/ Summer. Week lets only October and November. Angling Course September.
	Haystoun (Beat $1^1/_2$ miles)	Salmon Sea Trout	1 Feb. to 30 Nov.	Fraser's Salmon Fishing & Hire Ltd., 16 Kingsmuir Crescent, Peebles. Tel: (0721) 22960.	No spinning in autumn - fly only. No Sunday fishing. Rods limited to 6 per day. Part-time ghillie included in permit price. 8 named salmon pools.
	Kingsmeadow (Beat $3/_4$ mile)	Salmon Sea Trout	15 Feb. to 30 Nov.	Fraser's Salmon Fishing & Hire Ltd., 16 Kingsmuir Crescent, Peebles. Tel: (0721) 22960.	Spinning allowed 15 Feb to 14 Sept. Rods limited to 3 per day. Easy car access to beat. Part-time ghillie included in permit price. 5 named salmon pools.
	Glenormiston (Beat $1^1/_2$ miles)	Salmon Sea Trout	15 Feb. to 30 Nov.	Fraser's Salmon Fishing & Hire Ltd., 16 Kingsmuir Crescent, Peebles. Tel: (0721) 22960.	Fly only. Rods limited to 7 per day. Easy car access to beat.
	Galashiels	Trout	1 Apr. to 30 Sept.	Messrs. J. & A. Turnbull, 30 Bank Street, Galashiels. Tel: (0896) 3191. Kingsknowes Hotel, Galashiels. Tel: (0896) 58375. Anglers Choice, 23 Market Square, Melrose TD6 9PL. Tel: (0896) 823070.	No Sundays. Day tickets available on Saturdays. No spinning.
	Melrose	Trout Grayling	1 Apr.to 6 Oct. 7 Oct.to 15 Mar.	Melrose & District Angling Association Anglers Choice, 23 Market Square, Melrose. Tel: (0896) 823070.	No spinning. No ground baiting. No Sundays. Minnow fishing not permitted. Spinning reels of all types prohibited.

Water	Location	Species	Season	Permit available from	Other Information
Tweed cont.	Melrose (Ravenswood Tweedswood)	Brown Trout	1 Apr. to 30 Sept.	Anglers Choice, 23 Market Square, Melrose. Tel: (0896) 823070.	
	Melrose (Pavilion)	Salmon Sea Trout	1 Feb. to 30 Nov.	Anglers Choice, 23 Market Square, Melrose. Tel: 3070.	Fly only - 1 to 15 Feb. and 15 Sept. to 30 Nov. Feb. 16 to Sept. 14 fly and spinning.
	St. Boswells	Brown Trout Trout	1 Apr. to 30 Sept.	Dryburgh Abbey Hotel, St. Boswells. Tel: (0835) 22261. Anglers Choice, 23 Market Square, Melrose. Miss A. Laing, Newsagent, St. Boswells.	Fly only 1 Apr. to 1 May. No ground baiting. No bait fishing until May 1. No Sundays. No spinning tackle. No coarse fishing allowed outside season. Access to restricted beats by special permits only. Full details shown on permit.
Tweed (and Teviot)	Kelso Grayling		1 May-31 Aug. 1 Dec.-31 Jan.	Forrest & Sons, 35, The Square, Kelso. Tel: (0573) 224687. Intersport, 43, The Square, Kelso. Tel: (0573) 223381. Border Hotel, Woodmarket, Kelso. Tel: (0573) 224791.incl. Tweedside Tackle, 36-38 Bridge Street, Kelso. Tel: (0573) 225306.	Spinning restrictions. No maggots or ground bait. No fishing above Roxburgh Viaduct between 15 & 30 Sept. incl. Day/week/season. Tweedside Tackle have a computerised salmon letting facility on various beats on the Tweed.
	Kelso	Brown Trout Coarse Fish	1 Apr. to 30 Sept.	Forrest & Sons, 35, The Square, Kelso. Tel: (0573) 224687.	
Tweed	Cornhill	Salmon Sea Trout Brown Trout	1 Feb. to 30 Nov.	Tillmouth Park Hotel, Cornhill-on-Tweed, Northumberland TD12 4UU. Tel: (0890) 2255.	No Sundays. No worming. Boats and ghillies available. Special terms for residents.
	Ladykirk	Brown Trout	19 Mar. to 8 Oct.	Victoria Hotel, Norham, Tel: (0289) 82237.	No spinning. No ground baiting. Fly only above Norham Bridge to West Ford. No Sundays.
	Horncliffe (Tidal)	Trout, Grayling, Roach, Dace and Eel.		No permit required.	
Whiteadder & Dye & Tributaries	30 miles	Brown/ Rainbow Trout	15 Mar. to 30 Sept.	Whiteadder Angling Association Mr. Cowan, Crumstane, Duns. (Bailiff). Tel: (0361) 83235.	No Sundays. Fly only before 15 Apr. Worm from 15 Apr. only. Minnow from 1 May only. Tickets in advance. Size limit 8 inches. River stocked annually.
Whiteadder	Allanton	Trout	15 Mar to 30 Sept.	Berwick & District Angling Association. Mr. D. Cowan, 3 Church Street, Berwick. Tel: (0289) 330145.	Fly only before May. No spinning. No threadline. No maggot fishing. No ground baiting. 9 inch min. Max bag of 12 brown trout per day. No Sundays.

Water	Location	Species	Season	Permit available from	Other Information
LOCHS AND RESERVOIRS					
Acreknowe Reservoir	Hawick	Brown/ Rainbow Trout	15 Mar. to end Sept.	Porteous & Newcome, Howgate, Hawick. The Pet Shop, 1 Union Street, Hawick. Tel: (0450) 73543. Mr. R.A. Sutherland, 20 Longhope Drive, Hawick. Tel: (0450) 75150.	Ticket covers all other trout waters managed by Hawick Angling Club. Boat available from the Pet Shop. Fly fishing only.
Alemoor Loch	Hawick	Brown Trout Perch Pike		As Acreknowe	Bank fishing only.
Fruid Reservoir	Tweedsmuir	Brown Trout	1 Apr. to 30 Sept.	Waterkeeper, Victoria Lodge, Talla Reservoir. Tel: (08997) 2098 (8am to 8pm).	Fly fishing. Spinning and worm fishing. Sunday fishing. 2 boats and bank fishing.
Hellmoor Loch	Hawick	Brown Trout		As Acreknowe	No Boat. No competitions. Limit 6 trout.
Loch Lindean	Selkirk	Brown Trout	Apr. to Oct.	P. & E. Scott (Newsagent), 6 High Street, Selkirk TD7 4DA. Tel: (0750) 20749.	2 boats available.
Loch of the Lowes and St. Mary's Loch	Selkirk	Brown Trout	1 Apr. to 30 Sept.	St. Mary's A.C. per Sec. J. Miller, 25 Abbotsford Court, Colinton Road, Edinburgh. Gordon Arms Hotel, Yarrow. Mikes Tackle Shop, 48 Portobello High Street, Edinburgh. Countrylife, 229 Balgreen Road, Edinburgh. F. & D. Simpson, 28 West Preston Street, Edinburgh. Hook, Line & Sinker, 20 Morningside Road, Edinburgh.	Fly fishing only, until 30th April thereafter spinning and bait allowed.
		Pike Perch Eels	1 May to 30 Sept.	Bank Permits Tibbie Shiels Inn, St. Mary's Loch, Yarrow, Selkirk. Tel: (0750) 42231. Anglers Choice, 23 Market Square, Melrose. Rodono Hotel (Loch side).	Club fishing apply secretary or keeper. Sunday fishing. Weekly permits & rowing boats from keeper, Mr. Brown (0750) 42243. No float fishing. Loch of the Lowes is bank fishing only. River Tweed Protection Order applies. Club memberships available.
Megget Reservoir	Megget Valley	Trout	1 Apr. to 30 Sept.	Tibbie Shiels Inn, St. Mary's Loch, Yarrow, Selkirk. Tel: (0750) 42231	No bait fishing. 6 boats available. Max. bag limit 10 fish.
Peeblesshire Lochs	Tweed Valley	Brown/ Rainbow Trout	Apr. to Oct.	Tweed Valley Hotel, Walkerburn. Tel: (089 687) 636.	Stocked private lochans. Wild brown trout loch.
Portmore Game Fisheries	Peebles- Eddleston	Wild Brown Trout Rainbow Trout	1 Apr. to 31 Oct.	Portmore Game Fisheries at the Loch. Tel: (0968) 675684.	Average weight of fish caught: 2lbs. Popular flies: Lures at beginning; from May - dry & wet. Boats are available - contact: Steve McGeachie at above number.

74

Water	Location	Species	Season	Permit available from	Other Information
Synton Loch	Hawick	Brown Trout		As Acreknowe Reservoir.	Boats available From Pet Store, 1 Union Street, Hawick. Fly only.
Talla Reservoir	Tweedsmuir	Brown Trout	1 Apr. to 30 Sept.	Waterkeeper, Victoria Lodge, Talla Reservoir. Tel: (08997) 2098 (8am to 8pm).	Fly fishing only.
Upper Loch	Bowhill	Brown/ Rainbow Trout	1 Apr. to 28 Sept.	Buccleuch Estate Ltd., Estate Office, Bowhill, Selkirk. Tel: (0750) 20753.	Fly only. 2 rods per boat and limit of 8 fish per boat. Boat available on: Tues & Thurs all season; Mondays during June, July & Aug.
Watch Reservoir	Longformacus	Brown Trout Rainbow Trout	15 Mar.-30 Sept. All year	W.F. Renton, The Watch Fly Reservoir, Tel: (03617) 331 & (0289) 306028.	Sunday fishing. Fly only. Strictly no use of bait/maggots etc.
Whiteadder Reservoir	nr. Gifford	Brown Trout	1 Apr to 30 Sept.	Waterkeeper, Hungry Snout, Whiteadder Reservoir. Tel: (03617) 362 (8am to 8pm).	Bank fishing 1 June to 30 Sept. Sunday fishing. Fly fishing only. 4 boats are available.
Williestruther Loch	Hawick	Brown/ Rainbow Trout		As Acreknowe Reservoir.	Any legal method.
Wooden Loch	Eckford	Rainbow Trout	1 Apr.-31 Oct.	Mr. Graham Eckford Cottage, Eckford, Kelso. Tel: (083-55) 255.	1 boat. No bank fishing. Only rainbow trout after 30 Sept. Only 2 rods at any time. Advance booking necessary. No Sundays.

BORDERS
Sea Angling

The Scottish Borders provide some of the best sea angling in the UK. Based on Eyemouth, which has the largest fishing fleet in the South of Scotland, and the smaller fishing villages of Burnmouth and St. Abbs, the clear unpolluted waters are well stocked with a wide variety of sea fish. So clear is the water that one of the first Marine Reservations has been established off Eyemouth.

The rugged coastline with its unique fauna make a spectacular background to your day's fishing. It should be noted that sea angling is not permitted off St. Abbs Head National Reserve (Petticowick – Long Carr).

Eyemouth is only nine miles north of Berwick-upon-Tweed, just off the A.1. Its colourful boats, fish auction and sandy beach make it a popular resort during the summer. Well known for its excellent rock fishing, the town is also a useful point of access to shoreline to the north and south. Boat fishing has developed over the years due to the efforts of Eyemouth Sea Angling Club who now run a number of shore and boat competitions throughout the season.

The club operates the coast from Burnmouth harbour in the south to the harbour at St. Abbs in the north.

Types of fish: Shore – cod, mackerel, coalfish, flounder, plaice, sole, haddock, whiting, catfish, ling and wrasse. Boat – the same species can be caught as on shore but larger specimens.

Boats: A large number of fishing boats are usually available from Eyemouth, St. Abbs and Burnmouth for parties of anglers at weekends.

DUMFRIES AND GALLOWAY RIVERS AND LOCHS

Area Tourist Board
Dumfries and Galloway Tourist Board

Director of Tourism
Dumfries and Galloway Tourist Board
Douglas House,
Newton Stewart,
Wigtownshire DG8 6DQ.
Tel: Newton Stewart (0671) 2549

RIVER PURIFICATION BOARD
SOLWAY RIVER PURIFICATION BOARD
River's House, Irongray Road,
Dumfries DG2 0JE.
Tel: (0387) 720502.

RIVERS

Water	Location	Species	Season	Permit available from	Other Information
Annan	Hoddom & Kinmount Estates Ecclefechan	Salmon Sea Trout Brown Trout	25 Feb. to 15 Nov.	Miss Marsh, 1 Bridge End Cottage, Hoddom, Lockerbie DG11 1BE. Tel: (05763) 488.	No Sunday fishing. Fly water unless the spinning mark is covered.
	Halleaths Estate Lockerbie	Salmon Sea Trout	25 Feb. to 15 Nov.	Messrs. McJerrow & Stevenson, Solicitors, 55 High Street, Lockerbie, Dumfriesshire. Tel: (05762) 2123.	Limited number of tickets.
	Royal Four Towns Water Lockerbie	Sea Trout Brown Trout Herling Chub Grilse	25 Feb. to 15 Nov.	Clerk to the Commissioners, of Royal Four Towns Fishing Mrs. K. Ratcliffe, Clerk, 'Jay-Ar', Preston House Road, Hightae, Lockerbie. Tel: 0387 810220. Castle Milk Estates Office, Norwood, Lockerbie. Tel: 057 65 203.	Boats prohibited. No shrimps, prawns or maggots. No Sunday fishing.
	St. Mungo Parish	Salmon Sea Trout Brown Trout	15 Mar. to 6 Oct. 25 Feb. to 15 Nov.	Castle Milk Estates Office, Norwood, Lockerbie. Tel: 057 65 203.	Fly fishing only. No Sunday fishing.
	Warmanbie Estate	Salmon Sea Trout Brown Trout	25 Feb. to 15 Nov.	Warmanbie Hotel & Restaurant, Annan DG12 5LL. Tel: (0461) 204015.	Fly, spinning, worm all season. Access to many other stretches.
Bladnoch	Newton Stewart	Salmon	1 Mar. to 31 Oct.	Newton Stewart Angling Association Galloway Guns & Tackle, 36 Arthur Street, Newton Stewart. Tel: (0671) 3404. Palakona Guest House, Queen Street, Newton Stewart DG8 6JL. Tel: (0671) 2323.	
Cairn	Dumfries	Brown Trout Salmon Sea Trout	15 Mar.-31 Aug.	Dumfries & Galloway Angling Association, Secretary: D. Byers, 4 Bloomfield Edinburgh Road, Dumfries DG1 1SG. Tel: (0387) 53850.	Limited number of permits. No Sunday fishing. Restrictions depend on water level. Visitors Mon.-Fri. only.
Cree (and Pencill Burn)	Drumlamford Estate	Salmon Trout	April to October	The Keeper, The Kennels, Drumlamford Estate, Barrhill. Tel: (046 582) 256.	No Sunday fishing.

Water	Location	Species	Season	Permit available from	Other Information
	Newton Stewart	Salmon Sea Trout	1 Mar. to 14 Oct.	Newton Stewart Angling Association Galloway Guns & Tackle, 36 Arthur Street, Newton Stewart. Tel: (0671) 3404.	No Sunday fishing.
		Pike Perch	No close season	Palakona Guest House, Queen Street, Newton Stewart DG8 6JL. Tel: (0671) 2323.	No live bait.
Cross Waters of Luce	New Luce	Salmon Sea Trout	1 May to 31 Oct.	Stranraer & District Angling Association. The Sports Shop, 90 George Street, Stranraer. Tel: (0776) 2705.	No Sunday fishing. Live lobworm, branderings & magggots; fresh water baits. Day permits available for Piltanton Burn from Dunragit Angling Club.
Dee	Aboyne	Salmon Sea Trout	1 Feb. to 30 Sep.	Brooks House, Glen Tanar, Aboyne. Tel: (03398) 86451.	No Sunday fishing on Dee. Permits available for August only on Waterside & Ferrar Beats.
Black Water of Dee	Mossdale	Salmon.	11 Feb. to 31 Oct.	Local Hotels & Shops.	
		Trout Pike Perch	15 Mar. to 30 Sept.		
Esk	East Dumfriesshire	Salmon Sea Trout/ Herling Brown Trout	1 Feb.to 31 Oct. 1 May to 30 Sept. 15 Apr. to 30 Sept.	Esk & Liddle Fisheries Association per R.J.B. Hill, Secretary, Bank of Scotland Buildings, Langholm. Tel: (03873) 80428. George Graham, Hagg-on-Esk, Old School, Canonbie. Tel: (03873) 71416. Mrs. Pauline Wylie, Byreburnfoot, Canonbie. Tel: (03873) 71279.	Spinning allowed until 14 April and otherwise only when water is above markers at Skippers Bridge, Canonbie Bridge & Willow Pool. No Sunday fishing.
Kelhead Quarry	Dalry	Brown Trout	1 Apr. to 30 Sept.	Ken Bridge Hotel, New Galloway. Tel: (064-42) 211.	No Sunday fishing on Dalry A.A. waters. Fly only to 1 June.
Ken	New Galloway	Salmon Brown/ Rainbow Trout Perch Pike Roach	15 Mar. to 30 Sept.	Mr. Swain, Kenmure Arms Hotel, High Street, New Galloway. Tel: (06442) 240 or 360.	Boats available from hotel.
Liddle	Newcastleton Ticket	Salmon Sea Trout Brown Trout	15 Apr.-31 Oct. 1 May-30 Sept. 15 Apr.-30 Sept.	Secretary and J.D. Ewart, Tackle Agent, Newcastleton. Tel: (03873) 75257.	Spinning allowed when water is above markers at Newcastleton and Kershopelfoot Bridges. No Sunday fishing. Day tickets available.
Milk	Scroggs Bridge	Sea Trout Brown Trout	1 Apr. to 30 Sept.	Mr. Anthony Steel, Kirkwood, Lockerbie. Tel: (057 65) 212/200.	Fly fishing only. No Sunday fishing.
Minnoch	Newton Stewart	Salmon	1 Mar. to 30 Sept.	Galloway Guns & Tackle, 36 Arthur Street, Newton Stewart. Tel: (0671) 3404.	

Water	Location	Species	Season	Permit available from	Other Information
Nith	Dumfries	Salmon Sea Trout Brown Trout	25 Feb. to 30 Nov. 15 Mar. to 6 Oct.	Director of Finance, Nithsdale District Council, Municipal Chambers, Dumfries. Tel: (0387) 53166, ext. 230. Dumfries & Galloway Angling Association Secretary, D. Byers, 4 Bloomfield Edinburgh Road, Dumfries DG1 1SG. Tel: (0387) 53850	No Sunday fishing. Visitors fishing Mon. to Fri. only. Advance booking. Limited number of permits. Weekly permits from Mon.-Fri. Advance booking possible. Spinning restrictions.
	Thornhill	Salmon Sea Trout Brown Trout Grayling	25 Feb. to 30 Nov. 1 Apr. to 31 Sept. No close season	Drumlanrig Castle Fishings, The Buccleuch Estates Ltd., Drumlanrig Mains, Thornhill DG3 4AG. Tel: (08486) 283.	Lower, Middle & Upper beats. Average weight of fish caught: Salmon - 9lbs 8oz, Grilse - 6lbs, Sea Trout - 2lbs, Brown Trout - 8oz, Grayling 8oz. Popular flies: Stoats Tail, General Practitioner, Silver Doctor, Flying C, Silver Toby. Spinning. Worming (until 31 Aug, in Yellow Spate) Boats available. Weekly and daily lets up to 3 rods/beat.
		Salmon Sea Trout Brown Trout Grayling	25 Feb. to 30 Nov. 1 Apr. to 31 Sept. No close season	Drumlanrig Castle Fishings, The Buccleuch Estates Ltd., Drumlanrig Mains, Thornhill DG3 4AG. Tel: (08486) 283.	Nith Linns Average weight of fish caught: Salmon - 9lbs 8oz, Grilse - 6lbs, Sea Trout - 2lbs, Brown Trout - 8oz, Grayling 8oz. Popular flies: Stoats Tail, General Practitioner, Silver Doctor, Flying C, Silver Toby. Spinning. Worming (until 31 Aug, in Yellow Spate) Weekly and daily lets up to 4 rods/beat. *
		Salmon Sea Trout Brown Trout	25 Feb.-30 Nov. 1 Apr. to 30 Sept.	Mid Nithsdale Angling Assoc., Secretary, Mr. I.R. Milligan, 37 Drumlanrig Street, Thornhill DG3 5LS. Tel: (0848) 30555.	No day permits on Saturdays. Spinning & worming allowed, only in flood conditions. Advisable to book for autumn fishing.
Nith (and Tributaries Kello Crawick Euchan Mennock)	Sanquhar	Salmon Sea Trout Brown Trout Grayling	15 Mar. to 30 Nov. Jan., Feb.	Upper Nithsdale Angling Club. Pollock & McLean, Solicitors, 61 High Street, Sanquhar. Tel: (0659) 50241.	No Saturday/Sunday fishing. Visitors and residents. Day tickets - limit of 20 per day during months: Sept., Oct. & Nov. Week tickets - limit of 10 per week during season.
Tarf	Kirkcowan	Sea Trout Brown Trout	Easter - 30 Sept.	A. Brown, Three Lochs Caravan Park, Kirkcowan, Newton Stewart, Wigtownshire. Tel: (067183) 304.	
Upper Tarf	Nr. Newton Stewart	Salmon Trout	1 Mar.-14 Oct. 15 Mar.-6 Oct.	Palakona Guest House, Queen Street, Newton Stewart DG8 6JL. Tel: (0670) 2323.	Fly, spin or worm.
Urr	Castle Douglas	Salmon Sea Trout Brown Trout	25 Feb. to 30 Nov. 15 Mar. to 6 Oct.	Castle Douglas and District Angling Association Tommy's Sport Shop, King Street, Castle Douglas. Tel: (0556) 2851. Dalbeattie Angling Association Ticket Sec., M. McCowan & Son, 43 High Street, Dalbeattie. Tel: (0556) 610270.	

Water	Location	Species	Season	Permit available from	Other Information
White Esk	Eskdalemuir	Salmon Sea Trout	15 Apr.-30 Oct 15 Apr.-30 Sept.	Hart Manor Hotel, Eskdalemuir, by Langholm. Tel: (03873) 73217.	Fly and spinner only.

LOCHS AND RESERVOIRS

Water	Location	Species	Season	Permit available from	Other Information
Barend Loch	Sandyhills	Rainbow Trout	No close season	Barend Properties, Reception, Sandyhills, Dalbeattie. Tel: (038778) 663.	
Barscobe Loch	Balmaclellan	Brown Trout	15 Mar. to 6 Oct.	Sir Hugh Wontner, Barscobe, Balmaclellan, Castle Douglas. Tel: (064 42) 245/294.	Fly fishing only. Obtain permit first.
Black Esk Reservoir	Eskdalemuir	Brown Trout	1 Apr. to 30 Sept.	Hart Manor Hotel, Eskdalemuir, by Langholm. Tel: (03873) 73217.	Fly and spinner only.
Black Loch	Newton Stewart	Stocked Brown Trout	15 Mar.-30 Sept.	Forestry Commission, Creebridge. Tel: (0671) 2420. Clatteringshaws Wildlife Visitors Centre, New Galloway. Tel: (064 42) 285.	Fly only until 1 July. Sunday fishing.
Black Loch	Nr. Kirkcowan	(Stocked) Brown Trout Pike	15 Mar.-6 Oct. No close season	Palakona Guest House, Queen Street, Newton Stewart. Tel: (0671) 2323.	Any legal method permitted.
Bruntis Loch	Newton Stewart	Brown/ Rainbow Trout	15 Mar. to 30 Sept.	Newton Stewart Angling Association. Galloway Guns & Tackle, 36 Arthur Street, Newton Stewart. Tel: (0671) 3404.	Fly fishing only (fly & worm from June 1). Bank fishing only. Sunday fishing.
Carsfad Loch	Dalry	Brown Trout	1 April to 30 Sept.	P.O. Shop, Carsphairn. Tel: (06446) 283.	Obtain permit before fishing.
Clattering-shaws Loch	6 miles west of New Galloway	Brown Trout Pike Perch	Open all year for coarse fish	Clatteringshaws Wildlife Visitors Centre, New Galloway. Tel: (064 42) 285. Galloway Guns & Tackle, 36 Arthur Street, Newton Stewart. Tel: (0671) 3404. Kenmure Arms Hotel, High Street, New Galloway. Tel: (06442) 240.	Fly fishing, spinning or worm fishing permitted.
Craichlaw Loch	By Newton Stewart	Carp Tench Roach Bream Rudd	No close Season	Palakona Guest House, Queen Street, Newton Stewart DG8 6JL. Tel: (0671) 2323.	Non-toxic weights. Overnight fishing by arrangement only.
Culscadden Farm Pond	Garlieston	Roach Rudd Perch Carp Tench Bream	No close Season	Palakona Guest House, Queen Street, Newton Stewart DG8 6JL. Tel: (0671) 2323.	Baits: Maggots, sweetcorn, breads etc.
Dabton Loch	Thornhill	Perch	No close Season	The Buccleuch Estates Ltd., Drumlanrig Mains, Thornhill DG3 4AG. Tel: (08486) 283.	Average weight of fish: 8oz. Baits: Worm, Maggot. Bank fishing. Sunday fishing. Overnight fishing by arrangement.

Water	Location	Species	Season	Permit available from	Other Information
Dalbeattie Reservoir	Dalbeattie	Brown/ Rainbow Trout	15 Apr. to 30 Sept.	Dalbeattie Angling Assoc. M. McCowan & Son, 43 High Street, Dalbeattie. Tel: (0556) 610270.	Bank fishing. Fly only. Boats for hire.
Loch Dee	Castle Douglas	Brown Trout	15 Mar. to 6 Oct.	Forestry Commission, Creebridge. Tel: (0671) 2420. Forest Enterprise, 21 King Street, Castle Douglas. Tel: (0556) 3626. Clatteringshaws Wildlife Visitors Centre, New Galloway. Tel: (064 42) 285.	Fly fishing only, sunrise to sunset. Bank fishing only. Sunday fishing. Annual fly fishing competition in August.
Dindinnie Reservoir	Stranraer	Brown Trout	15 Mar. to 30 Sept.	Stranraer & District Angling Association. The Sports Shop, 90 George Street, Stranraer. Tel: (0776) 2705. Local hotels.	Fly fishing only. Sunday fishing.
Loch Dornal	Drumlamford Estate,	Coarse Stocked Trout	Apr. to Oct.	The Keeper, The Kennels, Drumlamford Estate, Barrhill. Tel: (046 582) 256.	Spinning allowed. Boats available. Fly fishing.
Loch Drumlamford	Drumlamford Estate	Stocked Trout	April to October	The Keeper, The Kennels, Drumlamford Estate, Barrhill. Tel: (046 582) 256.	Fly fishing only. Boats available.
Loch Dunskey	Portpatrick	Brown Trout	1 Apr. to 15 Sept.	Keeper, Dunskey Estate, Portpatrick. Tel: (077681) 364/211.	Fly only. Boat available.
Loch Ettrick	Closeburn	Rainbow Trout (stocked) Brown Trout	No close season 15 Mar to 30 Sept.	Gilchristland, Closeburn, Thornhill DG3 5HN. Tel: (0848) 30827/31204/ 31364.	Average weight of fish: $3/4$ to 1lb. Popular flies: Nymphs. Fly fishing only. 2 boats available.
Glendarroch Loch	by Newton Stewart	Roach Rudd Perch Carp Tench Bream	No close season	Palakona Guest House, Queen Street, Newton Stewart DG8 6JL. Tel: (0671) 2323.	Baits: Maggots, sweetcorn, breads etc.
Glenkiln Reservoir	Dumfries	Brown Trout (stocked) Rainbow Trout	1 Apr. to 30 Sept	Dumfries & Galloway Regional Council, Director of Water & Sewerage, Marchmount House, Dumfries DG1 1PW. Tel: (0387) 60756.	Enquiries to Mr. Ling at No. opposite.
Loch Heron	Nr. Newton Stewart	Perch Roach Pike	No close season	Palakona Guest House, Queen Street, Newton Stewart DG8 6JL. Tel: (0671) 2323. Three Lochs Caravan Site, by Newton Stewart.	Any legal method permitted.
Jericho Loch	Dumfries	Brown Trout Rainbow Trout Brook Trout	1 Apr. to 31 Oct.	Mouswald Caravan Park, Mouswald, by Dumfries. Tel: (038 783) 226. McMillan's Tackle Shop, Friars Vennel, Dumfries. Pattie's Tackle Shop, Queensberry Street, Dumfries. Thistle Stores, Locharbriggs, Dumfries. Club Bookings - contact: Jimmy Younger, Tel: (0387) 75247. Sunday tickets from:- Tourist Information Centre, Dumfries, Tel: (0387) 53862.	Bank fishing only. Fly fishing only. Popular flies: Lures, Nymphs, Traditionals. Sunday fishing.

Water	Location	Species	Season	Permit available from	Other Information
Loch Ken	West Bank Lochside Aird's (Viaduct)	Salmon Trout and course fish	Open all year for coarse fish	Shops, hotels in New Galloway	Surcharged if permits bought from bailiffs.
	New Galloway	Brown Trout Salmon Pike Perch Roach	15 Mar. to 30 Sept. All year round	Kenmure Arms Hotel, High Street, New Galloway. Tel: (06442) 240. Local shops.	Sunday fishing allowed except for Salmon. Worm & spinning permitted. Boats available.
Kettleton Reservoir	by Thornhill	Brown/ Rainbow Trout	1 Apr. to 30 Sept.	I.R. Milligan, 37 Drumlanrig Street, Thornhill.	Fly fishing only. Popular flies: Muddler, Black Pennel
Kirriereoch Loch	Newton Stewart	Brown Trout (stocked)	15 Mar. to 6 Oct.	Newton Stewart Angling Association. Galloway Guns & Tackle, 36 Arthur Street, Newton Stewart. Tel: (0671) 3404. Merrick Caravan Park, Glentrool. Tel: (0671) 84 280.	Fly fishing only (fly & worm after June 1). Bank fishing only. Sunday fishing.
Knockquassan Reservoir	Stranraer	Brown Trout	15 Mar. to 30 Sept.	Stranraer & District Angling Association. The Sports Shop, 90 George Street, Stranraer. Tel: (0776) 2705. Local hotels.	Bank fishing only. Fly and spinner. Sunday fishing.
Lairdmannoch Loch	Twynholm	Wild Brown Trout	1 Apr. to 30 Sept.	G.M. Thomson, & Co. Ltd., 27 King Street, Castle Douglas. Tel: (0556) 2701/2973.	Boat fishing only. Limited rods. Limited days. Self-catering Accom. Avail.
Lillies Loch	Castle Douglas	Brown Trout	15 Mar. to 6 Oct.	Forestry Commission, Creebridge. Tel: (0671) 2420. Forest Enterprise, 21 King Street, Castle Douglas. Tel: (0556) 3626.	Bank fishing only. Any legal method. Sunday fishing.
Lochenbreck Loch	Lauriston	Brown/ Rainbow Trout	1 Apr. to 30 Sept.	Watson McKinnel, 15 St. Cuthbert Street, Kirkcudbright. Tel: (0557) 30693. M. & E. Brown, 52 High Street, Gatehouse of Fleet. Tel: (0557) 814222. (shop hours: 6.30am-5pm).	8.30 am to 10 pm. Bank and fly fishing. Five boats. Sunday fishing.
Loch of the Lowes	Newton Stewart	Brown trout (stocked)	15 Mar. to 6 Oct.	Forestry Commission Creebridge. Tel: (0671) 2420. Clatteringshaws Wildlife Visitors Centre, New Galloway. Tel: (064 42) 285.	Fly only. Sunday fishing.
Loch Maberry	Drumlamford Estate	Coarse	Open all year	The Keeper, The Kennels, Drumlamford Estate, Barrhill. Tel: (046 582) 256.	Spinning & bait allowed. Boats available.
Morton Castle Loch	Thornhill	Stocked Brown/ Rainbow Trout	1 Apr. to 30 Sept.	The Buccleuch Estates Ltd., Drumlanrig Mains, Thornhill DG3 4AG. Tel: (08486) 283.	Average weight of fish: 2.25lbs Popular flies: Montanna, Damsel, P/T Nymph, Aces of Spades, Coachman (dry). Fly fishing only. Bank and boat fishing. Let on a daily basis for up to 3 rods.

Please mention this Pastime Publications Guide

Water	Location	Species	Season	Permit available from	Other Information
Morton Pond	Thornhill	Tench	No close season	The Buccleuch Estates Ltd., Drumlanrig Mains, Thornhill DG3 4AG. Tel: (08486) 283.	Average weight of fish: 2lbs. Baits: Bread, Sweetcorn. Bank fishing. Sunday fishing. Overnight fishing by arrangement.
Mossdale Loch	Mossdale Nr. New Galloway	Stocked Rainbow Trout Wild Brown Trout	15 Mar. to 30 Sept.	Mossdale Post Office, Mossdale, Castle Douglas DG7 2NF. Tel: (06445) 281.	Fly fishing only from boat. Boats available from Post Office. Sunday fishing.
Loch Nahinie	Drumlamford Estate	Stocked Trout	April to October	The Keeper, The Kennels, Drumlamford Estate, Barrhill. Tel: (046 582) 256.	Fly fishing only. Boats available.
Penwhirn Reservoir	Stranraer	Brown Trout	15 Mar. to 30 Sept.	Stranraer & District Angling Association. The Sports Shop, 90 George Street, Stranraer. Tel: (0776) 2705. Local hotels.	Fly fishing and spinning. Bank fishing. Sunday fishing.
Purdom Stone Reservoir	Hoddom & Kinmount Estates, Lockerbie	Brown Trout	1 Apr. to 15 Sept.	The Water Bailiff, 1 Bridge End Cottage, Hoddom, Lockerbie. Tel: Ecclefechan 488.	Fly fishing only.
Loch Roan	Castle Douglas	Brown/ Rainbow Trout	1 Apr. to 6 Oct.	Tommy's Sports King Street, Castle Douglas. Tel: (0556) 2851.	Fly fishing only. Shop, Four boats.
Loch Ronald	Nr. Newton Stewart	Pike Perch Roach	No close season	Palakona Guest House, Queen Street, Newton Stewart DG8 6JL. Tel: (0670) 2323.	Any legal method permitted.
Soulseat Loch	Stranraer	Brown/ Rainbow Trout	15 Mar. to 30 Sept.	Stranraer & District Angling Association. The Sports Shop, 90 George Street, Stranraer. Tel: (0776) 2705. Local hotels.	Fly, spinning and bait. Bank fishing and two boats. Sunday fishing.
Spa-wood Loch	Nr. Newton Stewart	Wild Brown Trout	15 Mar. to 30 Sept.	Palakona Guest House, Queen Street, Newton Stewart DG8 6JL. Tel: (0671) 2323.	Average weight of fish: 1lb 8oz. Fly only - guests only.
Loch Starburn	Thornhill	Stocked Brown/ Rainbow Trout	1 Apr. to 31 Aug.	The Buccleuch Estates Ltd., Drumlanrig Mains, Thornhill DG3 4AG. Tel: (08486) 283.	Average weight of fish: 2.2lbs. Popular flies: Montanna, Damsel, P/T Nymph, Ace of Spades, Coachman (dry). Fly fishing only. Bank fishing and beat fishing available. Let on a daily basis for up to 3 rods.
Loch Stroan	Castle Douglas	Pike Perch	Mar. to Oct.	Forest Enterprise, 21 King Street, Castle Douglas. Tel: (0556) 3626. Ticket machines both ends Raiders Road Forest Drive.	Bank fishing only. Any legal method. Sunday fishing.

Water	Location	Species	Season	Permit available from	Other Information
Loch Whinyeon	Gatehouse of Fleet	Brown Trout	1 Apr. to 30 Sept.	M. & E. Brown, 52 High Street, Gatehouse of Fleet. Tel: 0557 814 222. Watson McKinnel, 15 St. Cuthbert Street, Kirkcudbright. Tel: (0557) 30693. 8 am to 10 pm.	Bank and fly fishing only.
Woodhall Loch	Mossdale, Nr. New Galloway	Pike Perch Roach Brown Trout	Open all year	Mossdale Post Office, Mossdale, Castle Douglas DG7 2NF. Tel: (06445) 281.	Any legal method permitted.

DUMFRIES AND GALLOWAY

Sea Angling

Solway Firth to Mull of Galloway and Loch Ryan

An area of many headlands and off-shore reefs with strong tidal runs which can give rise to dangerous sea conditions with rising winds. Small boat anglers should always seek local advice before putting to sea. The Solway Firth area is noted for its many fine shore marks, many of which produce species such as bass, bullhuss and tope in far greater numbers than marks further north. Shore marks on the Kirkcudbrightshire coast regularly produce large cod during the winter months.

Kippford by Dalbeattie

Kippford is a well known yachting centre on the Solway Firth which offers some very good fishing, especially for flatfish.
Types of fish: Cod, flounder, plaice from the shore. Flatfish (including turbot), cod, tope, mackerel, and pollack from boats.
Bait: Lugworm can be dug locally. Cockles and mussels from the shore at low water.
Season for fishing: Best May-October. Some winter fishing for cod to 30lb.

Kirkcudbright

Kirkcudbright is a picturesque town with a very good but tidal harbour. It is approximately three miles from fishing grounds, which offer excellent tope as well as good general fishing. The coast is rugged and not recommended for dinghy or small boat fishing.
Types of fish: Cod, coalfish, conger, bass, plaice, flounders, pollack and dogfish from the shore. Cod,

coalfish, conger, dogfish, mackerel, haddock, tope, pollack, all types of flatfish and whiting from the boats. Local sea angling clubs hold regular outings and competitions, where visitors are welcome. Information in Harbour Square.
Tackle: Available from Patties, 109 Queensberry Street, Dumfries, Dumfriesshire. Tel: (0387) 52891.
Bait: Lugworm can be dug locally. Mussels available at low water.
Season for fishing: May- October. Some winter fishing.
Further information from:
Tourist Information Centre,
Tel: Kirkcudbright (0557) 30494.

Garlieston

Garlieston has a potentially good but undeveloped tidal harbour on the east side of the Machars Peninsula in Wigtownshire with several square miles of water, sheltered by the land from prevailing winds and therefore suitable for trailed and car-top dinghies. Access from the A75 Dumfries to Stranraer road is by the A714 and B7004 from Newton Stewart.
Types of fish: Mackerel, cod, pollack and coalfish from the shore. Mackerel, cod, pollack, ray, plaice, dab, flounder and coalfish from boats.
Bait: Lugworm may be dug and mussels gathered from the foreshore.
Season for fishing: June- September.

Isle of Whithorn

This picturesque old seaport on the souht-west corner of Wigtown Bay has an excellent redesigned harbour with a flourishing local sailing club. It tends to be busy in summer and is a port for 'Queenie' boats. The Isle Bay itself offers nearly a mile of sheltered water in all but severe weather conditions. There are many good rock fishing marks. Tope

festivals are held here twice a year, also shore and boat fishing competitions throughout the season. Local weather forecasts can be obtained from HM Coastguard Station in the centre of the village.
Types of fish: Cod, coalfish, dogfish, conger, pollack, mackerel, wrasse from the shore. Cod, rays, flatfish, spurdog, dogfish, mackerel, conger and tope from boats.
Boats: Craig Mills, Main Street, Isle of Whithorn DG8 8LN. Tel: (09885) 393.
Tackle: Available from A. McGhie, Radio Shop, George Street, Whithorn. J.M. William, Grocer & Harbour Master, The Harbour, Isle of Whithorn. Tel: (09885) 246.
Bait: Lugworm and ragworm, mussels and limpets can be gathered on the shore. Good bait can also be bought from E. McGuire, Burnside Cottage, Isle of Whithorn, at a reasonable price (order in advance).
Season for fishing: June-September.
Further information from:
Mr. E.C. McGuire, Burnside Cottage, Isle of Whithorn, Wigtownshire DG8 8LN. Tel: Whithorn (098- 85) 468.

Luce Bay

There are some good shore marks, namely Sandhead Sands for Flatfish, Dogfish and Bass in season, Terrally Bay for these species plus Codling, Whiting, Spurdogfish. Around East and West Tarbet bays at the Mull of Galloway good rock fishing may be had for Lesser Spotted Dogfish, Bull Huss, Spurdogfish, Conger Eels, Wrasse, Whiting, Pollack, Coalfish, Flatfish and Mackerel in season, normally from late April to December.
Boats: W. Carter, Castle Daly Angling Centre, Auchenmalg, Glenluce. Tel: 058 15 250. (Self drive boats for hire & hotel accommodation).

Port William

Port William is situated on the east side of Luce Bay and has a good though tidal harbour. It is the starting point for many anglers wishing to fish the lower part of Luce Bay. The once famous shore mark of Monreith Bay, still a good bass beach, lies just to the south of Port William.

Types of fish: Tope, spurdog, rays, cod, pollack, flatfish from boats. Bass, wrasse, codling and pollack from the shore.

Tackle: Available in village.

Bait: Lugworm, shellfish and molluscs along beach. Mackerel in bay.

Season for fishing: May- October.

Drummore

Drummore, the main port for anglers wishing to fish the western side of Luce Bay lies 5 miles north of the Mull of Galloway. Hotels and guest houses cater for anglers. There are many good shore marks on sandy beaches north of Drummore, while the Mull of Galloway provides excellent shore fishing over rocky ground. The Mull, the most southerly part of Scotland, is an area of very strong tides and is not recommended as a fishing area to anglers with small boats incapable of at least 10 knots, especially during ebb tides.

Types of fish: Pollack, wrasse from rocky shores, flatfish, bass, mullet and rays from sandy beaches. Pollack, coalfish, cod, whiting, wrasse, lesser, spotted dogfish, bullhuss, spurdog, tope, rays, conger from boats.

Boats: "On yer Marks" Ian or Sue Burrett, Cardrain Cottage, Drummore. Tel: (0776) 84 346.

Bait: All types available on shore at low tide. Mackerel from Mull of Galloway shore marks.

Port Logan

Port Logan is the small community which is situated about 7$\frac{1}{2}$ miles north of the Mull of Galloway on the west side of the Galloway Peninsula. An area with many good shore marks both to the north and south of the village. It is one of the few relatively easy launching sites on this coastline south of Portpatrick. A good alternative for the angler with his own boat when easterly winds prevent fishing in Luce Bay. Like the Mull of Galloway an area of strong tides, especially off Crammoc Head, to the south of Port Logan Bay.

Types of fish: As for the southern part of Luce Bay with occasional haddock. Herring in June and July.

Portpatrick

The small fishing port and holiday resort of Portpatrick lies on the west coast of Wigtownshire, 8 miles from Stranraer. There is good shore fishing from the many rocky points north and south of the resort, the best known being the Yellow Isle, $\frac{1}{2}$ mile north of the harbour. Sandeel Bay, a little further north, and Killintringan Lighthouse are also worth fishing.

Types of fish: Pollack, coalfish, plaice, flounder, codling, mackerel, dogfish, conger, wrasse, and tope occasionally.

Boats: Peter & Martin Green, 2 Eastcliff, Portpatrick. Tel: (0776) 81 534.

Bait: None sold locally. Lugworm and some ragworm can be dug east of the railway pier, Stranraer.

Season for fishing: May-December.

Further information from:
Mr R. Smith, 24 Millbank Road, Stranraer. Tel: Stranraer (0776) 3691.

Stranraer & Loch Ryan

Stranraer, at the head of Loch Ryan, offers the angler, as a rail and bus terminal, a good stepping off point for many sea angling marks and areas in this part of Scotland, with Sandhead on Luce Bay (8 miles) to the south, Portpatrick (8 miles) to the west and Lady Bay (8 miles) on the west side of Loch Ryan with Cairnryan (6 miles) and Finnart Bay (10 miles) on the opposite side of the loch. Best Shore marks being Cairnryan Village, South of Townsend Thoresen ferry terminal. Old House Point and Concrete Barges north of Cairnryan Village, Finnart Bay on East Mouth of Loch, Wig Bay, Jamiesons Point and Lady Bay on west side of Loch Ryan. Boats may be launched at Wig Bay Slipway, Lady Bay and at Stranraer Market Street.

Types of fish: Cod, pollack, mackerel, whiting, flatfish, (Gurnard, conger, dogfish thornback and occasional tope.

Boats: Roy Ferris, Kirkcolm, Tel: (0776) 853274. Mike Watson, Tel: (0776) 85 3225.

Tackle: The Sports Shop, George Street, Stranraer, Tel: (0776) 2705, (frozen bait stocked).

Bait: Excellent lugworms can be dug at low tide from the sands exposed to the east side of the railway pier at low tide (subject to conditions laid down by Loch Ryan S.A.A., who hold the lease).

Further information from:
Mr R. Smith, 24 Millbank Road, Stranraer, Tel: Stranraer (0776) 3691.

SCOTLAND FOR FISHING
A Pastime Publication

I/We have seen your advertisement and wish to know if you have the following vacancy:

Name ....

Address ....

....

Dates from pm ....

Please give date and day of week in each case....................................

To am ....

Number in Party ....

Details of Children ....

(*Please remember to include a stamped addressed envelope with your enquiry.*)

SCOTLAND FOR FISHING
A Pastime Publication

I/We have seen your advertisement and wish to know if you have the following vacancy:

Name ....

Address ....

....

Dates from pm ....

Please give date and day of week in each case ....

To am ....

Number in Party ....

Details of Children ....

(*Please remember to include a stamped addressed envelope with your enquiry.*)

Brown Trout

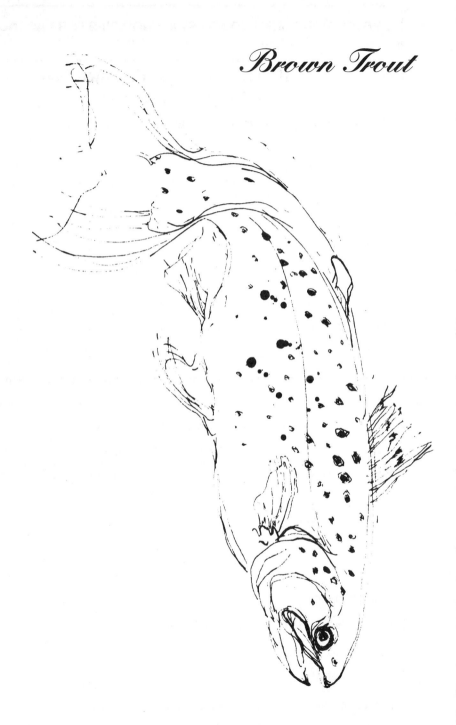

Constituent Area Tourist Boards

Ayrshire and Burns Country Tourist Board
Director of Tourism,
Ayrshire & Burns Country Tourist Board,
39 Sandgate, Ayr KA7 1BG.
Tel: Ayr (0292) 284196.

Ayrshire Valleys Tourist Board
Tourist Officer,
Ayrshire Valleys Tourist Board,
62 Bank Street,
Kilmarnock,
Ayrshire KA1 1ER.
Tel: (0563) 39090.

Clyde Valley Tourist Board
Tourism Officer,
Clyde Valley Tourist Board,
Horsemarket,
Ladyacre Road,
Lanark ML11 7LQ.
Tel: (0555) 2544

Tourist Information Centre
Tourist Officer,
Tourist Information Centre,
Promenade, Largs,
Ayrshire KA30 8BG.
Tel: Largs (0475) 673765

Isle of Arran Tourist Board
Area Tourist Officer,
Isle of Arran Tourist Board,
Information Centre, The Pier,
Brodick, Isle of Arran KA27 8AU.
Tel: Brodick (0770) 2140.

Greater Glasgow Tourist Board
Chief Executive,
Greater Glasgow Tourist Board,
39 St. Vincent Place,
Glasgow G1 2ER.
Tel: 041-227 4885/4880.

Other Tourist Organisations

**CUMBERNAULD AND KILSYTH
INVERCLYDE
MONKLANDS
EAST KILBRIDE
EASTWOOD**

**RIVER PURIFICATION BOARD
CLYDE RIVER PURIFICATION BOARD**
River House, Murray Road, East Kilbride, Tel:
East Kilbride 38181.

RIVERS

Water	Location	Species	Season	Permit available from	Other Information
Annick	Irvine	Salmon Sea Trout Brown Trout	15 Mar. to 31 Oct. 15 Mar. to 6 Oct.	Dreghorn Angling Club, Mr. S. Wallace, 14 Lismore Way, Dreghorn. Mr. R.W. Gillespie, 16 Marble Avenue, Dreghorn.	
Annick (and Glazert)	Kilmaurs	Salmon Sea Trout Brown Trout	15 Mar.to 31 Oct. 15 Mar. to 6 Oct.	Kilmaurs Angling Club, T.C. McCabe, 8 East Park Crescent, Kilmaurs. Mr. D. Dunn, 22 Habbieauld Road, Kilmaurs. Tel: (0563) 23846.	
Avon	Strathaven	Brown Trout Grayling	15 Mar.-6 Oct. No Close Season	Country Lines, 29 Main Street, The Village, East Kilbride. Tel: (03552) 28952. Sportsman Emporium, Hamilton. Tel: (0698) 283903. P. & R. Torbet, 15 Strand Street, Kilmarnock. Tel: (0563) 41734.	Any legal method.
Ayr	Craigie Park	Salmon Sea Trout Trout	10 Feb. to 31 Oct.	Gamesport (Ayr) Ltd., 60 Sandgate, Ayr. Tel: (0292) 263822.	No bait restriction. Fly, spin or worm.
	Failford	Salmon Sea Trout Trout	10 Feb. to 31 Oct.	Gamesport (Ayr) Ltd., 60 Sandgate, Ayr. Tel: (0292) 263822.	No Saturday or Sunday visitor permits.

Water	Location	Species	Season	Permit available from	Other Information
Ayr cont.	Mauchline	Salmon Sea Trout Brown Trout	15 Mar. to 31 Oct. 15 Mar. to 15 Sept.	Linwood & Johnstone Newsagent, The Cross, Mauchline. Tel: (0290) 50219.	
Ayr (Cessnock Lugar)	Mauchline	Salmon Sea Trout Brown Trout	11 Feb. to 31 Oct. 15 May-6 Oct.	Linwood & Johnstone Newsagents, The Cross, Mauchline. Tel: (0290) 50219.	
Ayr (Lugar)	Mauchline	Salmon Sea Trout Brown Trout	15 Mar. to 30 Oct. 15 Mar.-15 Sept.	Linwood & Johnstone Newsagents, The Cross, Mauchline. Tel: (0290) 50219.	
Cart	Busby	Brown Trout	15 Mar to 6 Oct.	Tackle & Guns, 920 Pollokshaws Road, Glasgow G41 2ET. Tel: 041-632 2005.	Average weight of fish caught: 8oz-10oz. Popular flies: small spider flies. Bait fishing allowed, no spinning.
Cessnock	Mauchline	Brown Trout	15 Mar. to 15 Sept.	Linwood & Johnstone, Newsagents, The Cross, Mauchline. Tel: (0290) 50219.	
Clyde	Motherwell, Lanark, Carstairs, Roberton & Crawford	Brown Trout Grayling Coarse	15 Mar. to 30 Sept. All year.	Country Lines, 29 Main Street, The Village, East Kilbride. Tel: (03552) 28952.	
Clyde	Thankerton & Roberton	Brown Trout Grayling	15 Mar. to 6 Oct. 7 Oct.-14 Mar.	B.F. Dexter, Secretary, Lamington & District Angling Improvement Association, 18 Boghall Park, Biggar. Waterbailiffs: Mr. McMahon at Wolfclyde Bridge & Mr. J. Grierson at Symington. W.P. Bryden, Newsagent, 153 High Street, Biggar. Tel: (0899) 20069. O'Hara Grocers, Thankerton. Wyndales Hotel, Symington.	Spinning with legal lures allowed from 1st May. Fly fishing at all times. Flies in normal use size 14. Ground baiting and keep nets are not allowed. No Sunday fishing.
Douglas (and Clyde)	Douglas Water	Brown Trout Grayling	15 Mar.-30 Sep. All year.	Permits widely available in tackle shops in Glasgow and Lanarkshire.	
Forth and Clyde Canal	Whole Canal	Pike Perch Roach	No close season	British Waterways, Rosebank House, Main Street, Camelon, Falkirk FK1 4DS. Tel: (0324) 612415.	
Garnock	Kilbirnie	Brown Trout Salmon Sea Trout	15 Mar. to 6 Oct. 15 Mar.-31 Oct.	Kilbirnie Angling Club I. Johnstone, 12 Grahamston Avenue, Glengarnock, KA14 3AF. Tel: (0505) 682154. R.T. Cycles, Glengarnock. Tel: (0505) 682191.	No Sunday fishing after July 1.
Garnock (and Lugton)	Kilwinning	Salmon Sea Trout Brown Trout	15 Mar. to 31 Oct. 15 Mar.-6 Oct.	The Craft Shop, 42 Main Street, Kilwinning. Tel: (0294) 58559.	No Saturday or Sunday fishing. No permits Friday, 14th Aug.
Gryfe	Bridge of Weir	Brown Trout Salmon Sea Trout	15 Mar.-6 Oct. 15 Mar.-31 Oct.	M. Duncan, Newsagent, Main Street, Bridge of Weir. Tel: (0505) 612477.	No Saturday or Sunday fishing.
Iorsa	Isle of Arran	Salmon Sea Trout	1 June to 15 Oct.	The Estate Office, Dougarie, Isle of Arran. Tel: (077084) 259.	

Water	Location	Species	Season	Permit available from	Other Information
Irvine	Hurlford and Crookedholm	Salmon Sea Trout Brown Trout	15 Mar. to 31 Oct. 15 Mar. to 6 Oct.	P. & R. Torbet, 15 Strand Street, Kilmarnock. Tel:(0563) 41734.	
	Kilmarnock	Salmon Sea trout Brown Trout	15 Mar. to 31 Oct. 15 Mar.-6 Oct.	McCririck & Sons, 38 John Finnie Street, Kilmarnock. Tel: (0563) 25577.	No Sunday fishing after 31st July.
Irvine (and Annick)	Dreghorn	Salmon Sea Trout Brown Trout	15 Mar. to 31 Oct. 15 Mar.-6 Oct.	Dreghorn Angling Club. Mr. S. Wallace, 14 Lismore Way, Dreghorn. Mr. R.W. Gillespie, 16 Marble Avenue, Dreghorn.	River Irvine only, extension of season for salmon and sea trout - 1 to 15 November. Fly only.
Irvine (and Cessnock)	Galston	Salmon Sea Trout Brown Trout	15 Mar. to 30 Nov. 15 Mar.-6 Oct.	Galston Angling Club, Sec. J. Steven, 12 Millands Road, Galston. Tel: Galston 820344. P. & R. Torbet, 15 Strand Street, Kilmarnock. Tel: (0563) 41734. Mr. MacRoberts (Newsagents), Wallace Street, Galston.	
Kelvin	Glasgow-Strathkelvin	Salmon Sea Trout	11 Feb. to 31 Oct.	Lawrence Angling, 268 Dumbarton Road, Glasgow G11 6TU. Tel: 041-339 1085.	Any legal bait permitted.
Machrie	Arran	Salmon Sea Trout	1 June to 15 Oct.	Margo M. Wilson, Boltachan House, Aberfeldy PH15 2LA. Tel: (0887) 820496.	No Sunday fishing. Booking: Nov.- Oct.
Rotten Calder	E. Kilbride	Brown Trout	15 Mar. to 6 Oct.	Country Lines, 29 Main Street, The Village, East Kilbride. Tel: (03552) 28952.	Any legal method.
Stinchar	Colmonell	Salmon Sea Trout	25 Feb. to 31 Oct.	Queen's Hotel, Colmonell. Tel: (046 588) 213.	No Sunday fishing.
White Cart	Waterfoot (Upstream)	Brown Trout	15 Mar. to 6 Oct.	Country Lines, 29 Main Street, The Village, East Kilbride. Tel: (03552) 28952.	

LOCHS AND RESERVOIRS

Water	Location	Species	Season	Permit available from	Other Information
Loch Arklet	Stirling & Trossachs	Brown Trout	30 Mar. to 28 Sept.	Strathclyde Reg. Council, Water Department, 419 Balmore Road, Glasgow, Tel: 041-355 5333. Or on location.	Fly fishing by rowing boat only. No live bait/spinning. Rowing boats supplied. 7 days fishing.
Loch Belston	Sinclairston	Brown/ Rainbow Trout	15 Mar. to 15 Sept.	Linwood & Johnstone, Newsagents, The Cross, Mauchline. Tel: (0290) 50219.	Boats available.
		Rainbow Trout	No close season	Gamesport (Ayr) Ltd., 60 Sandgate, Ayr. Tel: (0292) 263822.	

Water	Location	Species	Season	Permit available from	Other Information
Loch Bradan	Straiton	Brown Trout (Stocked)	15 Mar. to 30 Sept.	Forestry Commission, Straiton. Tel: (065 57) 637. Mr. R. Heaney, Tallaminnoch, Straiton. Tel: (065 57) 617.	Five Boats. Sunday fishing.
Loch Brecbowie	Straiton	Brown Trout	15 Mar. to 30 Sept.	Forestry Commission, Straiton. Tel: (065 57) 637. Mr. R. Heaney, Tallaminnoch, Straiton. Tel: (065 57) 617.	Fly fishing advised. Sunday fishing.
Burnfoot Reservoir	Nr. Fenwick	Brown/ Rainbow Trout	15 Mar. to 6 Oct.	Kilmaurs A.C., Mr. T.C. McCabe, 8 East Park Crescent, Kilmaurs. Mr. D. Dunn, 22 Habbieauld Road, Kilmaurs. Tel: (0563) 23846. Pages Newsagent, Main Street, Kilmaurs.	Average weight of fish caught: 1lb-5lbs. Popular flies: Butcher, Montanna, Nymph, Viva, Soldier Palmer. Any legal method - no swim feeders or floats.
Busbie Muir Reservoir	Ardrossan	Brown Trout	1 Apr. to 6 Oct.	Ardrossan Eglinton A.C., Alpine Stores, Dalry Road, Ardrossan.	Obtain permits before fishing. Average weight of fish caught: 8-12oz. Popular flies: Wickhams, Kate McLaren, Soldier Palmer, Grouse & Claret, Invicta, Blae & Black. Two boats, keys available from Alpine Store.
Camphill Reservoir	Kilbirnie	Brown Trout	1 Apr. to 6 Oct.	Kilbirnie A.C., I. Johnstone, 12 Grahamstone Avenue, Glengarnock KA14 3AF. Tel: (0505) 682154. R.T. Cycles, Glengarnock. Tel: (0505) 682191.	Fly only. Boat only.
Castle Semple Loch	Lochwinnoch	Pike Perch Roach Eels	No close season	Countryside Ranger Service, Castle Semple Country Park, Loch Winnoch, Renfrewshire. Tel: Lochwinnoch 842882.	Day permits for bank fishing. North shore only.
Dhu Loch	Straiton	Brown Trout	15 Mar. to 30 Sept.	Mr. R. Heaney, Tallaminnoch, Straiton. Tel: (065-57) 617.	Fly only.
Glen Finglas	Stirling & Trossachs	Brown Trout	30 Mar. to 28 Sept.	Strathclyde Reg. Council, Water Department, 419 Balmore Road, Glasgow, Tel: 041-355 5333. Or on location.	Fly fishing by rowing boat only. No live bait/spinning. Rowing boats supplied. 7 days fishing.
Loch Goin (between orange markers)	Nr. Eaglesham	Brown Trout	15 Mar. to 6 Oct.	Kilmaurs A.C., Mr. T.C. McCabe, 8 East Park Crescent, Kilmaurs. Mr. D. Dunn, 22 Habbieauld Road, Kilmaurs. Tel: (0563) 23846.	Average weight of fish caught: 8oz to 3lbs. Popular flies: traditional small flies. No other baits - fly only.
Craigendunton Reservoir	Nr. Kilmarnock	Rainbow/ Brown Trout	15 Mar. to 6 Oct.	Kilmarnock A.C., McCririck & Sons, 38 John Finnie Street, Kilmarnock. Tel: (0563) 25577.	Average weight of fish caught: Rainbow - 1lb 8oz, Brown - 12oz. Fly and spinning only; no live bait. Obtain permits before fishing.

Water	Location	Species	Season	Permit available from	Other Information
Harelaw Dam	Neilston	Brown Trout	15 Mar. to 6 Oct.	Doug Brown, 10 Garrioch Drive, Glasgow. Tel: 041 946 6060. Tackle & Guns, 920 Pollokshaws Road, Glasgow. Tel: 041-632 2005. Lawrence Angling, 268 Dumbarton Road, Glasgow G11 6TU. Tel: 041-339 1085.	Average weight of fish caught: 1lb 2oz. Popular flies: Black Pennel, Soldier Palmer, Sedges, and Dry Fly. Boats day or evening.
Loch Katrine	Stirling & Trossachs	Brown Trout	30 Mar. to 28 Sept.	Strathclyde Reg. Council, Water Department, 419 Balmore Road, Glasgow, Tel: 041-355 5333. Or on location.	Fly fishing by rowing boat only. No live bait/spinning. Rowing boats supplied. 7 days fishing.
Kilbirnie Loch	Kilbirnie	Brown/ Rainbow Trout	15 Mar. to 6 Oct.	Kilbirnie Angling Club, I. Johnstone, 12 Grahamston Avenue, Glengarnock KA14 3AF. Tel: (0505) 682154. R.T. Cycles, Glengarnock. Tel: (0505) 682191.	All legal methods. Boats available.
Lanark Loch	Lanark	Carp Tench	No close season		
Linfern Loch	Straiton	Pike	No close season	Mr. R. Heaney, Tallaminnoch, Straiton. Tel: (065 57) 617.	Sunday fishing. 1 May to mid-June no permits are available.
Mill Glen Reservoir	Ardrossan	Brown Trout	15 Mar. to 6 Oct.	Ardrossan Eglinton A.C., Alpine Stores, Dalry Road, Ardrossan. Obtain permits before fishing.	Average weight of fish caught: 8-12oz. Popular flies: Wickhams, Kate McLaren, Soldier Palmer, Grouse & Claret, Invicta, Blae & Black. Fly fishing only.
North Craig Reservoir	Kilmaurs	Brown/ Rainbow Trout	15 Mar. to 6 Oct.	Kilmaurs A.C., T.C. McCabe, 8 East Park Crescent, Kilmaurs. Mr. D. Dunn, 22 Habbieauld Road, Kilmaurs. Tel: (0563) 23846. Pages Newsagent, Main Street, Kilmaurs.	Average weight of fish caught: 1-5lbs. Popular flies: Butcher, Soldier Palmer, Blue Zulu, Baby Doll, Viva. Any legal method - no swim feeders or floats.
Penwhapple Reservoir	Nr. Girvan	Stocked Brown Trout Rainbow Trout	1 Apr. to 15 Sept.	Mrs. Stewart, Wee Lames Farm, Nr. Girvan. (1/4 mile from reservoir).	Fly fishing only. Average weight of fish caught: 12oz. Popular flies: Kate McLaren, Zulu, Invicta; traditional patterns. 4 boats available.
Prestwick Reservoir	Monkton	Rainbow Trout	15 Mar to 15 Nov.	Gamesport, Ayr. Kirk, Ayr. Newhall's Newsagent, Monkton. Wheatsheaf Inn, Monkton.	Average weight of fish caught: 1-4lbs. Popular flies: Butcher, Greenwell Glory. Worm fishing.
Raith Reservoir (Prestwick)	Monkton by Ayr	Rainbow Trout	15 Mar. to 15 Nov.	Gamesport (Ayr) Ltd., 60 Sandgate, Ayr. Tel: (0292) 263822.	
Loch Skelloch	Straiton	Brown Trout (Stocked)	15 Mar. to 30 Sept.	Mr. R. Heaney, Tallaminnoch, Straiton. Tel: (065 57) 617.	Fly fishing only. Boats available. Sunday fishing.

Please mention this Pastime Publications Guide

Water	Location	Species	Season	Permit available from	Other Information
Strathclyde Country Park Loch (and adjacent River Clyde)	Motherwell	Carp Bream Roach Pike Perch Dace	No close season	Booking Office, Strathclyde Country Park, 366 Hamilton Road, Motherwell. Tel: Motherwell 66155.	Regulations on permit. No fly fishing. Lead-free weights recommended.
		Grayling Trout	15 Mar. to 29 Sept.		
Loch Thom and compensations 6,7 & 8	Greenock	Brown Trout	15 Mar. to 6 Oct.	John M. Clark, Cornalees Farm, Greenock.	Fly and bank fishing only.

STRATHCLYDE SOUTH
Sea Angling

Loch Ryan to Ardrossan
The angling potential of much of the coast between Loch Ryan and Girvan remains unknown, the many rocky shores, small headlands and sandy beaches probably only attracting the anglers in an exploratory mood, or those seeking solitude in pursuit of their hobby.

Girvan
Girvan has a sheltered port and is a family holiday resort. From the end of the pier good fishing can be had for fair- sized plaice and flounders. Night fishing is good for rock cod. Just one mile to the south of the town lies the noted 'Horse Rock', only about 50 yards from the main Stranraer road. Access to the rock may be gained from about half-tide. Except during very high tides and during storms it is a good shore mark

providing access to water of about 20 feet on the sea-side even at low tide.
Types of fish: Haddock, plaice, hake, codling, rays, flounder, whiting, and gurnard (mostly from boat).
Boats: M. McCrindle, 7 Harbour Street, Girvan KA26 9AJ. Tel: (0465) 3219.
Baits: Lugworm and ragworm can be dug at beach nearby or fresh mackerel from boat.
Tackle: Available from Girvan Chandlers, 4 Knockcushon Street, Girvan KA26 9AG.
Season for fishing: March to October.

Ayr
Ayr is a popular holiday town on the estuaries of the Rivers Ayr and Doon, 32 miles south-west of Glasgow. Good shore fishing can be had on the Newton Shore, north of the harbour, from the harbour jetty and from the rocky coastline at the Heads of Ayr. Boat fishing in the bay can be very productive with good catches of cod, haddock, thornbacks,

spurdogs and flatfish. Tope have also been taken from around the Lady Isle.
Types of fish: Cod, mackerel, ling, plaice, dab and pollack are the main type of fish being caught in Ayr Bay over the past few year.
Tackle: Available from Gamesport, 60 Sandgate, Ayr.
Bait: Lugworm and ragworm from Ayr and Newton shore. Frozen bait can be purchased from Gamesport, 60 Sandgate, Ayr.

Prestwick
Prestwick is a pleasant seaside holiday town on the coast between Troon and Ayr. Shore fishing is best after dark. Temporary membership of Prestwick SAC can be obtained.
Types of fish: Shore – cod, flounder, plaice, dab, coalfish, dogfish and mullet. Boat – as above plus tope and rays, thornbacks and mackerel, except mullet.
Bait: Lugworm and ragworm can be dug on Prestwick shore.
Season for fishing: Shore – October-March. Boat – all year.

TO ASSIST WITH YOUR BOOKINGS
OR ENQUIRIES YOU WILL FIND IT HELPFUL
TO MENTION THIS

Pastime Publications Guide

Constituent Area Tourist Boards

Dunoon and Cowal Tourist Board
Area Tourist Officer,
Dunoon and Cowal Tourist Board,
Information Centre,
7 Alexandra Parade,
Dunoon, Argyll PA23 8AB.
Tel: Dunoon (0369) 3785.

**West Highlands & Islands of Argyll Tourist
Board,**
Area Tourist Officer,
West Highlands & Islands of Argyll Tourist board,
Albany Street, Oban,
Argyll PA34 1RN.
Tel: (0631) 63059.

Isle of Bute Tourist Board
Area Tourist Officer,
Isle of Bute Tourist Board,
15 Victoria Street, Rothesay,
Isle of Bute PA20 0AJ.
Tel: Rothesay (0700) 502151.

**RIVER PURIFICATION BOARD
CLYDE RIVER PURIFICATION BOARD**
Rivers House,
Murray Road,
East Kilbride G75 0LA.
Tel: East Kilbride 03552 38181.

RIVERS

Water	Location	Species	Season	Permit available from	Other Information
Aros	Mull	Salmon Sea Trout	End June to Mid Oct.	Tackle and Books, Main Street, Tobermory, Isle of Mull. Tel: (0688) 2336.	
Bellart	Mull	Salmon Sea Trout	June to End Oct.	Tackle & Books, Main Street, Tobermory, Isle of Mull. Tel: (0688) 2336.	No Sunday fishing.
Cur	13 miles from Dunoon	Salmon Sea Trout Brown Trout	1 Apr. to 31 Oct.	Purdies of Argyll, 112 Argyll Street, Dunoon. Tel: Dunoon 3232. Dunoon & District Angling Club.	Fishing all legal methods. Bookings, Hon. Sec., D. & D.A.C., "Ashgrove", 28 Royal Crescent, Dunoon PA23 7AH. Tel: (0369) 5732.
Douglas	Inveraray	Salmon Sea Trout	May to Mid-Oct.	Argyll Caravan Park, Inveraray, Argyll. Tel: (0499) 2285.	No Sunday fishing. Fly fishing only.
Euchar	Kilninver	Salmon Sea Trout Brown Trout	1 June to 15 Oct.	Mrs. Mary McCorkindale, 'Glenann' Kilninver, by Oban, Argyll. Tel: (085 26) 282.	No Sunday fishing.
		Salmon Sea Trout	Mid-July to Mid-Oct.	J.T.P. Mellor, Barncromin Farm,Knipoch, by Oban, Argyll. Tel: (085 26) 273.	(Tues, Wed & Thurs.)
	Kilninver (Lagganmore)	Salmon Sea Trout Brown Trout	June to 14 Oct.	Lt. Col. P.S. Sandilands, Lagganmore, Kilninver, by Oban. Tel: (085 26) 200.	Not more than 3 rods per day. Fly fishing only. No Sunday fishing.
Finnart	12 miles from Dunoon	Salmon Sea Trout Brown Trout	1 Apr. to 15 Oct.	Dunoon & District Angling Club. Purdie's of Argyll, 112 Argyll Street, Dunoon. Tel: Dunoon 3232.	Fishing all legal methods. Advanced bookings Hon. Sec., D.& D.A.C., "Ashgrove", 28 Royal Crescent, Dunoon PA23 7AH. Tel: (0369) 5732.
Forsa	Mull	Salmon Sea Trout	Mid-June to Mid-Oct.	Tackle and Books, Main Street, Tobermory. Tel: (0688) 2336.	No Sunday fishing.

Water	Location	Species	Season	Permit available from	Other Information
Grey	Islay	Salmon Sea Trout	July to October	Brian Wiles, Head Gamekeeper's House, Islay House Square, Bridgend. Tel: (049 681) 293.	Fly only. No night fishing.
Laggan	Islay	Salmon Sea Trout	July to October	Brian Wiles, Head Gamekeeper's House, Isle House Square, Bridgend. Tel: (049 681) 293.	Fly fishing only. No night fishing.
Machrie	Islay	Salmon Sea Trout Brown Trout	25 Feb. to 31 Oct.	Machrie Hotel, Port Ellen, Islay, Argyll PA42 7AN. Tel: (0496) 2310.	Own river. Loch by Arrangement.
Massan	6 miles from Dunoon	Salmon Sea Trout Brown Trout	1 Apr. to 31 Oct.	Dunoon & District Angling Club. Purdies of Argyll, 112 Argyll Street, Dunoon. Tel: Dunoon 3232.	All legal methods. Advanced booking Hon. Sec., D. & D.A.C., "Ashgrove", 28 Royal Crescent, Dunoon PA23 7AH. Tel: (0369) 5732.
Orchy	Dalmally	Salmon	11 Feb. to 15 Oct.	W.A. Church, Croggan Crafts, Dalmally, Argyll. Tel: (083 82) 201.	
Ruel	Glendaruel	Salmon Sea Trout	16 Feb. to 31 Oct.	Glendaruel Hotel, Clachan of Glendaruel, Argyll PA22 3AA. Tel: (036982) 274.	No Sunday fishing.
Sorn	Islay	Salmon Sea Trout	October	Brian Wiles, Head Gamekeeper's House, Islay House Square, Bridgend. Tel: (049 681) 293.	Fly fishing only. No night fishing.

LOCHS AND RESERVOIRS

Water	Location	Species	Season	Permit available from	Other Information
Loch A'Bharrain	Nr. Oban	Brown Trout	15 Mar. to 6 Oct.	D. Graham, Combe Street, Oban. Tack & Tackle Shop, Oban. Sports Centre, Oban. Anglers' Corner, Oban. Post Office, Kilmelford. Trading Post, Kilchrenan. Mr. Morrison, Ledaig Motors, Benderloch.	Standard trout flies wet or dry (12 & 14). Peaty loch with small fish.
Loch a'Chaorainn	Nr. Kilmelford	Brown Trout	15 Mar. to 15 Mar. to 6 Oct.	D. Graham, Combe Street, Oban. Tack & Tackle Shop, Oban. Sports Centre, Oban. Anglers' Corner, Oban. Post Office, Kilmelford. Trading Post, Kilchrenan. Mr. Morrison, Ledaig Motors,	Popular flies: imitations of natural flies. The loch contains trout up to Benderloch.2lbs.
Loch a'Cheigin	Nr. Kilmelford	Brown Trout	15 Mar. to 6 Oct.	D. Graham, Combe Street, Oban. Tack & Tackle Shop, Oban. Sports Centre, Oban. Anglers' Corner, Oban. Post Office, Kilmelford. Trading Post, Kilchrenan. Mr. Morrison, Ledaig Motors, Benderloch.	Popular flies: standard trout patterns, size 14.

Water	Location	Species	Season	Permit available from	Other Information
Loch a'Chlachain	Nr. Kilmelford	Brown Trout	15 Mar. to 6 Oct.	D. Graham, Combe Street, Oban. Tack & Tackle Shop, Oban. Sports Centre, Oban. Anglers' Corner, Oban. Post Office, Kilmelford. Trading Post, Kilchrenan. Mr. Morrison, Ledaig Motors, Benderloch.	Popular flies: standard trout flies, wet or dry (12 & 14).
Loch a'Chreachain	Nr. Kilmelford	Brown Trout	15 Mar. to 6 Oct.	D. Graham, Combe Street, Oban. Tack & Tackle Shop, Oban. Sports Centre, Oban. Anglers' Corner, Oban. Post Office, Kilmelford. Trading Post, Kilchrenan. Mr. Morrison, Ledaig Motors, Benderloch.	Popular flies: standard pattern trout flies sizes 12 & 14 also big lure type flies for the bigger trout.
Loch a'Cruaiche	Nr. Kilmelford	Brown Trout	15 Mar. to 6 Oct.	D. Graham, Combe Street, Oban. Tack & Tackle Shop, Oban. Sports Centre, Oban. Anglers' Corner, Oban. Post Office, Kilmelford. Trading Post, Kilchrenan. Mr. Morrison, Ledaig Motors, Benderloch.	Small weedy loch with small trout.
Loch a'Mhinn	Nr. Kilmelford	Brown Trout	15 Mar. to 6 Oct.	D. Graham, Combe Street, Oban. Tack & Tackle Shop, Oban. Sports Centre, Oban. Anglers' Corner, Oban. Post Office, Kilmelford. Trading Post, Kilchrenan. Mr. Morrison, Ledaig Motors, Benderloch.	Popular flies: standard trout flies, wet or dry (12 & 14). The loch contains small fat trout, frequently difficult to catch.
Loch a'Phearsain	Nr. Kilmelford	Brown Trout	15 Mar. to 6 Oct.	D. Graham, Combe Street, Oban. Tack & Tackle Shop, Oban. Sports Centre, Oban. Anglers' Corner, Oban. Post Office, Kilmelford. Trading Post, Kilchrenan. Mr. Morrison, Ledaig Motors, Benderloch.	Average weight of fish: 8oz to 1lb. Popular flies: standard patterns, sizes 12 & 14.
Loch an Daimh	Nr. Kilmelford	Brown Trout	15 Mar. to 6 Oct.	D. Graham, Combe Street, Oban. Tack & Tackle Shop, Oban. Sports Centre, Oban. Anglers' Corner, Oban. Post Office, Kilmelford. Trading Post, Kilchrenan. Mr. Morrison, Ledaig Motors, Benderloch.	The loch contains trout up to 6oz, but they are difficult to catch. Popular flies: standard trout flies, wet or dry (10 &14).
Loch an Losgainn Beag	Nr. Kilmelford	Brown Trout	15 Mar. to 6 Oct.	D. Graham, Combe Street, Oban. Tack & Tackle Shop, Oban. Sports Centre, Oban. Anglers' Corner, Oban. Post Office, Kilmelford. Treading Post, Kilchrenan. Mr. Morrison, Ledaig Motors, Benderloch.	Popular flies: standard trout flies, wet or dry (10 to 14). The loch contains very large trout that are difficult to catch. Reputed to fish best in the evening during June.

Water	Location	Species	Season	Permit available from	Other Information
Loch an Losgainn Mor	Nr. Kilmelford	Brown Trout	15 Mar. to 6 Oct.	D. Graham, Combe Street, Oban. Tack & Tackle Shop, Oban. Sports Centre, Oban. Anglers' Corner, Oban Post Office, Kilmelford. Trading Post, Kilchrenan. Mr. Morrison, Ledaig Motors, Benderloch.	Popular flies: standard trout flies, wet or dry (10 to 14). The loch contains trout of 6oz. but they are difficult to catch.
Loch Airigh-Shamhraidh	Musdale	Brown Trout	15 Mar. to 6 Oct.	D. Graham, Combe Street, Oban. Tack & Tackle Shop, Oban. Sports Centre, Oban. Anglers' Corner, Oban. Post Office, Kilmelford. Trading Post, Kilchrenan. Mr. Morrison, Ledaig Motors, Benderloch.	Popular flies: standard trout flies, wet or dry (12 & 14). Loch is full of easily caught trout.
Ardlussa Home Loch	Ardlussa	Salmon Sea Trout Brown Trout	20 July to 5 Oct.	C. Fletcher, Ardlussa, Isle of Jura. Tel: 049-682 323.	2 boats for 2 rods each.
Loch Aros Lake	Aros	Rainbow Trout	1 Apr. to 30 Nov.	Brown's Shop, Tobermory. Tel: (0688) 2020.	Popular flies: Butcher, Teal & Green, Soldier Palmer, Grouse & Claret (size 10 & 12). Bank fishing only. No spinning.
Loch Ascog	Argyll	Brown/ Rainbow Trout	15 Mar. to 5 Oct.	Kyles of Bute Angling Club. Several shops in Kames and Tighnabruaich.	Fly only.
Loch Assopol	Mull	Salmon Sea Trout Brown Trout	April to beg. Oct.	Argyll Arms Hotel, Bunessan, Isle of Mull. Tel: Fionnphort 240.	Fly and spinner only. No Sunday fishing.
Glen Astil Lochs (2)	Isle of Islay	Brown Trout	1 Apr. to 15 Oct.	I.G. Laurie, Newsagent, 19 Charlotte Street, Port Ellen, Isle of Islay. Tel: (0496) 2264.	£2.50 per rod per day. Fly only. No Sunday fishing. No catch limit. Permit covers all 5 lochs of Port Ellen Angling Club (see Loch Kinnabus).
Loch Avich	Taynuilt	Brown/ Rainbow Trout	15 Mar. to 6 Oct.	Mr. N.D. Clark, 11, Dalavich, By Taynuilt, Argyll PA35 1HN. Tel: Lochavich 209. W.A. Church, Croggan Crafts, Dalmally, Argyll. Tel: (083 82) 201.	5 boats available.
	Argyll	Brown/ Rainbow Trout	15 Mar. to 6 Oct.	Lochgilphead Tourist Office, Lochnell Street, Lochgilphead. Tel: (0546) 602344. Oban Tourist Office, Boswell House, Argyll Square, Oban. Tel: (0631) 63122.	Permits also available for pike fishing (no close season).
	Nr. Kilmelford	Brown Trout	15 Mar. to 6 Oct.	D. Graham, Combe Street, Oban. Tack & Tackle Shop, Oban. Sports Centre, Oban. Anglers' Corner, Oban. Post Office, Kilmelford. Trading Post, Kilchrenan. Mr. Morrison, Ledaig Motors, Benderloch.	Popular flies: standard patterns, sizes 12 & 14.

Water	Location	Species	Season	Permit available from	Other Information
Loch Awe	South Lochaweside by Dalmally	Salmon Sea Trout Brown Trout Rainbow Trout Perch Char Pike	11 Feb. to 15 Oct. 15 Mar. to 6 Oct. All year	Ardbrecknish House, by Dalmally, Argyll. Tel: (08663) 223/256. Boats, tackle and permits available. Clubs welcome.	
		Salmon Sea Trout Brown Trout Rainbow Trout Perch Char Pike	15 Mar. to 15 Oct. 15 Mar. to 6 Oct. All year	The Portsonachan Hotel, Nr.Dalmally, Argyll PA33 1BL. Tel: (086 63) 224/225/356/328.	
		Brown/ Rainbow Trout Salmon	15 Mar. 15 Oct.	Ford Hotel, Ford. Tel: (054 681) 273.	
	Taynuilt	Salmon Sea Trout Brown Trout Rainbow Trout	. 12 Feb. to 15 Oct. 15 Mar. to 6 Oct.	Mr. N.D. Clark, 11, Dalavich, By Taynuilt, Argyll PA35 1HN. Tel: Lochavich 209. D. Graham, Combe Street, Oban. Tack & Tackle Shop, Oban. Sports Centre, Oban. Anglers' Corner, Oban. Post Office, Kilmelford. Trading Post, Kilchrenan. Mr. Morrison, Ledaig Motors, Benderloch.	Boats available.
		Salmon Brown Trout Sea Trout Rainbow Trout Char Perch Pike	16 Mar. to 6 Oct. (No close season Pike)	Country Lines, 29 Main Street, The Village, East Kilbride. Tel: (03552) 28952.	Separate Pike permit available. Restrictions detailed on permit.
	Argyll	Brown/ Rainbow Trout	15 Mar. to 6 Oct.	Lochgilphead Tourist Office, Lochnell Street, Lochgilphead. Tel: (0546) 602344. Oban Tourist Office, Boswell House, Argyll Square, Oban. Tel: (0631) 63122. W.A. Church, Croggan Crafts, Dalmally, Argyll. Tel: (083 82) 201.	Permits also available for Pike fishing (no close season).
Ballygrant Loch	Ballygrant	Brown Trout	15 Mar. to 6 Oct.	Port Askaig Stores, Port Askaig, Isle of Islay. Tel: (049684) 245.	Average weight of fish caught: 8 - 16oz. Boats are available.
Barnluasgan Loch	Lochgilphead	Brown Trout	15 Mar. to 6 Oct.	Mr. A. MacVicar, Gartnagrenach, Achnamara.	Boat available.
Loch Bealach Ghearran	Nr. Minard Village	Brown Trout	15 Mar. to 6 Oct.	Mr. R. Hardie, No. 1, Nursery Cottages, Birdfield, Minard, Argyll. Mr. D. McNeil, Hydro Cottage, Lochgair. Forest District Office, Whitegates, Lochgilphead.	Average weight of fish caught: 8oz. Popular flies: most dark flies.

Water	Location	Species	Season	Permit available from	Other Information
Big Feinn Loch	Nr. Kilmelford	Brown Trout	15 Mar. to 6 Oct.	D. Graham, Combe Street, Oban. Tack & Tackle Shop, Oban. Sports Centre, Oban. Anglers' Corner, Oban. Post Office, Kilmelford. Trading Post, Kilchrenan. Mr. Morrison, Ledaig Motors, Benderloch.	The loch contains very large trout which are very difficult to catch. It fishes best at the beginning of the season in windy conditions. Popular flies: large salmon flies - Demons or Terrors.
Blackmill Loch	Nr. Minard Village	Brown Trout	15 Mar. to 6 Oct.	Mr. R. Hardie, No. 1, Nursery Cottages, Birdfield, Minard, Argyll. Mr. D. McNeil, Hyrdo Cottage, Lochgair. Forest District Office, Whitegates, Lochgilphead.	Average weight of fish caught: 8oz. Popular flies: most dark flies.
Cam Loch	Nr. Ford	Brown Trout	15 Mar. to 6 Oct.	Ford Hotel, Ford. Tel: Ford 273.	Average weight of fish caught: 8oz. Popular flies: most dark flies.
Coille Bhar	Lochgilphead	Brown Trout	1 Apr. to 6 Oct.	Mr. A. MacVicar, Gartnagrenach, Achnamara.	Two boats
Loch Crauch Maolachy	Nr. Kilmelford	Brown Trout	15 Mar. to 6 Oct.	D. Graham, Combe Street, Oban. Tack & Tackle Shop, Oban. Sports Centre, Oban. Anglers' Corner, Oban. Post Office, Kilmelford. Trading Post, Kilchrenan. Mr. Morrison, Ledaig Motors, Benderloch.	Stocked trout reach 2lbs or more. Standard patterns, sizes 12 & 14.
Dubh Loch	Kilninver Loch Leven	Trout Brown Trout	April to Mid-Oct.	J.T.P. Mellor, Barndromin Farm, Knipoch, by Oban. Tel: (085 26) 273.	Boat on loch.
Loch Dubh-Bheag	Nr. Kilmelford	Brown Trout	15 Mar. to 6 Oct.	D. Graham, Combe Street, Oban. Tack & Tackle Shop, Oban. Sports Centre, Oban. Post Office, Kilmelford. Trading Post, Kilchrenan. Mr. Morrison, Ledaig Motors, Benderloch.	Popular flies: standard trout patterns, sizes 12 & 14
Loch Dubh-Mor	Nr. Kilmelford	Brown Trout	15 Mar. to 6 Oct.	D. Graham, Combe Street, Oban. Tack & Tackle Shop, Oban. Sports Centre, Oban. Anglers' Corner, Oban. Post Office, Kilmelford. Trading Post, Kilchrenan. Mr. Morrison, Ledaig Motors, Benderloch.	Average weight of fish caught: 4oz. Popular flies: standard patterns, 10 & 12.
Dunoon Reservoir	Dunoon	Rainbow & Brook Trout	1 Mar. to 31 Nov.	Dunoon & District Angling Club. Purdies of Argyll, 112 Argyll Street, Dunoon. Tel: Dunoon 3232.	Fly fishing only.
Ederline Lochs 18 hill lochs	Ford	Wild Brown Trout	May to 6 Oct.	The Keeper, Keepers Cottage, Ederline, Ford, Lochgilphead. Tel: (054 681) 215.	Average weight of fish caught: 8oz. Fly only. Boats available on 5 lochs.

Water	Location	Species	Season	Permit available from	Other Information
Loch Ederline (& 3 smaller lochs)	Ford	Pike Perch	No close season	The Keeper Keepers Cottage, Ederline, Ford, Lochgilphead. Tel: (054 681) 215.	All baits allowed. 3 boats available.
Loch Fad	Bute	Brown Trout Rainbow Trout	15 Mar. to 6 Oct.	Bailiff at Loch. Tel: (0700) 504871.	Boats available. Whole day and evening tickets. No night fishing.
		Rainbow Trout Brown Trout	March to October	Carleol Enterprises Angling Holidays, 3 Alma Terrace, Rothesay. Tel: (0700) 503716.	Accommodation and permits are available.
Loch Fada	Isle of Colonsey	Brown Trout	15 Mar. to 30 Sept.	The Hotel, Isle of Colonsey, Argyll.	Fly fishing only. Boats are available.
Loch Finlaggan	Islay	Brown Trout	15 Mar. to 30 Sept.	Brian Wiles, Islay House Square, Bridgend, Isle of Islay, Argyll PA44 7NZ. Tel: (049 681) 293.	Two boats.
Forestry Hill Lochs	Ford	Brown Trout	15 Mar. to 6 Oct.	Ford Hotel, Ford, Argyll. Tel: (054-681) 273.	
Loch Frisa	North end of Mull	Brown Trout Sea Trout	Apr. to Oct.	Tackle and Books, Main Street, Tobermory, Mull. Tel: (0688) 2336.	1 Boat.
Loch Glashan	Nr. Lochgair Village	Brown Trout	15 Mar. to 6 Oct.	Mr. R. Hardie, No. 1, Nursery Cottages, Birdfield, Minard, Argyll. Mr. D. McNeil, Hydro Cottage, Lochgair. Forest District Office, Whitegates, Lochgilphead.	Average weight of fish caught: 12oz. Popular flies: most dark flies. One boat is available.
Loch Gleann A'Bhearraidh	Lerags by Oban	Brown Trout	15 Mar. to 6 Oct.	Cologin Homes Ltd., Lerags, by Oban, Argyll. Tel: (0631) 64501. The Barn Bar, Cologin, Lerags, by Oban.	One boat available.
Loch Gorm	Islay	Brown Trout	15 Mar. to 30 Sept.	Brian Wiles, Islay House Square, Bridgend, Isle of Islay, Argyll PA44 7NZ. Tel: (049 681) 293.	3 Boats available.
Loch Gully	Nr. Kilmelford	Brown Trout	15 Mar. to 6 Oct.	D. Graham, Combe Street, Oban. Tack & Tackle Shop, Oban. Sports Centre, Oban. Anglers' Corner, Oban. Post Office, Kilmelford. Trading Post, Kilchrenan. Mr. Morrison, Ledaig Motors, Benderloch.	The loch contains some good fat trout. Popular flies: standard patterns, 12 & 14.
Iasg Loch	Nr. Kilmelford	Brown Trout	15 Mar. to 6 Oct.	D. Graham, Combe Street, Oban. Tack & Tackle Shop, Oban. Sports Centre, Oban. Anglers' Corner, Oban. Post Office, Kilmelford. Trading Post, Kilchrenan. Mr. Morrison, Ledaig Motors, Benderloch.	Popular flies: standard patterns, 10 & 12.

Water	Location	Species	Season	Permit available from	Other Information
Inverawe Fisheries	Taynuilt	Rainbow Trout	Mar. to Dec.	Inverawe Fisheries, Taynuilt, Argyll. Tel: (08662) 446.	
Kinnabus Lochs (3)	Islay	Brown Trout Arctic Char	1 Apr. to 15 Oct.	I.G. Laurie, Newsagent, 19 Charlotte Street, Port Ellen, Isle of Islay Tel: (0496) 2264.	Fly only. No Sunday fishing. No catch limit. Ticket covers all five lochs. (see Glen Astil).
Lochgilphead Lochs	Lochgilphead	Brown Trout	15 Mar. to 6 Oct.	Lochgilphead and District A.C. c/o The Sports Shop, 31 Lochnell Street, Lochgilphead PA31 8JL. Tel: (0546) 602390.	10 lochs. Fly only. No Sunday fishing.
Loch Loskin	1 mile from Dunoon	Brown/ Sea Trout	1 Apr. to 30 Sept.	Dunoon & District Angling Club. Purdies of Argyll, 112 Argyll Street, Dunoon. Tel: Dunoon 3232.	Fly only. Boat only.
Loch Lossit	Ballygrant	Brown Trout	15 Mar. to 6 Oct.	Port Askaig Stores, Port Askaig, Isle of Islay. Tel: (049684) 245.	Average weight of fish caught: 8-16oz. Boats are available.
Loch Lussa	Campbeltown	Brown Trout	15 Mar. to 6 Oct.	MacGrory & Co., 16/20 Main Street, Campbeltown. Tel: (0586) 552132.	
Mishnish & Aros Lochs	Mull	Brown Trout	15 Mar. to 30 Sept.	Tobermory A.A., c/o Brown's Shop, Tobermory. Tel: (0688) 2020.	Average weight of fish caught: 12oz. Popular flies: Soldier Palmer, Teal & Green. No Spinners. 3 boats available. No Sunday fishing.
Loch na Curraigh	Nr. Kilmelford	Brown Trout	15 Mar. to 6 Oct.	D. Graham, Combe Street, Oban. Tack & Tackle Shop, Oban. Sports Centre, Oban. Anglers' Corner, Oban. Post Office, Kilmelford. Trading Post, Kilchrenan. Mr. Morrison, Ledaig Motors, Benderloch.	The loch has some fat 8oz-1lb trout that sometimes rise freely. The south-end is floating bog and fishing from this bank is not advised. Popular flies: standard trout flies, wet or dry (12 & 14).
Loch nam Ban	Nr. Kilmelford	Brown Trout	15 Mar. to 6 Oct.	D. Graham, Combe Street, Oban. Tack & Tackle Shop, Oban. Sports Centre, Oban. Anglers' Corner, Oban. Post Office, Kilmelford. Trading Post, Kilchrenan. Mr. Morrison, Ledaig Motors, Benderloch.	Fish upto 2lbs have been caught on occasion. Popular flies: standard trout flies, wet or dry (12 & 14).
Loch na Sailm	Nr. Kilmelford	Brown Trout	15 Mar. to 6 Oct.	D. Graham, Combe Street, Oban. Tack & Tackle Shop, Oban. Sports Centre, Oban. Anglers' Corner, Oban. Post Office, Kilmelford. Trading Post, Kilchrenan. Mr. Morrison, Ledaig Motors, Benderloch.	The loch has been damned to improve fishing. Popular flies: Standard trout pattern, sizes 12 & 14.

Water	Location	Species	Season	Permit available from	Other Information
Loch Nell	Nr. Oban	Salmon, Sea Trout Brown Trout Char	15 Mar. to 6 Oct. (Brown Trout)	D. Graham, Combe Street, Oban. Tack & Tackle Shop, Oban. Sports Centre, Oban. Anglers' Corner, Oban. Post Office, Kilmelford. Trading Post, Kilchrenan. Mr. Morrison, Ledaig Motors, Benderloch.	Popular flies: standard patterns Salmon and Sea Trout flies (8 & 10). Fly, spinning and Bubble & fly are permitted. Boat available.
Oude Reservoir	14 miles from Oban	Brown Trout	15 Mar. to 6 Oct.	D. Graham, Combe Street, Oban. Tack & Tackle Shop, Oban. Sports Centre, Oban. Anglers' Corner, Oban. Post Office, Kilmelford. Trading Post, Kilchrenan. Mr. Morrison, Ledaig Motors, Benderloch.	Bank fishing can be difficult because of the fluctuating water level. Popular flies: standard trout flies, wet or dry (12 & 14). A boat is often located on this loch for periods.
Powderworks Reservoir	Argyll	Brown/ Rainbow Trout	15 Mar. to 5 Oct.	Kyles of Bute A.C., c/o Kames Hotel. Tel: (0700) 811489.	Several shops in Kames and Tighnabruaich. Fly and bait only, no spinning.
Loch Quien	Bute	Brown Trout	1 Apr. to 4 Oct.	Bute Estate Office, Rothesay, Isle of Bute. Tel: (0700) 502627.	Fly only. Salmon and trout fishing in sea around Bute.
Loch Scammadale	Kilninver	Salmon Sea Trout Brown Trout	1 June to 15 Oct. 15 Mar.-6 Oct.	Mrs. McCorkindale 'Glenann', Kilninver, by Oban, Argyll. Tel: (085 26) 282.	No Sunday fishing.
Loch Seil	Kilninver	Sea Trout Brown Trout	Apr. to Mid-Oct.	J.T.P. Mellor, Barndromin Farm, Knipoch, by Oban, Argyll. Tel: (085 26) 273.	Boat on Loch.
Sior Lochs	Nr. Oban	Brown Trout	15 Mar. to 6 Oct.	D. Graham, Combe Street, Oban. Tack & Tackle Shop, Oban. Sports Centre, Oban. Anglers' Corner, Oban. Post Office, Kilmelford. Trading Post, Kilchrenan. Mr. Morrison, Ledaig Motors, Benderloch.	Popular flies: standard trout flies, wet or dry (12 & 14). The lochs fish best in April & May.
Loch Squabain	Mull	Salmon Sea Trout Brown Trout		Tackle & Books, Main Street, Tobermory, Mull. Tel: (0688) 2336.	Boat fishing only.
Loch Tarsan	8 miles from Dunoon	Brown Trout	1 Apr. to 30 Sept.	Dunoon & District Angling Club. Purdies of Argyll, 112 Argyll Street, Dunoon. Tel: Dunoon 3232.	Fly only
Tighnabruaich Reservoir (2 other lochs)	Tighnabruaich	Brown/ Rainbow Trout	15 Mar. to 5 Oct.	Kyles of Bute Angling Club. Several shops in Kames and Tighnabruaich, Argyll. Kames Hotel. Tel: (0700) 811489.	Motor boat available for sea fishing.
Torr Loch	North end of Mull	Wild Brown Trout Sea Trout Some Rainbow	April to Oct.	Tackle and Books, Main Street, Tobermory, Mull. Tel: (0688) 2336.	No Sunday fishing. 2 boats. Banks clear.
Loch Turamin	Isle of Colonsay	Brown Trout	15 Mar. to 30 Sept.	The Hotel, Isle of Colonsay, Argyll.	Fly fishing only. Boats are available.

Water	Location	Species	Season	Permit available from	Other Information
Wee Feinn Loch	Nr. Kilmelford	Brown Trout	15 Mar. to 6 Oct.	D. Graham, Combe Street, Oban. Tack & Tackle Shop, Oban. Sports Centre, Oban. Anglers' Corner, Oban. Post Office, Kilmelford. Trading Post, Kilchrenan. Mr. Morrison, Ledaig Motors, Benderloch.	A small loch that contains trout up to 2lbs. Popular flies: standard trout patterns, sizes 10 & 12.

STRATHCLYDE NORTH
Sea Angling

Isle of Bute Rothesay
The holiday resort of Rothesay, situated on the island of Bute, only a 30 minute crossing by roll- on/ roll-off ferry from Wemyss Bay, is sheltered from the prevailing south-westerly winds. Several boat hirers cater for sea anglers. There are also many excellent shore marks. The deep water marks at Garroch Head can be productive for both shore and boat anglers.
Types of fish: Shore – cod, coalfish, pollack, plaice, mackerel, wrasse. Boat – cod, pollack, plaice, mackerel, conger, spurdog, coalfish, wrasse and whiting.
Tackle: Available from Bute Arts & Tackle, 94- 96 Montague Street, Rothesay, Isle of Bute, Tel: (0700) 503598.
Bait: Bute Arts & Tackle, 94-96 Montague Street, Rothesay, Isle of Bute, Tel: (0700) 503598. Low water at Port Bannatyne for cockles, Lugworm and ragworm. Herring is also useful bait. Mussel bait can be obtained on shore.
Season for fishing: May-October.

Kilchattan Bay
Sheltered bay waters at the south end of the Isle of Bute renowned for its good all year round fishing.
Types of fish: Cod, pollack, plaice, mackerel, conger, dogfish, wrasse, whiting.
Bait: Worm, fresh cockle available locally.
Season for fishing: All year.

Mainland Ardentinny
Ardentinny is a small unspoiled village picturesquely situated on the west shore of Loch Long, 12 miles from Dunoon by car.
Types of fish: Cod, mackerel, from the shore. Cod, conger, haddock, ray, plaice, flounder, whiting, coalfish and mackerel from boats.

Bait: Cockles. mussels, lug and ragworm easily dug in bay.
Season for fishing: All year, winter for large cod.

Dunoon
Types of fish: Most of the shoreline around Dunoon provides catches of cod, coalfish, pollack, flounder, mackerel, plaice. Using ragworm & lugworm, cockle, mussel, razorfish & Peeler crab. Boat fishing takes mostly cod, pollack, coalfish, dogfish, dabs, plaice, flounder. Also conger over wrecks or rough ground at night.
Winter fishing: Also produces fair sized cod. Also haddock and whiting. So anglers can fish all year round from boat or shore.
Boats: Gourock skippers fish Dunoon waters. Approx. 3 miles from Dunoon is Holy Loch.
Bait: Can be bought at these shops most of the year or obtained in East Bay shore.

Tighnabruaich & Kames
Tighnabruaich, on the Kyles of Bute, is famed for its beauty and Highland scenery. Access to some good fishing banks on the west side of the Bute and around the Kyles.
Types of fish: Mackerel and coalfish from the shore. Cod, haddock, flatfish, whiting, dogfish, pollack, gurnard and several species of wrasse. Conger fishing can be arranged. The winter run of big cod is well known, haddock and whiting are also caught.
Bait: Supplies of fresh bait (lug, cockle, mussel, clams etc.) are locally available.
Boats: Motor dinghies available for hire. Local fishermen can take parties of anglers by arrangement. Contact: Andy Lancaster, Kames Hotel, Tel: (0700) 811489.
Season: Spring to Autumn, plus winter cod.

Loch Fyne
This is the longest sea-loch in Scotland, penetrating into the

Highlands from the waters of the lower Firth of Clyde. The depth of the water within the loch varies enormously with depth of around 100 fathoms being found not only at the seaward end but also at the head of the loch of Inveraray. Much of the shore angling potential remains unknown although access to both shores is made relatively easy by roads running down each side. Boat launching facilities are less easy to find because of the rugged shoreline. Best side is Inveraray to Furnace. Quarry is now out of bounds.
Types of fish: Mackerel, cod, pollack, flatfish, conger (at night).

Inveraray
Inveraray stands on its west shore near the head of Loch Fyne.
Types of fish: Cod, mackerel, pollack, coalfish, ling, dogfish, conger eel, hake and plaice.
Bait: Mussels and worms available from shore at low tide.
Season for fishing: June-September.

Tarbert (Loch Fyne)
The sheltered harbour and the adjacent coast of the loch near the lower end of the loch on the west shore are good fishing grounds for the sea angler.
Types of fish: Cod, mackerel, coalfish, and sea trout from the shore. Mackerel, cod, coalfish, rays, haddock and whiting from boats.
Boats: Evening out with the boats of the herring fleet can be arranged.
Tackle: Local shops.
Bait: There is an abundance of shellfish and worms on the mud flats.
Season for fishing: June, July and August.

Oban
Good catches can be occasionally taken in Kerrera Sound near the Cutter Rock and the Ferry Rocks. Fishing is much better off the south and west coasts of Kerrera Island, particularly near the Bach Island and Shepherds Hat, Maiden Island and

Oban Bay give good mackerel fishing in July and August. These places are very exposed and should only be attempted in good settled weather.
Types of fish: Boat – mackerel, dogfish, rays, pollack and occasionally cod and haddock. Heavy catches (mainly dogfish) have been taken in the entry to Loch Feochan during the past two seasons.
Bait: Mussels and lugworm, etc. can be dug from the Kerrera beaches.

Season for fishing: May- November.

Sea Life Centre
11 miles north of Oban on A828. Underwater observatory for seals and other fascinating sea creatures and fish. Ideal viewing conditions. Restaurant.

Isle of Islay
This is the southernmost of the islands. Several of the larger communities like Port Ellen and Port Askaig have good harbours.
Types of fish: Boat – cod, haddock, whiting, mackerel, dogfish, flounder, conger, skate.
Tackle: available from J. Campbell, sub-Post Office, Bridgend.
Bait: Lugworm plentiful on most beaches. Clam skirts from fish factory waste. Bait can be purchased from fishing boats at the piers.
Season for fishing: All year.

Constituent Area Tourist Boards

Edinburgh Marketing
Waverley Market,
3 Princes Street,
Edinburgh EH2 2QP.
Tel: 031-557 2727.

Forth Valley Tourist Board
Tourist Officer,
Forth Valley Tourist Board,
Burgh Hall, The Cross,
Linlithgow,
West Lothian EH49 7AH.
Tel: (0506) 84 3306.

**Loch Lomond, Stirling and Trossachs
Tourist Board**
Tourism Manager,
Loch Lomond, Stirling and Trossachs
Tourist Board,
41 Dumbarton Road,
Stirling FK8 2LQ.
Tel: Stirling (0786) 75019.

**St. Andrews and North East Fife
Tourist Board**
Tourism Manager,
St. Andrews and North East Fife Tourist Board,
2 Queens Gardens, St. Andrews,
Fife KY16 9TE.
Tel: St. Andrews (0334) 74609.

Kirkcaldy District Council
Tourist Officer,
Kirkcaldy District Council,
Information Centre,
South Street, Leven,
Fife KY8 4NT.
Tel: Leven (0333) 29464.

East Lothian Tourist Board
Tourism Director,
East Lothian Tourist Board,
Brunton Hall,
Musselburgh, EH21 6AE.
Tel: 031-665 3711.

**Other Tourist Organisations
MIDLOTHIAN**

**RIVER PURIFICATION BOARD
FORTH RIVER PURIFICATION BOARD**
Colinton Dell House,
West Mill Road, Colinton,
Edinburgh EH11 0PH.
Tel: 031-441 4691.

RIVERS

Water	Location	Species	Season	Permit available from	Other Information
Allan	Bridge of Allan	Salmon Sea Trout Brown Trout	15 Mar. to 31 Oct. 15 Mar. to 6 Oct.	Country Pursuits, 46 Henderson Street, Bridge of Allan. Tel: (0786) 834495.	
Almond	Cramond	Salmon Sea Trout Brown Trout	1 Feb. to 31 Oct. 15 Mar. to 6 Oct.	Country Life, Balgreen Road, Edinburgh. Tel: 031-337 6230. Post Office, Davidsons Mains, Edinburgh.	Mouth to Old Cramond Brig. East bank only.
	West Lothian	Salmon Sea Trout Brown Trout	1 Feb. to 31 Oct. 15 Mar. to 6 Oct.	Livingston Sports, Almondvale Centre, Livingston. Country Life, Balgreen Road, Edinburgh. Tel: 031-337 6230. 20 miles of river.	
Balvaig	Strathyre	Brown Trout Salmon	15 Mar. to 6 Oct.	Munro Hotel, Strathyre.	Average weight of fish caught: Trout - 1lb, Salmon - 8lbs. Popular flies: Peter Ross, Blue Zulu. Worm fishing allowed.

SCOTLAND FOR FISHING
A Pastime Publication

I/We have seen your advertisement and wish to know if you have the following vacancy:

Name ....

Address ....

....

Dates from pm ....

Please give date and day of week in each case ....

To am ....

Number in Party ....

Details of Children ....

(Please remember to include a stamped addressed envelope with your enquiry.)

SCOTLAND FOR FISHING
A Pastime Publication

I/We have seen your advertisement and wish to know if you have the following vacancy:

Name ....

Address ....

....

Dates from pm ....

Please give date and day of week in each case ....

To am ....

Number in Party ....

Details of Children ....

(Please remember to include a stamped addressed envelope with your enquiry.)

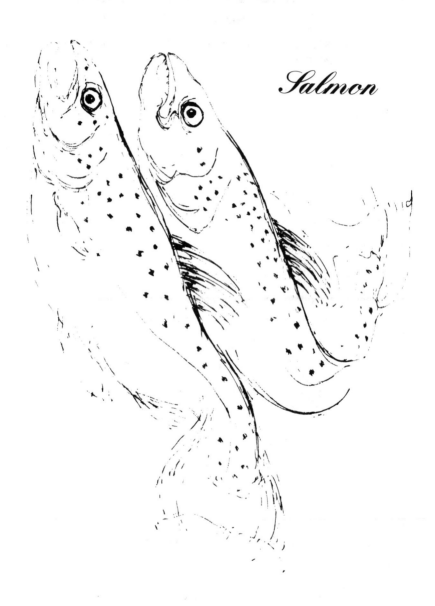

Salmon

Water	Location	Species	Season	Permit available from	Other Information
Devon	Dollar	Salmon Sea Trout Brown Trout	15 Mar. to 30 Oct. 15 Mar. to 5 Oct.	Devon Angling Association, R. Breingan, 33 Redwell Pl., Alloa. Tel: Alloa 215185. Scobbie Sports, 2/4 Primrose Street, Alloa. Tel: (0259) 722661. D.W. Black, The Hobby & Model Shop, 10-12 New Row, Dunfermline. Tel: (0383) 722582. D. Crockart & Son, 47 King Street, Stirling. Tel: (0786) 734433.	No Sunday fishing. Devonside Bridge upstream with excluded stretches. Fly fishing only from 15 Mar.-12 Apr.
	Hillfoots	Salmon Sea Trout Brown Trout	15 Mar. to 31 Oct. 15 Mar. to 6 Oct.	Country Pursuits, 46 Henderson Street, Bridge of Allan. Tel: (0786) 834495.	No Sunday fishing.
Eden	Cupar Area	Brown Trout Sea Trout Salmon	15 Mar.to 5 Oct. 15 Feb. to 31 Oct.	J. Caldwell, Newsagent & Fishing Tackle, Main Street, Methilhill, Fife.	All legal methods permitted.
Endrick	Drymen	Salmon Sea Trout Brown Trout	11 Feb. to 31 Oct. 15 Mar. to 6 Oct.	Loch Lomond Angling Improvement Association. R.A. Clement & Co. C.A., 29 St. Vincent Place, Glasgow. Tel: 041-221-0068.	Members only. No Sunday fishing. No worm fishing. Spinning restricted.
Esk	Musselburgh	Salmon Sea Trout Brown Trout	1 Feb. to 31 Oct. 15 Mar. to 6 Oct.	Givan Shop, 67 Eskside West, Musselburgh. Tel: 031-665 3371.	No Sunday fishing. Regulations on permit.
Esk	(North and South) Midlothian	Brown/ Rainbow Trout Grayling	15 Mar to 6 Oct. 7 Oct.-14 Mar. special winter permit.	Esk Valley Angling Improvement Association. Kevin Burns, 53 Fernieside Crescent, Edinburgh. Tel: 031-664 4685. F. & D. Simpson, 28/29 West Preston Street, Edinburgh EH8 9PZ. Tel: 031—667 3058. Country Life, Balgreen Road, Edinburgh. Tel: 031-337 6230. Laird & Dog Hotel, High Street, Lasswade.	Bailiffs at water. Fly rod and reel only to be used. Stocked at beginning of every month. Reductions for disabled, children and OAP's. Platform at Lasswade for disabled. Regulations on permit. Sunday fishing.
Forth	Stirling	Salmon Sea Trout Brown Trout	1 Feb.to 31 Oct. 15 Mar. to 6 Oct.	D. Crockart & Son, 47 King Street, Stirling. Tel: (0786) 73443. Mitchell's Tackle, 13 Bannockburn Road, Stirling. Country Pursuits, 45 Henderson Street, Bridge of Allan. Tel: (0786) 834495.	Information leaflet, maps, prices, rules, permits - Tel: (0786) 50403. No bait fishing before 1 Apr. or after 1 Sept.
	Gartmore Bridge- Buchlyvie (6¹/2m beat)	Salmon Sea Trout Brown Trout	1 Feb.-31 Oct.	Lawrence Angling, 268 Dumbarton Road, Glasgow G11 6TU. Tel: 041-339 1085.	Fishing by any legal method permitted.
Fruin	Helensburgh	Salmon Sea Trout Brown Trout	11 Feb. to 31 Oct. 1 Mar. to 6 Oct.	Loch Lomond Angling Improvement Association. R.A. Clement & Co. C.A., 29 St. Vincent Place, Glasgow. Tel: 041-221-0068.	Members only. Fly fishing only.

Water	Location	Species	Season	Permit available from	Other Information
Water of Leith	Edinburgh	Brown Trout	1 Apr. to 30 Sept.	Lothian Regional Council, Reception, George IV Bridge, Edinburgh. Tel: 031-229 9292, ext. 3286. Post Office, 36 Main Street, Balerno. Post Office, Bridge Road, Colinton, Edinburgh. Tel: 031-441 1003.	Fly fishing above Slateford Road Bridge. No spinning. Regulations on permit.
Leven	Dumbarton	Salmon Sea Trout Brown Trout	11 Feb. to 31 Oct. 15 Mar. to 6 Oct.	Loch Lomond Angling Improvement Association. R.A. Clement & Co. C.A., 29 St. Vincent Place, Glasgow. Tel: 041-221-0068. Various local tackle shops. Country Lines, 29 Main Street, The Village, East Kilbride. Tel: (03552) 28952.	Members may fish all Association waters. No Sunday fishing. Day tickets available.
	Markinch to Leven	Brown Trout Salmon Sea Trout	15 Mar. to 30 Sept. 11 Feb. to 15 Oct.	J. Caldwell, Newsagent & Fishing Tackle, Main Street, Methilhill, Fife.	
Teith	Callander	Salmon Sea trout Brown Trout	1 Feb. to 31 Oct.	J. Bayne, Main Street, Callander. Tel: (0877) 30218. Country Pursuits, 46 Henderson Street, Bridge of Allan. Tel: (0786) 834495. Season permits only.	Information leaflet, maps, prices, rules, permits: Tel: (0786) 50403. No Sunday fishing.
	Stirling (Blue Banks)	Salmon Sea Trout	1 Feb. to 31 Oct.	D. Crockart & Son, 47 King Street, Stirling, Tel: (0786) 73443.	
	Gart Farm by Callander	Salmon Sea Trout	1 Feb. to 31 Oct.	Country Pursuits, 46 Henderson Street, Bridge of Allan. Tel: (0786) 834495.	Season permits only.
Tyne	Haddington	Brown Trout Rainbow Trout Sea Trout	15 Mar. to 6 Oct.	East Lothian Angling Association. J.S. Main, Saddlers, 87 High Street, Haddington. Tel: (062 082) 2148. John Dickson & Son Ltd., 21 Frederick Street, Edinburgh EH2 2NE. Tel: 031-225 4218. Country Life, Balgreen Road, Edinburgh. Tel: 031-337 6230.	Twenty miles of river. No Sunday fishing. No threadlines. No spinning.
Union Canal	Edinburgh to Falkirk	Pike Perch Roach Carp Tench	No close season	Lothian Regional Council, Reception, George IV Bridge, Edinburgh. Tel: 031-229 9292, ext. 3286. Tourist Office, Linlithgow. Tel: (0506) 844600.	Regulations on permit.

Water	Location	Species	Season	Permit available from	Other Information
LOCHS AND RESERVOIRS					
Loch Achray	By Callander	Brown Trout Perch Pike	15 Mar. to 6 Oct.	Forestry Commission, Queen Elizabeth Forest Park Visitor Centre, Aberfoyle. Loch Achray Hotel, Trossachs. Tel: (08776) 229/240. Bayne's Fishing Tackle Shop, Callander.	Bank fishing only.
Loch Ard	Kinlochard	Brown Trout	15 Mar. to 6 Oct.	Altskeith Hotel, Kinlochard FK8 3TL. Tel: (08777) 266.	Average weight of fish caught: 12oz. Popular flies: Silver Butcher, Kate McLaren, Alexandra. Fly fishing only. Boats are available.
Loch Arklet	By Inversnaid	Brown Trout	15 Mar. to 27 Sept.	Strathclyde Water, 419 Balmore Road, Glasgow G22 6NU or at Loch Arklet.	Average weight of fish caught: 8 to 12oz. Popular flies: Silver Butcher, Grouse & Claret, Black Pennel, Greenwell's Glory. No live bait allowed. Rowing boats only are available.
Beecraigs Loch	Linlithgow	Brown Trout Rainbow Trout Brook Trout	1 Mar. to 31 Oct.	Beecraigs Country Park. Tel: Linlithgow 844516.	Fly fishing only. Boat fishing only.
Bonaly Reservoir	Edinburgh	Brown/ Rainbow Trout	1 Apr. to 30 Sept.	None Required.	
Bowden Springs	Linlithgow	Rainbow/ Brown Trout	3 Jan. to 23 Dec.	W. Martin, Bowden Springs Fishery, Linlithgow. Tel: Linlithgow 847269.	Bank and boat fishing. Fly fishing only. Minimum size 1 lb. Corporate days.
Cameron Reservoir	St. Andrews	Brown Trout	Mid-Apr. to End-Sept.	St. Andrews Angling Club, Secretary, Mr. P. Malcolm, 54 St. Nicholas Street, St. Andrews. Tel: (0334) 76347. The bailiff at the fishing hut on Cameron Reservoir.	Average weight of fish caught: 1lb. Fly fishing only. 6 boats are available.
Upper Carriston Reservoir	Nr. Markinch	Brown Trout	1 Apr. to 30 Sept.	J. Caldwell Newsagent & Fishing Tackle, Main Street, Methilhill, Fife.	Average weight of fish caught: 1lb to 1lb 8oz. Fly fishing only. Bank fishing only - maximum 20 anglers.
Carron Valley Reservoir	Denny	Brown Trout	13 Apr. to 19 Sept.	Director of Finance, Central Regional Council, Viewforth, Stirling. Tel: (0786) 442000.	Boat fishing only.
Clubbiedean Reservoir	Edinburgh	Brown/ Rainbow Trout	1 Apr. to 30 Sept.	Lothian Regional Council, Pentland Hills Regional Park H.Q., Boghall Farm, Biggar Road, Edinburgh. Tel: 031-445 5969.	Three boats. Bag limit 6 trout. Fly fishing only. Sessions: May to August.
Cocksburn Loch	Bridge of Allan	Brown Trout	1 Apr. to 6 Oct.	Country Pursuits, 46 Henderson Street, Bridge of Allan. Tel: (0786) 834495.	Average weight of fish caught: 8-12oz. Boat fishing only. Popular flies: small dark flies.

Water	Location	Species	Season	Permit available from	Other Information
Crosswood Reservoir	West Calder	Brown Trout Brook Trout Rainbow Trout	1 Apr. to 30 Sept.	Lothian Regional Council, Pentland Hills Regional Park H.Q., Boghall Farm, Biggar Road, Edinburgh. Tel: 031-445 5969. Dept. of Water & Drainage, Lomond House, Beveridge Square, Livingston. Tel: (0506) 414004.	Three boats available. 1 boat available - Boghall Farm. 2 boats available - Livingston. Fly fishing only.
Loch Drunkie	Aberfoyle	Brown Trout	15 Mar. to 6 Oct.	Forestry Commission Queen Elizabeth Forest Park Visitor Centre, Aberfoyle.	Bank fishing only.
Duddingston Loch	Edinburgh	Carp Perch	1 May to 30 Sept.	Historic Scotland, 20 Brandon Street, Edinburgh. Tel: 031-244 3085.	Bird Sanctuary. Bank fishing. Restricted area. No lead weights.
Loch Fitty	Kingseat, Dunfermline	Salmon Brown/ Rainbow Trout	1 Mar. to Xmas	The Fishing Lodge, Loch Fitty, Dunfermline, Fife. Tel: (0383) 620666.	Boat and Bank fly fishing. Day - 10am-5pm. Evenings - 5.30pm-dark. Reductions for single anglers, and 'Father & schoolboy Son'. Boats.
Gartmorn Dam Fishery	Nr. Alloa	Brown Trout	1 Apr. to 30 Sept.	Sept to April: Speirs Centre, 29 Primrose Street, Alloa FK10 1JJ. Tel: (0259) 213131. April to Sept: Visitor Centre, Gartmorn Dam Country Park, by Sauchie FK10 3AZ. Tel: (0259) 214319.	Average weight of fish caught: 1lb 4oz. Popular flies: Nymphs, Buzzers, Olives, Wickhams. Restricted bank spinning first six weeks. 9 boats available. Disabled anglers' wheelyboat. 2 sessions: 9am-5pm & 5pm-Dusk.
Gladhouse Reservoir	Midlothian	Brown Trout	1 Apr. to 30 Sept.	Lothian Regional Council, Pentland Hills Regional Park H.Q., Boghall Farm, Biggar Road, Edinburgh. Tel: 031-445 5969. Mrs. E. Kirk, Toxsidehill, Gorebridge. Tel: (087530) 262.	Average weight of fish caught: 1 to 2lbs. Local Nature Reserve. Double-sessions: May-August Day: 8am-4.30pm. Evening: 5pm-Sunset, plus 1 hour. Sunday fishing. Fly fishing only.
Glencorse Reservoir	Penicuik	Brown Trout Brook Trout Rainbow Trout	1 Apr. to 30 Sept.	Lothian Regional Council, Pentland Hills Regional Park H.Q., Boghall Farm, Biggar Road, Edinburgh. Tel: 031-445 5969.	Fly fishing only. 4 boats. Sessions: May to Aug.
Glen Finglas Reservoir	By Callander	Brown Trout	15 Mar. to 27 Sept.	Strathclyde Water, 419 Balmore Road, Glasgow G22 6NU or at Glen Finglas.	Average weight of fish caught: 8 to 12oz. Popular flies: Silver Butcher, Grouse & Claret, Black Pennel, Greenwell's Glory. No live bait allowed. Rowing boat only, are available.
Loch Glow	Cleish Hills, Nr. Kelty	Brown Trout	15 Mar. to 6 Oct.	Tackle shops in Dunfermline, Cowdenbeath, Kelty & Kinross.	Fly, bait & spinning. Regularly stocked with brown trout; some tagged fish. Further information Mr. J.W. Mill, Tel: (0383) 722128.

Water	Location	Species	Season	Permit available from	Other Information
Harlaw Reservoir	Balerno	Brown/ Rainbow Trout	1 Apr. to 30 Sept.	Day tickets: Fleming's Grocery Shop, 42 Main Street, Balerno. Tel: 031-449 3833. Season Permits: Dalmeny Estate Office, South Queensferry, West Lothian.	Average weight of fish caught: 1-2lbs. Fly fishing only. Bank fishing only. Season tickets issued by ballot - applications must be in by 1st March.
Harperrig Reservoir	West Calder	Brown Trout	1 Apr. to 30 Sept.	Dept. of Water & Drainage, Lomond House, Beveridge Square, Livingston. Tel: (0506) 414004.	Bank fishing permits from machine at reservoir. Correct coins required for machine, 50p 10p 5p denominations. Four boats and bank fishing. No Sunday fishing. Fly fishing only.
Hopes Reservoir	Gifford	Brown Trout	1 Apr. to 30 Sept.	Lothian Regional Council, Dept. of Water & Drainage, Alderston House, Haddington. Tel: (062 082) 4131, ext. 217.	2 boats.
Loch Katrine	Stronach -lachar	Brown Trout	15 Mar. to 27 Sept.	Strathclyde Water, 419 Balmore Road, Glasgow G22 6NU or at Stronachlachar.	Average weight of fish caught: 8 to 12oz. Popular flies: Silver Butcher, Grouse & Claret, Black Pennel, Greenwell's Glory. No live bait allowed. Rowing boats only are available.
Lake of Menteith	Port of Menteith	Rainbow Trout	4 Apr. to 30 Oct.	Lake of Menteith Fisheries Ltd., Port of Menteith, Perthshire. Tel: (08775) 664.	28 boats are available. No bank fishing.
Lindores Loch	Newburgh	Brown/ Rainbow Trout	15 Mar. to 30 Nov.	F.G.A. Hamilton, The Byre, Kindrochet, St. Fillans PH6 2JZ. Tel: (076 485) 337.	Two sessions. 9 am - 5 pm 5 pm - 10 pm
Linlithgow Loch	Linlithgow	Brown/ Rainbow Trout	15 Mar. to 6 Oct.	Tel: (0831) 288921.	Average weight of fish caught: 1lb 8oz. Popular flies: black lures, Green Peter, Grouse & Claret, Buzzers. Fly fishing only. 12 boats are available.
Lochore	Ballingry	Brown/ Rainbow Trout	15 Mar. to 6 Oct.	Hobby & Model Shop, Dunfermline. Lochore Meadows Country Park, Crosshill, Lochgelly, Fife. Tel: (0592) 860086.	Reductions for clubs and groups. Sessions: Day - 9 am-5 pm. Evening - 5 pm-dusk. Fly fishing and spinning. Bait fishing from bank from 1 July.
Loch Lomond	Balloch to Ardlui	Salmon Sea Trout Brown Trout Pike Roach Perch	11 Feb. to 31 Oct. 15 Mar.-6 Oct. No close season	Loch Lomond Angling Improvement Association R.A. Clement & Co, C.A., 29 St. Vincent Place, Glasgow. Tel: 041-221-0068. Country Lines, 29 Main Street, The Village, East Kilbride. Tel: (03552) 28952. Local hotels, shops & tackle dealers.	Boats for hire locally. No Sunday fishing. Day permits available.
	Ardlui	Salmon Sea Trout Brown Trout Pike	11 Feb. to 31 Oct. 15 Mar. to 6 Oct.	Ardlui Hotel, Loch Lomond. Tel: 030 14 243.	Popular flies: Silver Victor, Mallard, Claret. Other baits: Toby, Rapala, Sprat. Boats are available.

Water	Location	Species	Season	Permit available from	Other Information
Loch Lomond cont.	Balmaha	Salmon Sea Trout Pike	Mar to Oct. All year.	MacFarlane & Son, The Boatyard, Balmaha. Tel: 036 087 214.	Boats and outboard motors are available.
	By Drymen	Salmon Sea Trout Brown Trout	11 Feb. to 31 Oct. 15 Mar. to 6 Oct.	Rowardennan Hotel, Rowardennan.	Average weight of fish caught: Salmon - 9lbs, Sea Trout - 3 lbs, Brown Trout - 1lb 12oz. Other baits: Toby for trawling.
	Inverbeg	Salmon Sea Trout Brown Trout Pike Perch	11 Feb. to 31 Oct. 15 Mar. to 6 Oct. All Year.	Inverbeg Caravan Park, Inverbeg. Tel: 043 686 267.	Popular flies: March Brown, Peter Ross. Live bait allowed.
Maltings Fishery	West Barns, Dunbar EH42 1RG.	Brown/ Rainbow Trout	All year for Rainbow.	Dunbar Trout Farm Tel: (0368) 63244. (Or at the fishery).	Fly only. Maximum fly size no. 10 long shank.
Morton Fishery	Mid Calder	Brown/ Rainbow Trout	6 Mar. to 30 Oct.	Morton Fishery, Morton Reservoir, Mid Calder, W. Lothian. Tel: (0506) 882293.	Fly fishing only. Advance bookings. Double sessions May-Aug, 9 am-5 pm, 5 pm-dusk. Bag limits 3-6 fish per rod.
North Third	By Cambus -barron	Rainbow/ Brown Trout	15 Mar. to 31 Oct.	North Third Trout Fishery, "Greathill", Cambusbarron, Stirling. Tel: Stirling (0786) 71967.	Fly fishing only. Boat and bank. Day/season permits available. Advance bookings advisable. Fishery record for rainbow trout 19lbs. Loch stocked in 1992 with American brook trout.
Loch Ore	Ballingry	Brown/ Rainbow Trout	15 Mar. to 6 Oct.	Lochore Meadows Country Park, Crosshill, Lochgelly, Fife. Tel: (0592) 860086.	Average weight of fish caught: 1lb 4oz. Spinning and bait from bank (check of dates). Boats are available.
Lochan Reoidhe	Aberfoyle	Brown Trout	15 Mar. to 6 Oct.	Forestry Commission Queen Elizabeth Forest Park Visitor Centre, Aberfoyle.	Fly fishing only. Limited rods. Boat available. Advance bookings accepted.
Selm Muir Loch	Nr. Livingston	Rainbow Trout	All year	Selm Muir Loch.	Average weight of fish caught: 1lb 4oz. Popular flies: Montana Nymph, small black lures. Other baits: maggots, sweetcorn, no spinning.
Swan's Water Fishery	Stirling	Rainbow/ Brown Trout	All year for Rainbow	Swan's Water Fishery.	Average weight of fish caught: 1lb 12oz. Popular flies: Viva, Black Pennel. Fly fishing only. 2 boats are available.
Threipmuir Reservoir	Balerno	Brown/ Rainbow Trout	1 Apr. to 30 Sept.	Day tickets: Flemings, Grocer, 42 Main Street, Balerno. Tel: 031-449 3833. Season permits: Dalmeny Estate Office, South Queensferry, West Lothian.	Average weight of fish caught: 1-2lbs. Fly fishing only. Bank fishing only. Season tickets issued by ballot - applications must be in by 1st March.

Water	Location	Species	Season	Permit available from	Other Information
Loch Venachar	Callander	Brown Trout	15 Mar. to 6 Oct.	J. Bayne, Main Street, Callander. Tel: (0877) 30218.	Boats for hire.
		Salmon Sea Trout Brown Trout	1 Feb. to 31 Oct. 15 Mar. to 6 Oct.	Country Pursuits, 46 Henderson Street, Bridge of Allan. Tel: (0786) 834495.	Season permits only.
Loch Voil	Balquhidder	Brown Trout Salmon Sea Trout Char	15 Mar. to 6 Oct.	Stronvar Country House Hotel, Balquhidder FK19 8PB. Tel: (08774) 688.	Hotel Guests only. Advanced bookings necessary.
				C.M. Oldham & I.T. Emslie, Muirlaggan, Balquidder, Lochearnhead FK19 8PB. Tel: (08774) 219.	Popular flies: Blae & Black, Kate McLaren, Grouse & Claret, Black Spider, Greenwell's Glory, Butcher, Professor (size 12). Other baits: spinners, rapala, toby, kynoch killer for salmon. 5 boats are available.

FORTH AND LOMOND (CLYDE COAST)

Sea Angling

Helensburgh

Helensburgh is a small seaside town on the Firth of Clyde at the southern end of the Gareloch, easily reached by train or car.
Types of fish: Shore and boat – cod, flounder, coalfish, conger, rays, dogfish, whiting, dab, haddock, pollack and mackerel.
Bait: Ragworm, lugworm, may be dug locally. Mussels and crabs can be gathered from the shore.
Season for fishing: All year, especially winter for large cod.

Garelochhead

Garelochhead is the village at the head of the Gareloch, with the whole shoreline within easy reach. Upper and lower Loch Long and Loch Goil are only a few miles away.
Types of fish: Cod, coalfish, pollack, dab, flounder, plaice, whiting, haddock, pouting, rays, mackerel, spurdog, lesser spotted dogfish.
Bait: Garelochhead – cockles and mussels. Roseneath – lugworm, ragworm and cockles. Rhu – ragworm. Kilcreggan – ragworm. Coulport – cockles.
Season for fishing: December-March, migratory cod – June onwards.

Arrochar, Loch Long

The village lies at the northern end of the loch, and has waters sheltered by the high surrounding hills.

Types of fish: Shore – cod, conger, pollack, coalfish and rays. Boat – cod, haddock, whiting, conger, pollack, coalfish, mackerel, dogfish and rays.
Bait: Fresh herring and mackerel, mussels and cockles usually available from the pier. Artificial baits, lures etc. available from shops in village.
Season for fishing: All year.

Clynder

Clynder is the fishing centre on the sheltered west side of the Gareloch and one mile north of the popular Rhu Narrows.
Types of fish: Shore: cod and mackerel. Boat: cod, conger, rays, plaice, flounders, dogfish, whiting, pouting and mackerel.
Boats: C. Moar (0436) 831336;
Bait: Cockles, mussels, lug, ragworm, can be dug.\
Season for fishing: All year, winter for large cod.

FORTH AND LOMOND (EAST COAST)

Anglers going afloat from Fife and Forth Harbours are advised to contact the coastguard at Fifeness for weather information. Tel: Crail (0333) 50666 (day or night).

Tayport

Tayport, on the Firth of Tay opposite Dundee, in the northern-most part of Fife, enjoys good shore fishing in sheltered waters. There are no hotels but there is a modern caravan and camping site with showers, laundry etc.

Types of fish: Cod, flounder and plaice from shore, with occasional sea trout (permit required).
Bait: Lugworm, ragworm, mussels, cockles and crabs available locally at low water.
Season for fishing: April- January.

St. Andrews

St. Andrews is a leading holiday resort with sea angling as one of its attractions. Fishing is mainly from boats, but good sport can be had from the rocks between the bathing pool and the harbour.
Tackle: Messrs. J. Wilson & Sons (Ironmongers), 169-171 South Street, St. Andrews, KY16 9EE, Tel: 0334 72477.
Bait: Excellent supplies of Lugworm, ragworm and large mussels can be gathered on the beach.

Boarhill and Kings Barns

Good beach fishing for cod and flatfish.

Anstruther

It is a fishing village with plenty of good boat and beach fishing. A very rocky coastline but can be very rewarding with good catches of cod, saithe, flounder, wrasse, and whiting. Be prepared to lose tackle.
Types of fish: Cod, saithe, wrasse, flounder, ling, conger and mackerel.
Boats: Plenty charter boats with local skippers who know all the hot spots.
Bait: Lug, rag, white rag, cockle, crab, mussel which can be dug locally.
Season: Boat – May-October. Beach – September-January.

Pittenweem

The nerve centre of the East Neuk with a large deep water harbour which boats can enter or leave at any stage of the tide. The European Cod Festival is now held here each year and produces large catches of cod. The harbour wall is very popular with young and old alike, with some good catches.

Types of fish: Cod, saithe, flounder, wrasse, ling, conger, whiting, mackerel from boats. Cod, saithe, flounder, wrasse and whiting from beach.
Bait: Lug, rag, can be dug locally.
Season: Beach – September-January.

Leven

A holiday resort with about 2 miles of lovely sandy beaches. Beach fishing is very popular with some very good catches.

Types of fish: Flounder, cod, bass, mullet, saithe.
Boats: No charter boats.
Bait: Lug available locally.
Season: July-January.

Buckhaven

A small town on the north side of the Firth of Forth, which is renowned for its boat and beach fishing. The Scottish Open Beach Competition is fished from Buckhaven to Dysart each year with large entries from all over Scotland.

Types of fish: Cod, saithe, flounder, whiting, mackerel from beach. Cod, saithe, flounder, whiting, ling, mackerel and wrasse from boat.
Bait: Lug available at Leven.
Boats: No charter hire.
Season: Boat – June-November. Beach – October-January.

Kirkcaldy

Beach fishing at east and west end of town.
Types of fish: Cod, flatfish, saithe, mackerel.
Bait: Beach off bus station.

Pettycur and Kinghorn

Rock and beach fishing off Pettycur Harbour and Kinghorn Beach.
Types of fish: Saithe, flatfish.
Boats: Small boats can be launched from beaches.
Bait: Plenty locally. Local caravan sites.

Burntisland

Permission required to fish the beach from harbour to swimming pool.
Types of fish: Saithe, flatfish, small cod.
Boats: None locally.
Bait: Lug available locally.

South Queensferry

A picturesque burgh overshadowed by the Forth Bridges. There are 3 launching slips in the area, but currents can be dangerous and local advice should be obtained before setting out in dinghies.
Types of fish: Cod, whiting, coalfish, mackerel, flounder from boat and shore in season.
Bait: Lugworm, ragworm, mussel, cockle, clams and crabs at low water in the area.
Season for fishing: May to October.

Edinburgh

Scotland's capital city, on the south of the Forth estuary, has several miles of shoreline. Most of this is sandy, and can produce good catches of flatfish, although codling, Ray's bream, whiting, eels and mackerel can be taken in season from the shore. Best marks are at Cramond, round the mouth of the River Almond, and the Seafield to Portobello area.
Bait: Lugworm, ragworm, mussels, cockles and clams from most beaches at low water.
Season for fishing: All year round.

Musselburgh

This town stands on the estuary of the River Esk, 6 miles to the east of Edinburgh, overlooking the Firth of Forth. It has a small but busy harbour at Fisherrow, catering mainly for pleasure craft.
Boats: Enquiries should be made at the harbour. Best shore marks range from Fisherrow harbour to the mouth of the Esk.
Bait: Lugworm, ragworm, mussels, cockles and clams at low water.

Cockenzie

Mullet can be caught around the warm water outfall to the east of Cockenzie Power station and around the harbour. Other species include flatfish, codling and mackerel.

North Berwick

There is good boat fishing out of North Berwick and the coastline between the town and Dunbar is good for shore fishing.
Types of fish: Cod, haddock, plaice, mackerel and coalfish.
Bait: Mussels, crabs and shellfish of various types available at low water.
Further information from: Information Centre, Quality Street. Tel: North Berwick (0620) 2197 January-December.

Dunbar

The coastline from Dunbar to Eyemouth is very popular for rock and beach fishing.
Types of fish: Cod, haddock, flounder, coalfish, mackerel, wrasse and whiting.
Boats: Details can be obtained from The Tourist Information Centre, Dunbar.
Bait: Mussels, lug and ragworm available at low water, and also from tackle dealers.
Season for fishing: Best April to October.
Further information from: Information Centre, Town House, High Street. Tel: Dunbar (0368) 63353 January-December.

Constituent Area Tourist Boards

City of Dundee Tourist Board
Director,
City of Dundee Tourist Board,
Tourism Information Department,
4 City Square,
Dundee DD1 3BA.
Tel: Dundee (0382) 23141, ext. 4384

Perthshire Tourist Board
Director of Tourism,
Perthshire Tourist Board,
45 High Street, Perth PH1 5TJ.
Tel: Perth (0738) 27958.

Angus Tourist Board
Tourist Manager,
Angus Tourist Board,
Market Place, Arbroath,
Angus DD11 1HR.
Tel: Arbroath (0241) 76680.

RIVER PURIFICATION BOARD
TAY RIVER PURIFICATION BOARD
1 South Street,
Perth PH2 8NJ.
Tel: Perth (0738) 27989.

RIVERS

Water	Location	Species	Season	Permit available from	Other Information
Braan	Amulree	Brown Trout	15 Mar. to 6 Oct.	Post Office, Amulree.	Fly fishing only.
	Cochill Burn	Brown Trout	15 Mar to 6 Oct.	Kettles of Dunkeld, Atholl Street, Dunkeld. Tel: (0350) 727556.	Fly fishing only.
Dean	Strathmore	Brown Trout	15 Mar. to 6 Oct.	Strathmore Angling Improvement Association, Mrs. A.J. Henderson, 364 Blackness Road, Dundee. Tel: (0382) 68062.	
	Devon Hillfoots, Tillicoultry to Crook of Devon	Salmon Sea Trout Brown Trout	15 Mar. to 31 Oct. 15 Mar.-6 Oct.	Country Pursuits, 46 Henderson Street, Bridge of Allan. Tel: (0786) 834495.	Fly fishing only from: 15 March to 12 April.
Dochart	Killin	Brown Trout	15 Mar. to 6 Oct.	J. Lewis, Tackle Dealer, Killin, Perthshire. Tel: (056 72) 362.	All legal lures permitted. Fly only on lower beat.
Earn	Crieff	Salmon Sea Trout Brown Trout	1 Feb. to 15 Oct. 15 Mar.-6 Oct.	Crieff Angling Club. Mr. R. Kelly, 39 King Street, Crieff. Tel: (0764) 3871.	No shrimp, prawn, diving minnow or floats. No bait before 1st May.
Earn	By Crieff	Salmon Sea Trout Brown Trout	1 Feb. to 31 Oct. 15 Mar.-6 Oct.	Country Pursuits, 46 Henderson Street, Bridge of Allan. Tel: (0786) 834495.	(Lower Strowan Beat) Permit available for season only (day per week throughout season).
Ericht	Bridge of Cally	Salmon Brown Trout	1 Jan.-15 Oct. 15 Mar.-6 Oct.	Bridge of Cally Hotel, Blairgowrie, Perthshire. Tel: (025 086) 231.	Fly fishing only after 15 April.
	Craighall	Salmon Brown Trout	15 Jan.-15 Oct. 15 Mar.-6 Oct.	A.L. Rattray, Craighall, Blairgowrie PH10 7JB. Tel: (0250) 874749 or (0738) 30926.	Subject to availability.
Garry	Blair Atholl	Brown Trout	15 Mar. to 6 Oct.	Highland Shop, Blair Atholl. Tel: (0796) 481303.	Any legal method permitted.

Water	Location	Species	Season	Permit available from	Other Information
Isla	Strathmore	Brown Trout	15 Mar. to 6 Oct.	Strathmore Angling Improvement Association, Mrs. A.J. Henderson, 364 Blackness Road, Dundee. Tel: (0382) 68062.	
Lochay	Killin	Brown Trout Pike Perch	15 Mar. to 6 Oct.	J. Lewis, Tackle Dealers, Main Street, Killin, Perthshire. Tel: (056 72) 362.	Fly only on upper beat.
Lunan	Arbroath	Sea/ Brown Trout	15 Mar to 6 Oct.	Arbroath Cycle and. Tackle Centre, 274 High Street, Arbroath. Tel: (0241) 73467.	Fly, bait or spinning.
Lyon	Aberfeldy	Salmon	15 Jan. to 15 Oct.	Fortingall Hotel, Fortingall, by Aberfeldy. Tel: (0887) 830367.	No Sunday fishing. Max. 5 rods on each of 2 beats. Maps, tackle etc. available. (6 miles single bank).
	Tirinie Fishings	Salmon Brown Trout	15 Jan.-15 Oct. 15 Mar.-6 Oct.	Coshieville Hotel, By Aberfeldy PH15 2NE.	Max. 4 rods. No bait fishing. No Sunday fishing. Boat & ghillie available for hire.
South Esk	Kirriemuir	Salmon Sea Trout	16 Feb. to 31 Oct.	H. Burness, Kirriemuir Angling Club, 13 Clova Road, Kirriemuir. Tel: (0575) 73456.	No permits on Saturdays. No Sunday fishing. Fly only in parts in low water. Booking advisable.
Tay	Aberfeldy	Brown Trout Grayling	15 Mar. to 6 Oct.	Jamiesons Sports Shop, 41 Dunkeld Street, Aberfeldy. Tel: (0887) 20385.	Fly only until 1st May.
		Salmon Brown Trout	15 Jan.-15 Oct. 15 Mar.-6 Oct.	Weem Hotel, Weem, by Aberfeldy. Tel: (0887) 820381.	Salmon - any legal means. Trout - fly or small mepps only.
		Salmon Sea Trout	15 Jan. to 15 Oct.	Country Pursuits, 46 Henderson Street, Bridge of Allan. Tel: (0786) 834495.	(Killiechassie Beat) 4 rods maximum. Ghillie available. No prawns/shrimps after 1 Sept.
		Salmon Sea Trout	15 Jan. to 15 Oct.	Country Pursuits, 46 Henderson Street, Bridge of Allan. Tel: (0786) 834495.	(Derculich Beat) Maximum 3 rods. Ghillie available. No bait.
		Salmon Sea Trout	15 Jan. to 15 Oct.	Country Pursuits, 46 Henderson Street, Bridge of Allan. Tel: (0786) 834495.	(Lower Farleyer) 4 rods maximum. Ghillie Available. No Prawns/ shrimps after 1 Sept.
		Salmon Sea Trout	15 Jan. to 15 Oct.	Country Pursuits, 46 Henderson Street, Bridge of Allan. Tel: (0786) 834495.	(Moness Beat) Maximum 3 rods. Boat & ghillie available. No prawns/shrimps after 1 Sept.
	Grandtully	Salmon Brown Trout Grayling	15 Jan.-15 Oct. 15 Mar. to 6 Oct.	Grantully Hotel, Strathtay, Perthshire. Tel: (0887) 840207.	Fly or spinning. Boat & ghillie available. Booking advisable. Rod hire and tackle. 5-rod beat.
		Salmon Sea Trout	15 Jan. to 15 Oct.	Country Pursuits, 46 Henderson Street, Bridge of Allan. Tel: (0786) 834495.	(Findyate Beat) Maximum 3 rods. Boat & ghillie available. No prawns/shrimps after 1 Sept. Good Spring beat.

Water	Location	Species	Season	Permit available from	Other Information
Tay cont.	Grandtully	Salmon Sea Trout	15 Jan. to 15 Oct.	Country Pursuits, 46 Henderson Street, Bridge of Allan. Tel: (0786) 834495.	(Clochfoldich Beat) Maximum 3 rods. Boat & ghillie available. No prawns/shrimps after 1 Sept. Good Spring beat.
	Dalguise	Salmon	15 Jan. to 15 Oct.	The Manager, Burnside, Dalguise, by Dunkeld. Tel: (0350) 727593.	1½ miles both banks.
	Dunkeld	Salmon Brown Trout	15 Jan.-15 Oct. 15 Mar.-6 Oct.	Stakis Hotels Ltd., Dunkeld House Hotel, Dunkeld. Tel: (0350) 727771.	Two boats with two rods. Experienced ghillies. 8 bank rods. Tuition. No salmon fishing on Sundays. Booking advisable.
		Brown Trout Grayling	15 Mar. to 6 Oct.	Kettles of Dunkeld, Atholl Street, Dunkeld. Tel: (0350) 727556.	Fly fishing only. Tackle hire.
		Salmon Sea Trout	15 Jan. to 15 Oct.	Country Pursuits, 46 Henderson Street, Bridge of Allan. Tel: (0786) 834495.	(Upper Newtyle Beat) Maximum 5 rods. Boat and ghillie available. No prawns/shrimps after 1 Sept.
		Salmon Sea Trout	15 Jan. to 15 Oct.	Country Pursuits, 46 Henderson Street, Bridge of Allan. Tel: (0786) 834495.	(Lower Newtyle Beat) Maximum 5 rods. Boat & ghillie available. No prawns/shrimps after 1 Sept.
	Stanley	Salmon Sea Trout Brown Trout	15 Jan.-13 Oct. 12 Mar.- 6 Oct.	Tayside Hotel, Stanley, Nr. Perth. Tel: (0738) 828249.	Day permits available May-July. Ghillies by arrangement. Advisable to book in advance.
	Perth	Salmon Sea Trout Flounder Roach	15 Jan. to 15 Oct.	Director of Leisure & Recreation, Perth & Kinross District Council, 3 High Street, Perth. Tel: (0738) 39911, (Monday to Friday). Tourist Information Centre, 45 High Street, Perth PH1 5TJ. Tel: (0738) 38353 Weekends & public holidays.	Advisable to book in advance. Only 20 permits per day. Only 2 permits in advance by any one person. No weekly permits.
	Ballinluig	Salmon	15 Jan. to 15 Oct.	Jim Trittow, Port of Tay Cottage, Ballinluig.	(Upper Kinnaird Beat) Average weight of fish caught: 12lbs. Other baits: prawns, worms. Boats are available.
Tilt	Blair Atholl	Salmon	End-May to 15 Oct.	The Highland Shop, Blair Atholl. Tel: (0796) 481303.	(Private Beat, 3 miles) Booking advised. Fly or spinning only.
Tummel	Pitlochry to Ballinluig	Brown Trout Grayling	15 Mar. to 6 Oct.	Atholl Sports, Atholl Road, Pitlochry.	Five miles of river, both banks. Map and rules on permits.
		Brown Trout Grayling	15 Mar. to 6 Oct. 7 Oct.-14 Mar.	Mitchells of Pitlochry, 23 Atholl Road, Pitlochry. Tel: (0796) 472613.	Permits available 7 days per week - 15 Jan. to 15 Oct.
	Tummel (Upper) Kinloch Rannoch	Brown Trout	15 Mar. to 6 Oct.	E.M. Beattie (Sec.), 2 Schiehallion Place, Kinloch Rannoch. Tel: (0882) 632261. Local shops & hotels.	Average weight of fish caught: 12oz. Other baits: spinning and live.

Water	Location	Species	Season	Permit available from	Other Information
LOCHS AND RESERVOIRS					
Loch Bainnie	Spittal of Glenshee	Brown Trout	18 Mar. to 11 Aug.	Invercauld Estates Office, Braemar AB35 5XQ. Tel: Braemar 41224.	Boat available from: Mr. R. Hepburn, Gamekeeper, Wester Binzean, Glenshee. Tel: Glenshee 206. No spinning or use of live bait.
Ben Vrackie Loch	By Pitlochry	Brown Trout	15 Mar. to 30 Sept.	Mr. Seaton, Gamekeeper's House, Baledmund Estate, Pitlochry.	Average weight of fish caught: 8oz. Any legal method permitted.
Blair Walker Pond	Blair Atholl	(Stocked) Brown/ Rainbow Trout	15 Mar. to 6 Oct.	The Highland Shop, Blair Atholl. Tel: (0796) 481303.	Fly only.
Butterstone Loch	Dunkeld	Rainbow/ Brown Trout	1 Apr. to 31 Oct.	The Bailiff, Lochend Cottage, Butterstone, by Dunkeld. Tel: (0350) 724238.	Fly fishing only. 15 Boats. Day Session: 9 am-5 pm. Evening: 5.30 pm-dusk.
Castlehill Reservoir	Glendevon	Brown Trout	1 Apr. to 30 Sept.	Fife Reg. Council, Craig Mitchell House. Flemington Road, Glenrothes. Tel: (0592) 754411). Glendevon Treatment Works. Tel: (0259) 781453.	Fly fishing only. Boat £10 inc. 2 rods. Bank £3.
Loch Dochart	by Crianlarich	Salmon Brown Trout	1 Feb. to 6 Oct.	Portnellan House, by Crianlarich FK20 8QS. Tel: (08383) 284.	Popular flies: Black Pennel, Black & Peacock, Mullard, Claret. Any legal method permitted. Boats available.
Dunalastair Loch	Kinloch Rannoch	Brown Trout	15 Mar. to 6 Oct.	Lassintullich Fisheries. Tel: (0882) 632238.	Five boats. No bank fishing. Fly fishing only.
Loch Earn	Lochearnhead	Brown Trout	15 Mar. to 6 Oct.	Clachan Cottage Hotel, Lochside, Lochearnhead. Tel: (05673) 247. Lochearnhead Holiday Centre. Tel: (05673) 221.	Fishing Mon. to Sun. Fly rod, Fly reel and any legal method, max. B.S. 4lbs. Min. taking size 8". Prohibited baits: diving minnow.
		Brown/ Rainbow Trout	Mar. to Oct.	St. Fillans Post Office, St. Fillans.	Average weight of fish caught: 12oz-2lbs. The loch is regularly stocked.
Loch Eigheach	Moor of Rannoch	Brown Trout	15 Mar. to 6 Oct.	Rannoch & District Angling Club, John Brown, The Square, Kinloch Rannoch. Tel: (0882) 632268.	Bank fishing only.
Errochty Dam	Nr. Blair Atholl	Brown Trout Pike	15 Mar. to 6 Oct. No close season	The Highland Shop, Blair Atholl. Tel: (0796) 481303.	Any legal method permitted.
Loch Faskally	Pitlochry	Salmon	Mar., May to Oct.	Mr. D. McLaren, Pitlochry Boating Station, Loch Faskally, Pitlochry. Tel: (0796) 472919/472759	Any legal lure for salmon Boats available. Cafe facilities.
		Brown Trout Pike Perch	Mar. to Sept.		
Glendevon Lower Reservoir)	Glendevon	Brown Trout	1 Apr. to 30 Sept.	Fife Regional Council, Craig Mitchell House. Flemington Road, Glenrothes. Tel: (0592) 754411. Glendevon Treatment Works. Tel: (025981) 453.	Fly fishing only. No Sunday fishing. Bank fishing allowed on Lower Glendevon. Boat £10 incl. 2 rods. Bank £3.

Water	Location	Species	Season	Permit available from	Other Information
Glenfarg	Glenfarg	Brown Trout	1 Apr. to 30 Sept.	Fife Regional Council, Craig Mitchell House, Flemington Road, Glenrothes. Tel: (0592) 754411. Glenfarg Treatment Works. Tel: (05773) 561.	Fly fishing only. No Sunday fishing. Boat available.
Heathery-ford	Just off Junction 6 on M90 at Kinross.	Brown/ Rainbow Trout	Mid-March to Dec.	Kinross Trout Fishery, office on site, Tel: (05778) 64212.	All bank fishing, top quality trout. Trout master water. Fly fishing only.
Holl	Lomond Hills	Brown Trout	1 Apr. to 30 Sept.	Fife Regional Council, Craig Mitchell House, Flemington Road, Glenrothes. Tel: (0592) 754411.	Fly fishing only. No Sunday fishing. Boat available.
Loch lubhair	Nr. Crianlarich	Salmon Brown Trout	1 Feb. to 6 Oct.	Portnellan House, by Crianlarich FK20 8QS. Tel: (08383) 284.	Popular flies: Black Pennel, Black & Peacock, Mullard, Claret. Any legal method permitted. Boats are available.
Loch Kinardochy	Tummelbridge	Brown Trout	15 Mar. to 6 Oct.	Mitchells of Pitlochry, 23 Atholl Road, Pitlochry PH16 5BX. Tel: (0796) 472613.	Fly fishing from boat only. Advance booking recommended.
Lochan-na-Laraig	Killin	Trout	15 Mar. to 6 Oct.	J. Lewis, Tackle Dealers, Main Street, Killin. Tel: (056 72) 362.	All legal lures.
Loch Lee	Glen Esk	Brown Trout Arctic Char	1 May to 12 Aug.	Head Keeper, Invermark, Glenesk, by Brechin DD9 7YZ. Tel: (0356) 670208.	Average weight of fish caught: 8oz to 12oz. Popular flies: any small dark flies. 3 boats - 3 rods per boat. No Sunday fishing. No bank fishing.
Loch Leven	Kinross	Brown Trout (Loch Leven strain)	2nd Apr. to 6th Oct.	Lochleven Fisheries, The Pier, Kinross. Tel: (0577) 863407.	Fly and boat fishing only.
Lintrathen Reservoir	Kirriemuir	Brown Trout	1 Apr. to 6 Oct.	Lintrathen Angling Club Jack Yule, 61 Hillrise, Kirriemuir, Angus DD8 4JS. Tel: (05756) 327. Club bookings: Dr. Parratt, 91 Strathearn Road, Broughty Ferry, Dundee. Tel: (0382) 77305. (Not after start of season).	18 boats. Sunday fishing. Max. catch 24 fish per boat. Tel. for details of sessions and backwater dam. Bank fishing only.
Monikie	Monikie	Brown Trout	Beg. Apr. to 6 Oct.	Tel: Newbigging 300.	Average weight of fish caught: 1lb 4oz. Popular flies: Bibio, Kate McLaren, Ace of Spades. Boats: (10) Island Pond, (4) North Pond, (4) Crombie. Fly only. Boat only.
Loch Nan Ean	Dalmunzie	Brown Trout	18 Mar. to 11 Aug.	Invercauld Estates Office, Braemar AB35 5XQ. Tel: Braemar 41224.	No spinning or use of live bait permitted.

Water	Location	Species	Season	Permit available from	Other Information
Loch Rannoch	Kinloch Rannoch	Brown Trout	15 Mar. to 6 Oct.	Loch Rannoch Conservation Association, Cuilmore Cottage, Kinloch Rannoch. Loch Rannoch Hotel. Tel: (0882) 632201. Bunrannoch Hotel, Tel: (0882) 632367.	Fly fishing only. 6 am - 10 pm. 15 foot open boats. No live bait. Ghillie service. Rod hire. Small tackle shop.
		Brown Trout Pike Perch	15 Mar. to 6 Oct.	E.M. Beattie (Sec.), 2 Schiehallion Place, Kinloch Rannoch. Tel: (0882) 632261.	Local shops and hotels. Average weight of fish caught: 8oz to 1lb. No live bait allowed. Boats are available from: Dunalastair or Loch Rannoch hotels.
Rescobie Loch	Forfar	Brown/ Rainbow Trout	15 Mar. to 31 Oct.	Bailiff, Rescobie Loch, South Lodge, Reswallie, By Forfar DD8 2SA. Tel: (030781) 384.	Fly fishing only. Bank & Boat.
Sandy-knowes Fishery	Bridge of Earn	Rainbow Trout	1 Mar. to 30 Nov.	E. Christie, The Fishery Office, Sandyknowe Fishery, Bridge of Earn. Tel: (0738) 813033.	Bank fly fishing only. Session times 10 am-2 pm, 2 pm-6 pm, 6 pm-10 pm. Bag limit - 4 trout per session. Open 7 days. No Sunday evenings.
Loch Tay	Killin	Brown Trout	15 Mar. to 5 Oct.	J. Lewis, Tackle Dealers, Main Street, Killin. Tel: (056 72) 362.	All legal lures permitted.
		Salmon	15 Jan.- 15 Oct.	Clachaig Hotel, Killin. Tel: (056 72) 270.	3 boats available with outboards.
	Milton Morenish	Salmon Trout	15 Jan.-15 Oct. 15 Mar.-6 Oct.	Loch Tay Highland Lodges, Milton Morenish, by Killin. Tel: (056 72) 323.	Sixteen boats available. Ghillie and rod hire. Special offers for mid-week fishing.
	Kenmore	Salmon Brown Trout Rainbow Trout	15 Jan.-15 Oct. 15 Mar. to 15 Oct.	Kenmore Hotel, Kenmore, by Aberfeldy. Tel: (0887) 830205.	Boats available on Loch Tay. Ghillie service, rod hire to residents. Fishing for two miles on River Tay.
Loch Tummel	West of Pitlochry	Trout Pike Perch	Apr. to Oct.	Queen's View Visitor Centre, Strathtummel, by Pitlochry PH16 5NR.	
Loch Turret	Crieff	Brown Trout	1 Apr. to 30 Sept.	The Director, Central Scotland Water Development Board, Balmore, Torrance, Glasgow G64 4AJ. Tel: (0360) 205. Mr. R. Kelly, 39 King Street, Crieff. Tel: (0764) 3871.	Four boats with outboards. Fly only.

TAYSIDE
Sea Angling

Arbroath
Situated on the east coast of Angus, 17 miles north-east of Dundee, Arbroath is easily accessible by road and rail. It is the centre for commercial fishing, and famous for its smokies. Pleasure boats ply for short cruises to local sea cliffs and caves, from the harbour. There are about 10 boats between 15ft and 35ft used for lobster and crab fishing, taking out parties for sea angling.
Types of fish: Cod, coalfish, mackerel, flounder, conger, plaice, haddock and pollack.
Boats: Available through local fishermen and part time lobster and crab fishermen at reasonable prices.

Dundee
Dundee is situated on the estuary of the River Tay and has sea fishing in the city centre, while Broughty Ferry, a suburb of Dundee, Easthaven and Carnoustie, all within easy reach by road and rail, have sea fishing from rocks, piers or from boats. There are good marks around the Bell Rock about 12 miles offshore.
Types of fish: Cod, flatfish from shore plus cod, haddock, coalfish, ling, pouting and plaice from boats.
Tackle: available from Shotcast Ltd., 8 Whitehall Crescent, Dundee.
Tel: Dundee 25621.
Bait: Available locally.
Season for fishing: All year.

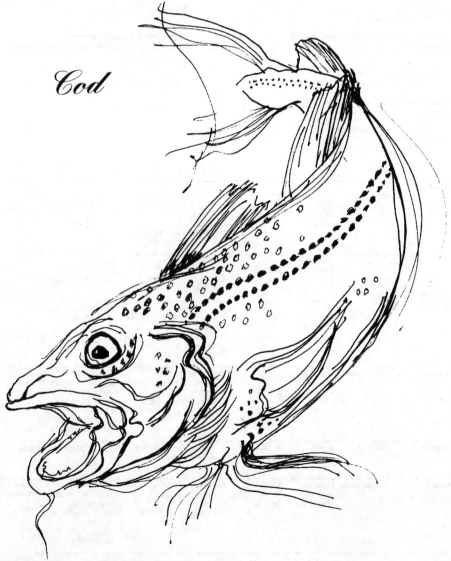

Cod

Constituent Area Tourist Boards

Aviemore and Spey Valley Tourist Board
Area Tourist Officer,
Aviemore and Spey Valley Tourist Board,
Grampian Road, Aviemore,
Inverness-shire PH22 1PP.
Tel: Aviemore (0479) 810363.

Banff and Buchan Tourist Board
Tourism Manager,
Banff and Buchan Tourist Board,
Collie Lodge,
Banff AB4 1AU.
Tel: Banff (026 12) 2789.

Kincardine and Deeside Tourist Board
Tourist Officer,
Kincardine and Deeside Tourist Board,
45 Station Road, Banchory,
Kincardineshire AB31 3XX.
Tel: Banchory (033 02) 2066.

City of Aberdeen Tourist Board
Director,
City of Aberdeen Tourist Board,
St. Nicholas House, Broad Street,
Aberdeen AB9 1DE.
Tel: Aberdeen (0224) 632727.

Gordon District Tourist Board
Director,
Gordon District Tourist Board,
St. Nicholas House, Broad Street,
Aberdeen AB9 1DE.
Tel: Aberdeen (0224) 632727.

Moray District Council
Chief Tourist Officer,
Moray District Council,
17 High Street, Elgin,
Morayshire IV30 1EG.
Tel: Elgin (0343) 542666.

RIVER PURIFICATION BOARD
NORTH EAST RIVER PURIFICATION BOARD
Greyhope House,
Greyhope Road, Torry,
Aberdeen AB1 3RD.
Tel: Aberdeen (0224) 248338.

RIVERS

Water	Location	Species	Season	Permit available from	Other Information
Avon	Ballindalloch	Salmon Sea Trout	11 Feb. to 30 Sept.	Delnashaugh Inn, Ballindalloch, Banffshire AB37 9AJ. Tel: Ballindalloch 255.	No prawn. Fly fishing Sept. No lead attached to fly.
	Tomintoul	Salmon Sea Trout	Feb. to end Sept.	Gordon Arms Hotel, Tomintoul, Banffshire AB37 9ET. Tel: (08074) 206.	No prawn. Fly fishing Sept. No lead attached to fly.
Bogie	Huntly	Salmon Sea Trout Brown Trout	11 Feb. to 31 Oct. 1 Apr. to 6 Oct.	Clerk of Fishings, Huntly Fishings Committee, P.O. Box 2, Royal Bank Buildings, 27/29 Duke Street, Huntly. Tel: (0466) 792291.	Permit covers Bogie, Deveron and Isla.
Carron	Stonehaven	Brown Trout Sea Trout Salmon	1 May to 31 Aug.	Davids Sports Shop, 31 Market Square, Stonehaven. Tel: Stonehaven 62239.	Visitors permits for Sea pool to railway viaduct. For further information: Mr. D. MacDonald, 93 Forest Park, Stonehaven AB3 2GF. Tel: (0569) 64717.
Clunie	Braemar	Brown Trout	15 Mar. to 20 Sept.	Invercauld Estates Office, Braemar AB35 5XQ. Tel: Braemar 41224.	Tourist Information Centre, Braemar. Fly fishing only.
Cowie	Stonehaven	Salmon Sea Trout Brown Trout	1 May to 31 Aug.	Davids Sports Shop, 31 Market Square, Stonehaven. Tel: Stonehaven 62239.	Visitors permits for Sea pool to railway viaduct. For further information: Mr. D. MacDonald, 93 Forest Park, Stonehaven AB3 2GF. Tel: (0569) 64717.

Water	Location	Species	Season	Permit available from	Other Information
Dee	Aboyne	Salmon Sea Trout	1 Feb. to 30 Sept.	Brooks House, Glen Tanar, Aboyne. Tel: (03398) 86451.	No Sunday fishing. Permits available from Aug. only on Waterside & Ferrar beats.
Deveron	Huntly	Salmon Sea Trout Brown Trout	11 Feb. to 31 Oct. 1 Apr. to 6 Oct.	Clerk of Fishings, Huntly Fishings Committee, P.O. Box 2, Royal Bank Buildings, 27/29 Duke Street, Huntly. Tel: (0466) 792291.	Permits cover Deveron, Bogie and Isla.
		Salmon Sea Trout Brown Trout	11 Feb. to 31 Oct.	Castle Hotel, Huntly AB54 4SH. Tel: (046679) 2696.	Fishing on other private beats on Deveron & Don.
	Turriff	Salmon Sea Trout Brown Trout	11 Feb. to 31 Oct.	Turriff Ang. Assoc., I. Masson, The Cross, 6 Castle Street, Turriff. Tel: (0888) 62428.	No day tickets. Six weekly available to visitors. Restrictions on spinning.
Don	Glenkindie	Salmon Brown Trout	11 Feb.-31 Oct. 15 Mar.-1 Oct.	Glenkindie Arms Hotel, Glenkindie, by Alford. Tel: Glenkindie 41288.	May to Sept. fly only.
	Manar Fishings	Salmon Sea Trout Brown Trout	11 Feb. to 31 Oct. 1 Apr.-30 Sept.	J.J. Watson 44 Market Place, Inverurie. Tel: (0467) 20321.	No worm, shrimp or prawn. Limit of 8 rods per day.
	Kemnay	Salmon Brown Trout	11 Feb. to 31 Oct.	F.J. & S.L. Milton, Kemnay House, Kemnay, Aberdeenshire AB51 9LH. Tel: Kemnay 42220	Advance booking essential. Fly or spinning only.
	Strathdon	Salmon Brown Trout	11 Feb. to 31 Oct.	Bellabeg Shop, Strathdon. Tel: (09756) 51211.	Fly & spinning only.
	Kintore	Salmon Sea Trout Brown Trout	11 Feb. to 31 Oct.	Kintore Arms Inn, Kintore. Tel: (0467) 32216. J.A. Copland, Newsagent, 2 Northern Road, Kintore. Tel: (0467) 32210.	No worm till 1 Apr. No natural minnow. No shrimp or prawn. Reductions for school children and OAP's.
	Inverurie	Salmon Sea Trout Brown Trout	11 Feb. to 31 Oct. 1 Apr.-30 Sept.	J.J. Watson, 44 Market Place, Inverurie. Tel: (0467) 20321.	No worm till 1 Apr. No natural minnow. No shrimp or prawn. Reductions for school children and OAP's.
Dulnain	Grantown- on-Spey	Salmon Sea Trout Brown Trout	11 Feb. to 30 Sept. 15 Mar. to 30 Sept.	Strathspey Angling Assoc., Mortimer's, 3 High Street, Grantown-on-Spey. Tel: (0479) 2684.	Visitors resident in Grantown, Cromdale, Duthill, Carrbridge, Dulnain Bridge and Nethy Bridge areas. 12 miles of river.
Findhorn	Forres	Salmon Sea Trout	11 Feb. to 30 Sept.	J. Mitchell, Tackle Shop, 97D High Street, Forres. Tel: (0309) 672936.	Popular flies: all shrimp, Stoats Tail, Dunkeld, Munro Killer. Spinning or worming allowed. Some private beats available.
Gairn	Nr. Ballater	Brown Trout	15 Mar. to 20 Sept.	Invercauld Estates Office, Braemar AB35 5XQ. Tel: Braemar 41224. Countrywear, Bridge Street, Ballater.	Fly fishing only.
Isla	Huntly	Salmon Sea Trout Brown Trout	11 Feb. to 31 Oct. 1 Apr. to 6 Oct.	Clerk of Fishings, Huntly Fishings Committee, P.O. Box 2, Royal Bank Buildings, 27/29 Duke Street, Huntly. Tel: (0466) 792291.	Permit covers Isla, Deveron and Bogie.

Water	Location	Species	Season	Permit available from	Other Information
Muckle burn	By Forres	Salmon Sea Trout	11 Feb. to 30 Sept.	J. Mitchell, Tackle Shop, 97D High Street, Forres. Tel: (0309) 672936.	Reductions for juniors
Spey	Aberlour	Salmon Sea Trout Brown Trout	11 Feb. to 30 Sept.	J.A.J. Munro, 93-95 High Street, Aberlour. Tel: Aberlour 871428.	3 tickets per hotel, (Aberlour, Lour & Dowans or 6 day tickets, first come first served.) One fish above bridge (9 am-5 pm), one fish below bridge (9 am-midnight), other fish sold for club funds. No day tickets on Saturday or local holidays.
	Grantown on-Spey	Salmon Sea Trout Brown Trout	11 Feb. to 30 Sept. 15 Mar. to 30 Sept.	Strathspey Angling Assoc., Mortimer's 3 High Street, Grantown-on-Spey. Tel: (0479) 2684.	7 miles both banks. No prawn. No Sunday fishing. Visitors must reside in Grantown, Cromdale, Duthil, Carrbridge, Dulnain Bridge and Nethy Bridge.
	Nethy Bridge Boat of Garten	Salmon Sea Trout Brown Trout	11 Feb. to 30 Sept.	Abernethy Angling Improvement Assoc. Boat of Garten. Allen's, Deshar Road, Boat of Garten. Tel: 372.	
	Boat of Garten	Salmon Sea Trout Brown Trout	11 Feb. to 30 Sept. 15 Mar. to 30 Sept.	Abernethy Angling Improvement Assoc. Craigard Hotel, Boat of Garten. Tel: Boat of Garten 206. Allen's, Deshar Road, Boat of Garten. Tel: 372.	
	Aviemore	Salmon Sea Trout Brown Trout	11 Feb. to 30 Sept.	Rothiemurchus Estate, Inverdruie, Aviemore PH22 1QH. Tel: (0479) 810703. Kinrara Estate Office, Aviemore. Tel: (0479) 810240/811252. Lynwilg Hotel. Tel: (0479) 810207.	3 beats plus Lochan Mor.
	Aviemore	Salmon Sea Trout Brown Trout	11 Feb. to 30 Sept.	Abernethy Angling Improvement Assoc., Speyside Sports, 64 Grampian Road, Aviemore. Tel: (0479) 810656.	
	Kincraig	Brown Trout Salmon Sea Trout	11 Feb. to 30 Sept.	Alvie Estate Office, Kincraig, by Kingussie. Tel: (0540) 651255/651249. Dalraddy Caravan Park, Aviemore. Tel: (0479) 810330.	Fly fishing or spinning.
Ugie	Peter-head	Salmon Sea Trout Brown Trout	11 Feb. to 31 Oct.	Dicks Sports, 54 Broad Street, Fraserburgh. Tel: (0346) 24120. Robertson Sports, 1-3 Kirk Street, Peterhead AB4 6RT. Tel: (0779) 72584.	Bag limit - 8 fish per day. Fly, spinning or worm entire season. No shrimps, prawns or illegal baits.
Ury	Inverurie	Salmon Sea Trout Brown Trout	11 Feb. to 31 Oct. 1 Apr. to 30 Sept.	J.J. Watson, 44 Market Place, Inverurie AB5 9XN. Tel: (0467) 20321.	No worm till 1 Apr. No natural minnow. No shrimp or prawn. Reductions for school children and OAP's. Sunday fishing - trout only.

Water	Location	Species	Season	Permit available from	Other Information
Ythan	(Estuary) Newburgh	Salmon Sea Trout	11 Feb. to 31 Oct.	The Ythan Fishery, Mrs. Forbes, 3 Lea Cottages, Newburgh, Ellon, Aberdeenshire AB41 0BN. Tel: (03586) 89297.	Limited fishing available. Details from Mrs. Forbes.
	Fyvie	Salmon Sea Trout	11 Feb. to 31 Oct.	Fyvie Angling Assoc., Local shop, hotel, cafe, bank.	No shrimps or prawns. No worming May to August.

LOCHS AND RESERVOIRS

Water	Location	Species	Season	Permit available from	Other Information
Aboyne Loch	Aboyne	Pike Perch		The Warden, Aboyne Loch, Holiday Park. Tel: (03398) 86244.	Fishing parties restricted on Sat. and Sun. afternoons.
Loch Alvie	Aviemore	Brown Trout Pike	15 Mar. to 6 Oct.	Alvie Estate Office, Kincraig, by Kingussie. Tel: (0540) 651255/651249. Dalraddy Caravan Park, Aviemore. Tel: (0479) 810330.	1 Boat. Fly fishing or spinning only.
Avielochan	Aviemore	Rainbow/ Brown Trout	1 Apr. to 30 Sept.	Mortimer's, 3 High Street, Grantown-on-Spey. Tel: (0479) 2684. Mrs. MacDonald, Avielochan, Aviemore. Tel: (0479) 810847.	Bank fishing only. Spinning area designated. No Sunday fishing. 10am-6pm & 6pm-10pm.
Loch of Blairs	Forres	Brown/ Rainbow Trout	30 Mar. to 30 Sept.	J. Mitchell, Tackle Shop, 97D High Street, Forres. Tel: (0309) 672936.	Average weight of fish caught: 1lb 8oz. Popular flies: lures, conventional wet flies, dry flies. Two sessions. Boat fishing. Fly only. Sunday fishing. 3 boats available.
Loch Dallas	Boat of Garten	Brown/ Rainbow Trout	1 Apr. to 30 Sept.	Mortimer's 3 High Street, Grantown-on-Spey. Tel: (0479) 2684. Allan's Store, Boat of Garten. Tel: (0479) 83 372.	Fly fishing only (10am-6pm). Boat fishing. No Sunday fishing. 1 boat (2 rods).
Loch Ericht	Dalwhinnie	Brown Trout	15 Mar. to 6 Oct.	Badenoch Angling Association, Loch Ericht Hotel, Dalwhinnie. Tel: (05282) 257.	Boat & bank fishing.
Glenlatterach Reservoir	By Elgin	Stocked Brown Trout	1 May to 30 Sept.	Warden at Millbuies, Tel: (034 386) 234.	Fly fishing only. 3 boats available. Bank fishing.
Loch Insh	Kincraig	Salmon Sea Trout Brown Trout Char Pike	11 Feb. to 30 Sept.	Alvie Estate Office, Kincraig, by Kingussie. Tel: (0540) 651255/651249. Dalraddy Caravan Park, Aviemore. Tel: (0479) 810330.	One boat. Boat fishing only. Fly fishing or spinning.
		Salmon Sea Trout Brown Trout Arctic Char Pike	May to Sept.	Loch Insh Watersports, Boat House, Kincraig. Boat are available.	
Loch Lochindorb	by Forres	Brown Trout	15 Mar. to 6 Oct.	J. Mitchell, Tackle Shop, 97D High Street, Forres. Tel: (0309) 672936.	Average weight of fish caught: 4oz to 1lb. Popular flies: black flies. Spinning and worming allowed. Boat and bank fishing.

Please mention this Pastime Publications Guide

Water	Location	Species	Season	Permit available from	Other Information
Loch McLeod	Nr. Grantown on Spey	Brown/ Rainbow Trout	1 Apr. to 30 Sept.	Strathspey Estate Office, 14 The Square, Grantown-on-Spey. Tel: (0479) 2529.	Bank fishing only. No fishing on Sundays. 2 rods per day. Fly fishing only (10am-6pm).
Millbuies Loch	By Elgin	Brown/ Rainbow Trout	Easter to Mid-Oct.	Moray District Council, Dept. of Leisure & Libraries, High Street, Elgin. Warden at Millbuies. Tel: 034 386 234.	Boat fishing. Fly fishing only. Four boats available.
Loch Mor	Dulnain Bridge	Brown/ Rainbow Trout	Apr. to Sept.	Mortimer's 3 High Street, Grantown-on-Spey. Tel: (0479) 2684.	Fly fishing only.
Loch Na Bo	Lhanbryde	Brown Trout	1 Apr. to 30 Sept.	D. Kinloch, Gardener's Cottage, Loch-na-Bo, Lhanbryde, Elgin. Tel: (0343 84) 2214.	Fly fishing only.
Rothiemurchus Estate (Fish farm, Loch, Loch Pityoulish, Lily Loch	Aviemore	Rainbow Trout Brown Trout Pike	Check with manager, Aviemore.	Rothiemurchus Fish Farm, by Aviemore PH22 1QH. Tel: (0479) 810703.	Stocked rainbow trout loch. Open all year except when frozen.
Loch Saugh	Fettercairn/ Drumtochty Glen	Brown Trout	15 Mar. to 6 Oct.	Brechin Angling Club, W.G. Balfour, 9 Cookston Crescent, Brechin DD9 6BP. Tel: (0356) 622753. Ramsay Arms Hotel, Fettercairn. Tel: (05614) 334. Drumtochty Arms Hotel, Auchenblae AB30 1XR. Tel: (0561) 320210. David Rollston-Smith, Fishing Tackle, Guns & Sport, 180 High Street, Montrose. Tel: (0674) 72692.	
Glen Tanar Loch	Glen Tanar	Rainbow Trout	Apr. to Oct.	Brooks House, Glen Tanar, Aboyne. Tel: (03398) 86451.	2 boats. Boat fishing by day or evening, April to October.
Loch Vaa	Aviemore	Brown/ Rainbow Trout	1 Apr. to 30 Sept.	Mortimer's 3 High Street, Grantown-on-Spey. Tel: (0479) 2684.	Boat fishing only. 2 boats - 2 rods per boat. Fly fishing only. No Sunday fishing. Fishing 10am-6pm only.
Loch Vrotichan	Cairnwell	Brown Trout	18 Mar. to 11 Aug.	Invercauld Estates Office, Braemar AB35 5XQ. Tel: Braemar 41224. Ballater A.A., 59 Golf Road, Ballater. Tel: Ballater 55365. Tourist Information Centre, Braemar. Tourist Information Centre, Ballater.	Fly fishing only.

NORTH EAST AND SPEY VALLEY

Sea Angling

Moray Firth
The Moray Firth has always been famous for its fishing grounds and most of the towns along the south coastline depend largely on commercial fishing for their prosperity; cod, haddock, flatfish of many kings, pollack, coalfish and mackerel being landed.

Nairn
Nairn is set on the pleasant coastal plain bordering the southern shore of the Moray Firth. There is a beautiful stretch of sands to the east. Most fishing is done from two small piers at the entrance to the tidal harbour.
Types of fish: Mackerel, small coalfish, pollack, dab and cod.
Boats: One or two, privately owned, will often take a passenger out. Enquiries should be made at the harbour.
Tackle: P. Fraser, 41 High Street, Nairn. Tel: (0667) 53038.
Bait: Lugworm available on the beach at low water. Mackerel etc. mostly taken on flies.

Lossiemouth and Garmouth
Lossiemouth, a small, prosperous town, is a unique combination of white fish centre, seaside, shops and hotels. The angler will find unlimited sport of a kind probably new to him, for of the east and west beaches sea trout and finnock abound, and spinning for these into the sea, especially into the breakers, is a magnificent sport.
Types of fish: Sea trout, conger from the pier, coalfish, flatfish, 6$^{1}/_{2}$ miles of shore fishing. Haddock, cod, plaice and coalfish from boats. Shore fishing – sea trout between harbour and Boar's Head Rock and at the old cement works Garmouth.
Bait: Lugworm on the west beach and the harbour at low water. Also plenty of mussels to be collected. Spinners, Pirks.
Season for fishing: Migratory fish season, October. Best months – late July, early August.

Buckie
Buckie is a major commercial fishing port on the eastern side of Spey Bay. It has become increasingly popular over the last few years as a tourist area and is well supplied with hotels, golf courses and caravan sites. It offers a varied coastline in the form of sandy beaches and quite spectacular rugged cliff formations.
Types of fish: Cod, coalfish, conger, pollack, mackerel, haddock, whiting, flatfish.
Bait: Lugworm, ragworm, mussels, cockles and crabs freely available along the shoreline eastwards.
Season for fishing: April-October. Winter months best for cod.

Portknockie
Portknockie is a quaint little fishing village to the west of Cullen Bay. The small harbour is used by two small mackerel boats.
Types of fish: Excellent rock fishing here for cod, coalfish, and some mackerel from the piers. Good boat fishing for haddock, ling and gurnard.
Boats: There are no boats for hire as such, although it is possible to get out in two small (18ft) mackerel boats.
Bait: Lugworm and mussels in the harbour at low water.
Further information from:
Tourist Information Centre, 17 High Street, Elgin, IV30 1EG. Tel: (0343) 542666/543388.

Portsoy
One of the numerous small towns that line the Banffshire coast. It is a former seaport but the harbour is silting up.
Types of fish: Coalfish and mackerel from the small pier and some good rock fishing east and west for cod. From boats, mackerel, cod, haddock, plaice, coalfish and dab.
Bait: Some lugworm at low water mark.

Gardenstown and Crovie
These are traditional fishing villages. Mackerel are plentiful, June-September. Anglers would be well advised to follow local boats which are fishing commercially.
Types of fish: From shore – coalfish, pollack, flatfish, conger. From boats – mackerel, cod, haddock, flounder, plaice, conger, dab, catfish, gurnard and ling.
Bait: Available on beach, but local people prefer to use flies.

Fraserburgh
Situated on the north-east shoulder of Scotland, Fraserburgh has the Moray Firth to the west and north and the North Sea to the east. The Burgh was primarily given over to the herring and white fish industry, but has developed as a holiday resort with the decline of commercial fishing in the North Sea. Tickets and permits for game fishing from the beaches can be had at Weelies, Grocer, College Bounds.

Types of fish: Shore – cod, coalfish and mackerel. Boat – as shore.
Bait: Mussels and lugworm can be dug from the beach.
Season for fishing: May- October.

Peterhead
Peterhead is an important fishing port situated north of Buchan Ness, the most easterly point of Scotland. Excellent breakwaters, 1900ft and 2800ft long, are the main shore marks for holiday anglers. Access to the breakwaters is dependent on weather conditions and can be restricted when vessels are being worked. A safety access procedure has been agreed with the North Breakwater Sea Angling Society to whom further queries should be directed However passengers are at times taken out by private boats.
Types of fish: From the pier – mackerel, coalfish, dab and cod. From boats – cod, haddock, dabs, ling, coalfish and mackerel.
Boats: There are a number of privately owned boats which will sometimes take out passengers. Enquiries should be made at the harbour.
Tackle: Available from Robertsons Sports, 1 Kirk Street, Peterhead. Tel: Peterhead 72584.
Bait: Lugworm can be dug from shore at low water while mussels can be gathered from the rocks.

Stonehaven
Stonehaven is a holiday resort 15 miles south of Aberdeen on main road and rail routes. Magnificent catches of cod and haddock are taken regularly by boat. Anglers obtain great co-operation from angling boat skippers and local professional fishermen. On either side of Stonehaven there are good rock fishing marks which should be approached with care especially during strong easterly winds.
Types of fish: Cod, haddock, pollack, coalfish, flounder, catfish and mackerel from the shore. Cod, haddock, coalfish, pollack, ling, catfish, plaice and other flatfish, ballan wrasse, cuckoo wrasse, whiting and Norway haddock from boats.
Boats: Boats are available from skipper: A. McKenzie, 24 Westfield Park, Stonehaven, Tel: (0569) 63411.
Bait: Mussels available if ordered from skippers of boats.
Season for fishing: All year.
Further information from:
Information Centre, 66 Allardice Street, Tel: (0569) 62806 Easter-October.

Constituent Area Tourist Boards

Fort William and Lochaber Tourist Board
Area Tourist Officer,
Fort William and Lochaber Tourist Board,
Cameron Centre, Cameron Square,
Fort William,
Inverness-shire PH33 6AJ.
Tel: Fort William (0397) 703781.

**Isle of Skye and South West Ross
Tourist Board**
Area Tourist Officer,
Isle of Skye and South West Ross Tourist Board,
Tourist Information Centre, Portree,
Isle of Skye IV51 9BZ.
Tel: Portree (0478) 2137.

**Inverness, Loch Ness and Nairn
Tourist Board**
Area Tourist Officer,
Inverness, Loch Ness and Nairn Tourist Board,
Castle Wynd, Inverness IV2 3BG.
Tel: Inverness (0463) 234353.

**RIVER PURIFICATION BOARD
HIGHLAND RIVER PURIFICATION BOARD**
Strathpeffer Road,
Dingwall IV15 9QY.
Tel: Dingwall 62021.

RIVERS

Water	Location	Species	Season	Permit available from	Other Information
Brogaig	North Skye	Salmon Sea Trout Brown Trout	1 Mar. to 31 Oct.	Jansport, Wentworth Street, Portree, Skye. Tel: (0478) 2559.	
Coe	Glencoe	Salmon Sea Trout	15 Apr. to 15 Oct.	National Trust for Scotland, Achnambeithach Farm, Glencoe. Tel: (08552) 311.	No Sunday fishing.
Croe		Salmon Sea Trout	1 Mar. to 30 Sept.	National Trust for Scotland, Morvich Farm, Inverinate, By Kyle. Tel: Glenshiel (059981) 219.	Fly fishing only.
Farrar	Struy	Salmon Brown Trout	June-15 Oct. 15 Mar. to 30 Sept.	Culligran Estate, Glen Strathfarrar, Struy, Nr. Beauly IV4 7JX. Tel: (046376) 285.	Fly fishing only.
Garry (upper)	Garry Gualach to Poulary Bridge	Salmon Brown Trout	15 Mar.-14 Oct. 15 Mar.-6 Oct.	Garry Gualach, Invergarry. Tel: (08092) 230.	Fly only 1 May to end of season.
Glass	Struy	Salmon Brown Trout	June-15 Oct. 15 Mar.-30 Sept.	Culligran Estate, Glen Strathfarrar, Struy, Nr. Beauly IV4 7JX. Tel: (046376) 285.	Fly fishing only.
Lealt	North Skye	Salmon Sea Trout Brown Trout	1 Mar. to 31 Oct.	Jansport, Wentworth Street, Portree, Skye. Tel: (0478) 2559.	
Lochy	Fort William	Salmon Sea Trout	May to Sept.	Rod & Gun Shop, 18 High Street, Fort William. Tel:(0397) 702656.	
Moriston	Glen-moriston Estuary beat	Salmon	15 Jan. to 15 Oct.	A. MacKintosh, Head Gamekeeper. Tel: (0320) 51219.	Fly & spinning only.
	Dundreggan Beat	Salmon Brown Trout	1 May-end Sept. Mar.to Sept.	A. MacKintosh, Head Keeper. Tel: (0320) 51219.	Fly and spinning only.

Water	Location	Species	Season	Permit available from	Other Information
Nairn	Nairn/ Culloden Moor	Salmon Sea Trout	11 Feb. to 30 Sept.	Nairn Angling Association P. Fraser, High Street, Nairn. Clava Lodge Holiday Homes, Culloden Moor, Inverness IV1 2EJ. Tel: (0463) 790228,	
Nevis	Fort William	Salmon Sea Trout		Rod & Gun Shop 18 High Street, Fort William. Tel: (0397) 702656.	
Polloch	Strontian	Salmon Sea Trout Brown Trout	1 May to 31 Oct.	The Centre, Strontian. Post Office, Strontian.	Average weight of fish caught: Salmon - 6lbs, Sea Trout - 1lb, Brown Trout - 1lb. Popular flies: dark flies. Worm & spinning allowed. No prawn fishing.
Snizort	Skye	Salmon Sea Trout Brown Trout	1 Jul. to 15 Oct.	Skeabost House Hotel, Skeabost, Isle of Skye. Tel: (047 032) 202.	Discounts for residents.
Staffin	North Skye	Salmon Sea Trout Brown Trout	1 Mar. to 31 Oct.	Jansport, Wentworth Street, Portree, Skye. Tel: (0478) 2559.	
Strontian	Strontian	Salmon Sea Trout Brown Trout	1 May to 31 Oct.	The Centre, Strontian. Post Office Strontian.	Average weight of fish caught: Salmon - 6 to 10lbs, Sea Trout - 1lb. Popular flies: Blue Charm, Hair Fly. Worm (if river in spate) & spinning. No prawns.

LOCHS

Water	Location	Species	Season	Permit available from	Other Information
Ardtornish Estate Waters	Morvern	Salmon Sea Trout Brown Trout	Apr.-Oct.	Ardtornish Estate Office, Morvern, by Oban, Argyll. Tel: (0967) 421288.	Six boats for hire.
Loch Arkaig	Fort William	Sea Trout Brown Trout Salmon (occasional) Pike	Mar.-Oct.	Locheil Estate Fishings, West Highland Estates Office, 33 High Street, Fort William. Tel: (0397) 702433.	
Loch Beannachran	Glen Strathfarrar	Brown Trout	15 Mar. to 6 Oct.	Glen Affric Hotel, Cannich. Tel: Cannich 214.	Fly fishing only. 1 boat. No bank fishing.
Loch Benevean (Bheinn a' Mheadhoin)	Glen Affric	Brown Trout	15 Mar. to 6 Oct.	Glen Affric Hotel, Cannich. Tel: Cannich 214.	Fly fishing only. 6 Boats available. No bank fishing.
Loch Dochfour	Inverness	Brown Trout	15 Mar. to 6 Oct.	Dochfour Estate Office, Dochgarroch, by Inverness. Tel: Dochgarroch 218. Dochgarroch Shop & Post Office, Dochgarroch, by Inverness.	No Sunday fishing. Bank fishing only.
Loch Doilet	Strontian	Salmon Sea Trout Brown Trout	1 May to 31 Oct.	George Fisher, Polloch Lodge, Strontian.	Average weight of fish caught: Salmon - 6lbs, Sea Trout 1lb. Popular flies: black flies. Worm and spinning permitted. No prawns. Boats available from: (0967) 2408 or (0967) 2412.
Glenmoriston Hill Lochs (21)	Glenmoriston	Brown Trout	May to Oct.	Mr. A. Mackintosh (Gamekeeper), Levishie, Glenmoriston, Tel: (0320) 51 219 (Eve.)	1 boat available.

Please mention this Pastime Publications Guide

Water	Location	Species	Season	Permit available from	Other Information
Guisachan Hill Lochs	Tomich	Brown Trout	Apr. to Sept.	Tomich Hotel, Tomich, by Beauly. Tel: (04565) 399.	Fly fishing only. Rainbow Trout on 2 lochs.
Loch Inchlaggan & Loch Garry	Invergarry	Brown Trout Arctic Char	May-Sept.	Garry Gualach, Invergarry. Tel: (08092) 230.	Boats available. Loch Inchlaggan fly only.
Loch Insh	Kincraig	Salmon Trout Arctic Char Pike	May to September	Loch Insh Watersports, Boat House, Kincraig. Boats are available.	
Loch Lundavra	Nr. Fort William	Brown Trout	15 Apr. to 30 Sept.	Mrs. A. MacCallum, Lundavra Farm, Fort William. Tel: (0397) 702582.	Average weight of fish caught: 8oz. Popular flies: Black Pennel, Bloody Butcher, Peter Ross. Fly fishing only. 2 boats available. Bank fishing.
Loch Lungard	Glen Cannich	Brown Trout	15 Mar. to 6 Oct.	Glen Affric Hotel, Cannich. Tel: Cannich 214.	Fly fishing only. No bank fishing. Boats available from Loch Mullardoch.
Loch Mealt	North Skye	Brown Trout Arctic Char	15 Mar. to 30 Sept.	Jansport, Wentworth Street, Portree, Skye. Tel: (0478) 2559.	
Loch Monar	Glen Strathfarrar	Brown Trout	15 Mar. to 6 Oct.	Glen Affric Hotel, Cannich. Tel: Cannich 214.	Fly fishing only. Boat for hire. No bank fishing.
Loch Morar (and hill lochs)	Morar	Salmon Sea Trout Brown Trout Arctic Char	15 Mar. to 6 Oct.	The Morar District Salmon Fishery Board, Superintendant, David de-Gernier. Tel: (0687) 2388.	6 boats for hire, and ghillie if required.
Loch Mullardoch	Cannich	Brown Trout	15 Mar. to 6 Oct.	Glen Affric Hotel, Cannich. Tel: Cannich 214.	Fly fishing only. 4 boats. No bank fishing.
Loch Ness	Glenmoriston	Salmon Trout	15 Jan.	Mr. A. MacKintosh (Gamekeeper), Levishie, Glenmoriston. Tel: (0320) 51219 (Eve.)	1 boat available.
Loch Ruthven	Farr	Brown Trout	15 Mar. to 6 Oct.	J. Graham & Co., 37/39 Castle Street, Inverness. Tel: (0463) 233178.	Fly fishing only.
Loch Sheil	Glenfinnan	Salmon Sea Trout	Apr.-Oct.	The Stage House, Glenfinnan, Inverness-shire. Tel: (0397) 83246.	4 boats available with outboards. Advance bookings only.
South Skye Fishings (various lochs)	South Skye	Sea Trout Brown Trout	Apr.-Oct.	Fearann Eilean Iarmain, Eilean Iarmain, Isle of Skye. Tel: (047 13) 266.	
Storr Lochs (and hill lochs)	North Skye	Brown Trout	1 Apr. to 30 Sept.	Jansport, Wentworth Street, Portree, Skye. Tel: (0478) 2559.	Further info: Sec., Portree Angling Assoc., Hillcroft, Treaslane, By Portree.
Tomich Hill Lochs	Tomich	Brown Trout	15 Mar. to 6 Oct.	Caledonian Hotel, Beauly. Tel: (0463) 782278.	Fly fishing only. boats available.

Water	Location	Species	Season	Permit available from	Other Information
Whitebridge Lochs (Knockie, Bran & Killin)	Whitebridge	Brown Trout	Mar.-Oct.	Whitebridge Hotel, Stratherrick, Gorthleck, Inverness-shire. Tel: Gorthleck 226.	Boats available. Fly fishing only.

GREAT GLEN AND ISLE OF SKYE

Sea Angling

Isle of Eigg
The Isle of Eigg lies 5m SW of Skye.
Types of fish: Pollack, conger, spurdog, skate, cod, mackerel.
Season for fishing: Summer-Autumn.

Isle of Skye
The many lochs and bays around the beautiful Isle of Skye provide ideal facilities for sea angling. There is a great variety of fish, most of which can be caught from the shore because of the deep water found close inshore off rocky shores and headlands. Local residents are very knowledgeable about fishing in their own area. Loch Snizort has now been found to hold a number of large common skate and anglers could well contact these during a session there.

Isle of Skye (Portree)
Portree, the capital of Skye, is situated half way up the east coast of the island. There is a very good harbour and good fishing marks in and round it. Ample free anchorage and berthing available for visiting craft. Slipping, re- fuelling and watering facilities are easily accessible.
Types of fish: Cod, haddock, whiting, coalfish, pollack and mackerel.

Boats: Greshornish House Hotel, Edinbane, by Portree, Isle of Skye. Tel: (047082) 266, has one boat available.
Bait: Unlimited mussels and cockles available in tidal area of Portree Bay.
Season for fishing: May-September.

Isle of Skye (Camastianavaig by Portree)
To reach this sheltered bay which lies 4 miles south east of Portree, turn off the A850 to Braes. Although local tactics are the use of feathers, bottom fishing with trace or paternoster has yielded heavy bags with skate of $62^{1}/_{2}$lbs, cod 6lbs, whiting 3lbs, haddock 3lbs, spurdog 12lbs, gurnard 2lbs, pollacks 12lbs, coalfish 14lbs, all from boats.
Types of fish: Shore – coalfish, pollack, wrasse and mackerel. Boat – cod, haddock and spurdog.
Tackle: Obtainable at Portree.
Bait: Lugworm at Broadford Bay and Balmeanac Bay. Cockles and mussels at Portree Loch.
Season for fishing: June- October.

Isle of Skye (Uig)
Uig, a picturesque village amidst some of the finest scenery in the north west, has excellent fishing on its doorstep. Loch Snizort and small islands at its entrance, together with the Ascrib Islands opposite, are well worth fishing. Fishing can be arranged as far round the coast as Score Bay, known to some ring net

fishermen as the 'Golden Mile'.
Types of fish: Shore – coalfish, mackerel, pollack, conger and dogfish. Boat – coalfish, mackerel, pollack, conger, whiting, haddock, dogfish, flatfish, skate, cod and gurnard.
Boats: Available locally at Uig, Waternish and Kilmuir.
Season for fishing: May-September.

Isle of Skye (Skeabost Bridge)
Skeabost Bridge is situated 5 miles from Portree at the south east end of Loch Snizort.
Types of fish: There is no shore fishing but many types of sea fish can be caught from boats.
Bait: Available locally.
Season for fishing: July- October.

Kyle of Lochalsh
The village of Kyle, on the mainland opposite Kyleakin on the Isle of Skye, is a railhead and a car ferry link with Skye and the Hebrides.
Types of fish: Conger, coalfish, pollack and whiting from the harbour. Boat – pollack, cod, coalfish, mackerel and whiting.
Tackle: Available from John MacLennan & Co., Marine Stores, Kyle of Lochalsh. IV40 8AE. Tel: (0599) 4208.
Bait: Mussels from Fishery Pier and clams and cockles at spring tides.
Season for fishing: June-September.

TO ASSIST WITH YOUR BOOKINGS OR ENQUIRIES YOU WILL FIND IT HELPFUL TO MENTION THIS

Pastime Publications Guide

Constituent Area Tourist Boards

Caithness Tourist Board
Area Tourist Office,
Caithness Tourist Board,
Whitechapel Road, Wick,
Caithness KW1 4EA.
Tel: Wick (0955) 2596.

Ross and Cromarty Tourist Board
Area Tourist Officer,
Ross and Cromarty Tourist Board,
Information Centre, North Kessock,
Black Isle, Ross-shire IV5 1XB.
Tel: Kessock (0463 73) 505.

Sutherland Tourist Board
Area Tourist Officer,
Sutherland Tourist Board,
The Square, Dornoch,
Sutherland IV25 3SD.
Tel: Dornoch (0862) 810400.

RIVER PURIFICATION BOARD
HIGHLAND RIVER PURIFICATION BOARD
Strathpeffer Road,
Dingwall IV15 9QY.
Tel: Dingwall 62021.

RIVERS

Water	Location	Species	Season	Permit available from	Other Information
Alness	Alness	Salmon Sea Trout	5 May to 16 Oct.	Novar Estates, Estate Office, Evanton, Ross-shire. Tel: (0349) 830205.	Fly fishing only. 6 beats on rotation. 4 rods per beat.
Beauly	Muir of Ord	Salmon Sea Trout Brown Trout	May to Sept.	Ord House Hotel, Muir of Ord. Tel: (0463) 870492.	
Blackwater	Strathpeffer	Salmon Sea Trout	Apr. to end Sept.	Further info. from: Craigdarroch Lodge Hotel, Contin, by Strathpeffer. Tel: Strathpeffer 21265.	
Upper Blackwater	Contin	Salmon Brown Trout	1 June-30 Sept. 1 Apr.-30 Sept.	John MacMillan Newsagent, The Square, Strathpeffer. Tel: (0997) 421346.	Popular flies: Black Brahan, G.P., Stoats Tail, Red Shrimp & standard trout patterns. Fly fishing. Spinning only in high water. 1 boat available.
Brora (Lower)	Brora	Salmon Sea Trout	1 Feb. to 15 Oct.	Mr. & Mrs. Hammond, Sciberscross Lodge, Strath Brora, Rogart. Tel: (0408) 641246.	Popular flies: Orange, black, red Waddingtons, Willie Gunn.
Conon	Contin	Salmon Sea Trout	26 Jan. to 30 Sept.	Coul House Hotel, Contin, by Strathpeffer. Tel: Strathpeffer 421487.	Lower/middle/upper Brahan, lower Fairburn beats various times. Ghillies, boats. Fly (& spinning until end May).
	Maryburgh	Brown/ Rainbow Trout Pike	15 Mar. to 15 Oct.	Seaforth Highland Estate, Brahan, Dingwall. Tel: (0349) 61192.	Stocked pond. Loch fishing and river in the lower, middle and upper Conon. Fishing available in the stocked pond and loch all year round.
	Muir of Ord	Salmon Sea Trout Brown Trout	May to Sept.	Ord House Hotel, Muir of Ord. Tel: (0463) 870492.	
	Strathpeffer	Salmon Brown Trout	1 Apr. to 30 Sept.	Further info. from: Craigdarroch Lodge Hotel, Contin, by Strathpeffer. Tel: Strathpeffer 21265.	

Water	Location	Species	Season	Permit available from	Other Information
Conon cont.	Dingwall	Salmon Sea Trout	25 Jan. to 30 Sept.	The Sports & Model Shop, Tulloch Street, Dingwall. Tel: (0349) 62346.	Popular flies: Greenwell's Glory, Peter Ross, Black Pennel. Fly fishing only. Thigh waders only.
Lower Conon	Contin	Salmon Sea Trout	26 Jan. to 30 Sept.	Dingwall & District A.C., c/o Sports & Model Shop, Tulloch Street, Dingwall. Tel: (0349) 62346.	Fly only. Thigh waders only.
Upper Conon	Strathconon	Salmon Brown Trout	1 Apr. to 30 Sept.	John MacMillan Newsagent, The Square, Strathpeffer. Tel: (0997) 421346.	Popular flies: Stoats Tail, Red Shrimp, Munro Killer, Black Brahan & standard trout patterns. Fly fishing with spinning during periods of high water.
Doinard	Durness	Salmon Sea Trout		Cape Wrath Hotel, Durness, Sutherland. Tel: 097 181 274.	Please phone in advance, especially in high season.
Glass	Evanton	Brown Trout	15 Mar. to 6 Oct.	Novar Estates, Estate Office, Evanton, Ross-shire. Tel: (0349) 830205.	Fly fishing only.
Halladale	Forsinard (2 mile upper beat)	Salmon	11 Jan. to 30 Sept.	Forsinard Hotel, Forsinard KW13 6YT. Tel: (06417) 221.	Fly fishing only (spate river).
	Forsinard to Melvich Bay	Salmon	11 Jan. to 30 Sept.	Mrs. J. Atkinson, 8 Sinclair Street, Thurso, Caithness.	Lodge also available.
Helmsdale	Helmsdale	Salmon Sea Trout	11 Jan. to 30 Sept.	Strathullie Crafts & Fishing Tackle, Dunrobin Street, Helmsdale KW8 6AH. Tel: (043 12) 343.	Association beat. Fly fishing only.
Kerry	Gairloch	Salmon Sea Trout	May to Oct.	Creag Mor Hotel, Charleston, Gairloch. Tel: (0445) 2068.	Maximum 4 rods daily. Fly fishing only.
Kirkaig	Lochinver	Salmon	1 May to 15 Oct.	Inver Lodge Hotel, Lochinver IV27 4LU. Tel: (05714) 496.	
Kyle of Sutherland	Bonar Bridge	Salmon Sea Trout	1 June to 30 Sept.	Dunroamin Hotel, Bonar Bridge IV24 3EB. Tel: (08632) 236.	
Okyel	Sutherland	Salmon Sea Trout	End June to 30 Sept.	Inver Lodge Hotel, Lochinver IV27 4LU. Tel: (05714) 496.	2 top beats only (3 miles).
Thurso	Thurso/ Halkirk	Salmon	11 Jan. to 5 Oct.	Thurso Fisheries Ltd., Thurso East, Thurso. Tel: (0847) 63134.	Fly fishing only.
Torridon	Torridon	Salmon Sea Trout	1 May. to 31 Oct.	Loch Torridon Hotel, Torridon, by Achnasheen. Tel: (044 587) 242.	Fly fishing only.
Ullapool	Ullapool	Salmon Sea Trout Brown Trout	May to 30 Sept.	Lochbroom Hardware Shop, Shore Street, Ullapool. Tel: (0854) 612356.	
Weaster	by Wick	Salmon Sea Trout Brown Trout	1 Mar. to 31 Oct.	Mrs. G. Dunnet, Auckhorn Lyth, by Wick KW1 4UD. Tel: (095583) 208.	

Water	Location	Species	Season	Permit available from	Other Information
Wick	Wick	Salmon Sea Trout Brown Trout	11 Feb. to 21 Oct.	Hugo Ross Tackle Shop, 16 Breadalbane Crescent, Wick. Tel/Fax: (0955) 4200.	Fly/worm fishing. Spate river with good holding pools.

LOCHS

Water	Location	Species	Season	Permit available from	Other Information
Loch A'chroisg	Achnasheen	Brown Trout Pike Perch	No close season	Ledgowan Lodge Hotel, Achnasheen. Tel: (044 588) 252.	Free to residents.
Loch a'Ghriama	Overscaig	Brown Trout	30 Apr. to 30 Sept.	Overscaig Lochside Hotel, Loch Shin, by Lairg IV27 4NY. Tel: 054 983 203.	Boats available. No Sunday fishing.
Loch an Lascaigh	Torridon	Salmon Sea Trout Brown Trout	1 May to 31 Oct.	Loch Torridon Hotel, Torridon, by Achnasheen, Wester Ross IV22 2EY. Tel: (044 587 242.	
Loch an Ruthair	by Kinbrace	Brown Trout	Apr. to end Sept.	Head Keeper, Achentoul Estate, Kinbrace. Tel: (04313) 227.	Average weight of fish caught: 8 to 12oz. Popular flies: Soldier Palmer, Black pennel. Bait fishing and spinning allowed. 2 boats available.
	Loch Achall by Ullapool	Salmon Sea Trout Brown Trout	1 May to 30 Sept. 15 Mar.-6 Oct.	Lochbroom Hardware Shop, Shore Street, Ullapool. Tel: (0854) 612356.	Popular flies: Soldier Palmer, Butcher, Grouse & Claret. 3 boats available. Bank fishing.
Loch Achonachie	Strathconon	Salmon Brown Trout	1 Apr. to 30 Sept.	John MacMillan Newsagent, The Square, Strathpeffer. Tel: (0997) 421346.	Popular flies: standard loch patterns. Spinning, trolling & fly fishing permitted. 2 boats are available.
Loch Ascaig	Helmsdale	Salmon Sea Trout Brown Trout	1 June to 30 Sept. 15 Mar.-6 Oct.	M. Wigan, Borrobol, Kinbrace KW11 6UB. Tel: (04313) 264/252 or 071-289 5126 (Jan. to Mar.)	Popular flies: Loch Ordie, Soldier Palmer, Fly fishing only. 3 boats available.
Loch Badagyle	Nr. Achiltibuie	Sea Trout Brown Trout Arctic Char	1 Apr. to 30 Sept.	Polly Estates Ltd., Inverpolly, Ullapool IV26 2YB. Tel: 085 482 452.	Fly fishing only. No Sunday fishing. Boats with or without motors are available.
Loch Badanloch (& other hill lochs)	Kinbrace	Brown Trout	15 Mar. to 6 Oct.	Richard McNicol, Badanloch, Kinbrace, Sutherland. Tel: (043 13) 232.	Average weight of fish caught: 8oz. Popular flies: Loch Ordie, Black Pennel, Soldier Palmer. 6 boats. Fly only. Sunday fishing.
Loch Beannach	Lairg	Brown Trout	30 Apr. to 30 Sept.	Boat permits: R. Ross (Fishing Tackle), Main Street, Lairg IV27 4DB. Tel: (0549) 2239.	Average weight of fish caught: 1lb. Popular flies: Kate McLaren, Loch Ordie. Strictly fly fishing only. Boats available from above.
Loch Beannach -arain (Scardroy)	Strathconon	Brown Trout	1 Apr. to 30 Sept.	John MacMillan Newsagent, The Square, Strathpeffer. Tel: (0997) 421346.	Average weight of fish caught: 8oz. Fly and spinning permitted. 2 boats available.
Bad an Scalaig	Nr. Gairloch	Brown Trout Pike	Mar. to Oct.	Wildcat Stores, Gairloch.	Spinning allowed for Pike. 2 boats are available.
Loch Bad na H-Achlaise (Green Loch)	Nr. Achiltibuie	Brown/ Sea Trout	1 Apr. to 30 Sept.	Polly Estates Ltd., Inverpolly, Ullapool IV26 2YB. Tel: 085 482 452.	Fly fishing only. No Sunday fishing.

Water	Location	Species	Season	Permit available from	Other Information
Loch Bad na H Erba	Sciberscross	Wild Brown Trout	1 Apr. to 15 Oct.	Mr. & Mrs. Hammond, Sciberscross Lodge, Strath Brora, Rogart IV28 3YQ. Tel: (0408) 641246.	Average weight of fish caught: 12oz. Popular flies: Black Pennel, Ke-He, Loch Ordie, Dunkeld. Boats are available.
Black Loch	Nr. Achiltibuie	Brown Trout	1 Apr. to 30 Sept.	Polly Estates Ltd., Inverpolly, Ullapool IV26 2YB. Tel: 085 482 452.	Fly fishing only. No Sunday fishing. Boat available.
Loch Borralan	Ledmore	Brown/ Rainbow Trout Arctic Char	15 Mar. to 6 Oct.	The Alt Bar, The Altnacealgach, Ledmore, by Lairg. Tel: 085 486 220.	Any legal method permitted. Boat & bank fishing.
Loch Borralie	Durness	Brown Trout	Apr. to End Sept.	Cape Wrath Hotel, Durness, Sutherland. Tel: 097 181.274.	Limestone loch. Fly fishing only. Boats available. Please phone in advance, especially in high season.
Loch Brora	Brora	Salmon Sea Trout Brown Trout	Apr. to Oct.	Rob Wilson Rods & Guns, Rosslyn Street, Brora. Tel: Brora 621373.	Boats available.
		Salmon Sea Trout Brown Trout Char	1 May to 15 Oct.	Mr. & Mrs. Hammond, Sciberscross Lodge, Strath Brora, Rogart IV28 3YQ. Tel: (0408) 641246.	Popular flies: General Practitioner, Stoats Tail, Dunkeld. Boats available with outboard, if required.
Loch Caise	Forsinard	Brown Trout	1 May to 30 Sept.	Forsinard Hotel, Forsinard. Tel: (06417) 221.	
Loch Caladail	Durness	Brown Trout	Apr. to End Sept.	Cape Wrath Hotel, Durness, Sutherland. Tel: 097 181 274.	Limestone loch. Fly fishing Only. Boats available. Please phone in advance, especially in high season.
Loch Calder	Thurso	Brown Trout	15 Mar. to 6 Oct.	Harper's Fishing Tackle, 57 High Street, Thurso. Tel: (0847) 63179. Pentland Sports, Thurso. Loch Watten Hotel, Watten.	Average weight of fish caught: 12oz to 1lb (fish upto 7lbs). Popular flies: Bibio, Black Pennel, Kate McLaren. Spinning & bait fishing permitted, but fly fishing preferred. Boats available.
Caol Loch	Forsinard	Brown Trout	1 May to 30 Sept.	Forsinard Hotel, Forsinard. Tel: (06417) 221.	Boat & bank fishing. Use standard pattern loch flies.
Cape Wrath & hill lochs (30 plus)	Durness	Brown Trout	Apr. to End Sept.	Cape Wrath Hotel, Durness, Sutherland. Tel: 097 181 274.	Please phone in advance, especially in high season.
Col Loch Beg		Wild Brown Trout	1 Apr. to 15 Oct.	Garvault Hotel, by Kinbrace. Tel: Kinbrace 224.	Average weight of fish caught: 8oz. Popular flies: Loch Ordie, Black Spider, Black Pennel. Fly fishing only.
Col Loch Mhor		Wild Brown Trout	1 Apr. to 15 Oct.	Garvault Hotel, by Kinbrace. Tel: Kinbrace 224.	Average weight of fish caught: 8oz. Popular flies: Loch Ordie, Black Spider, Black Pennel. Fly fishing only.
Loch Cracail	By Bonar Bridge	Brown Trout	May to 31 Oct.	Dunroamin Hotel, Bonar Bridge, Sutherland. Tel: (08632) 236.	1 boat available.

Water	Location	Species	Season	Permit available from	Other Information
Loch Craggie	Tongue	Brown Trout	15 Mar. to 6 Oct.	Ben Loyal Hotel, Tongue. Tel: Tongue 216. Post Office, Tongue. Tel: Tongue 201.	Fly fishing only. Boat available.
		Brown Trout	Mar. to Sept.	Altnaharra Hotel, By Lairg IV27 4UE.	Average weight of fish caught: 8oz to 1lb. Popular flies: Pennel, Goats Toe, Zulu. Boat available.
Loch Croispol	Durness	Brow Trout	Apr. ton End Sept.	Cape Wrath Hotel, Durness, Sutherland. Tel: 097 181 274.	Limestone loch. Fly fishing only. Boats available. Please phone in advance, especially in high season.
Loch Culag (and numerous other lochs)	Lochinver	Brown Trout	Mid-May to 6 Oct.	Inver Lodge Hotel, Lochinver, Sutherland. Tel: Lochinver 496.	7 lochs with boats. 2 lochs for residents of hotel only. (Check for details).
The Dam Lochs	Nr. Ullapool	Brown Trout	15 Mar. to 6 Oct.	Ullasport, West Argyle Street, Ullapool. Tel: (0854) 612621.	Fly fishing only.
Loch Damph	Torridon	Salmon Sea Trout Brown Trout	1 May to 31 Oct.	Loch Torridon Hotel, Torridon, by Achnasheen, Wester Ross IV22 2EY. Tel: 044 587242.	Fly fishing only. No Sunday fishing. 2 boats are available.
Loch Doir na H-Airbhe (Stac Loch)	Nr. Achiltibuie	Brown/ Sea Trout	1 Apr. to 30 Sept.	Polly Estates Ltd., Inverpolly, Ullapool IV26 2YB. Tel: 085 482 452.	Fly fishing only. No Sunday fishing.
Dornoch & District A.C. (7 lochs)	Dornoch	Salmon Sea Trout Brown Trout	15 Mar. to 6 Oct.	Dornoch & District A.A., William A. McDonald, Castle Street, Dornoch. Tel: (0862) 810301.	No Sunday fishing. Fly fishing only. 7 boats available.
Lochan Dubh na H-Amaite	Sciberscross	Wild Brown Trout	1 Apr. to 15 Oct.	Mr. & Mrs. Hammond, Sciberscross Lodge, Strath Brora, Rogart IV28 3YQ. Tel: (0408) 641246.	Average weight of fish caught: 1lb. Popular flies: Black Pennel, Ke-He, Loch Ordie, Dunkeld. Boats are available.
Dunnet Head Loch	Dunnet Head (B855)	Brown Trout	May to Oct.	Dunnet Head Tearoom, Brough Village, Dunnet Head. Tel: (084 785) 774.	Loch well stocked. Fly from bank only. No Sunday fishing. Sea fishing from rocks.
Fionn Loch	Gairloch	Salmon Brown Trout	Mid-May to 6 Oct.	Inver Lodge Hotel, Lochinver, Sutherland. Tel: Lochinver 496. K Guns, Gairloch. Tel: (0445) 2400.	Fly only.
Forsinard Loch (& many others)	Forsinard	Brown Trout	1 May. to 30 Sept.	Forsinard Hotel, Forsinard, Sutherland. Tel: Halladale 221.	Fly fishing only. Bank & boat fishing (5 boats).
	Kyle of Tongue	Salmon Sea Trout Sea Bass	11 Feb. to 31 Oct.	Ben Loyal Hotel, Tongue. Tel: Tongue 216. Post Office, Tongue. Tel: Tongue 201.	No Sunday fishing. Bank fishing only.
Loch Ganneigh		Wild Brown Trout	1 Apr. to 15 Oct.	Garvault Hotel, by Kinbrace. Tel: Kinbrace 224.	Average weight of fish caught: 8oz. Popular flies: Loch Ordie, Black Spider, Black Pennel. Fly fishing only.

Water	Location	Species	Season	Permit available from	Other Information
Loch Glascarnoch	Aultguish	Brown Trout Pike	Mar to Sept. All year	Tel: (09975) 254 to obtain permission.	
Loch Glass	Head of River Glass	Brown Trout	15 Mar. to 6 Oct.	Novar Estates, Estate Office, Evanton, Ross-shire. Tel: (0349) 830205.	Bank fishing only. Any legal method.
Garbh Loch	Forsinard	Brown Trout	1 May to 30 Sept.	Forsinard Hotel, Forsinard. Tel: (06417) 221.	Bank & boat fishing. Popular flies: Black Pennel, Ke-He, Invicta.
Golspie A.C. Waters (Loch Brora Loch Lundie Loch Horn Loch Buidhe)		Salmon Sea Trout Brown Trout	1 Apr. to 15 Oct.	Golspie A.C., Lindsay & Co., Main Street, Golspie. Tel: (0408) 683212.	Fly fishing only. Bank & boat fishing. No Sunday fishing.
Loch Heilan	Castleton	Brown Trout	May to Sept.	H.T. Pottinger, Greenland Mains, Castleton, Thurso. Tel: (0847) 82210.	Boats are available.
Hill Loch (32)	Around Assynt	Brown Trout	15 Mar. to 6 Oct.	Tourist Information Centre, Lochinver.	Mainly fly fishing, there are 6 lochs where spinning or bait can be used. Bank fishing only.
Loch Hope	Nr. Tongue	Salmon Sea Trout	18 June to 30 Sept.	Ian MacDonald, The Keepers House, Hope, by Lairg. Tel: 084 756 272.	Fly fishing from boats only. 3 rods per boat.
		Salmon Sea Trout	Mid-Apr.to Sept. June to Sept.	Altnaharra Hotel, by Lairg IV27 4UE.	Average weight of fish caught: Salmon - 8lbs, Sea Trout - 3lbs. Popular flies: Salmon - Invicta, Pennel. Sea Trout - Peter Ross. Other baits: Toby, sprat. 6 boats are available.
Lochs Kernsary Tournaig Goose Ghiuragarstidh	Gairloch	Brown Trout	15 Mar. to 6 Oct.	National Trust for Scotland, Inverewe Visitor Centre, Poolewe, Ross-shire. Tel: (044 586) 229.	
Kyle of Tongue & local lochs	Tongue & Farr	Salmon Sea Trout Brown Trout		Tongue Stores & P. Office, Main Street, Tongue. Tel: 084 755 201.	Sunday fishing for brown trout only. Boats available from: Woodside Cottage.
Loch Lagain	By Bonar Bridge	Brown Trout	May to 31 Oct.	Dunroamin Hotel, Bonar Bridge, Sutherland. Tel: (08632) 236.	1 boat available.
Loch Laro	By Bonar Bridge	Brown Trout	May to 31 Oct.	Dunroamin Hotel, Bonar Bridge, Sutherland. Tel: (08632) 236.	
Leckmelm Hill Lochs	Ullapool	Brown Trout	May to Sept.	Leckmelm Holiday Cottages, Leckmelm, Ullapool. Tel: (0854) 2471.	Bank fishing only. No Sunday fishing.
Loch Loyal	Tongue	Salmon Sea Trout Brown Trout	15 Mar. to 6 Oct.	Ben Loyal Hotel, Tongue. Tel: Tongue: 216. Post Office, Tongue. Tel: Tongue 201.	Fly fishing only. Bank or boat fishing.
		Brown Trout	Mar. to Sept.	Altnaharra Hotel, By Lairg IV27 4UE.	Average weight of fish caught: 8oz to 1lb. Popular flies: Pennel, Goats Toe, Zulu. 1 boat available.

Water	Location	Species	Season	Permit available from	Other Information
Loch Lurgainn	Nr. Achiltibuie	Brown/ Sea Trout	1 Apr. to 30 Sept.	Polly Estates Ltd., Inverpolly, Ullapool IV26 2YB. Tel: 085 482 452.	Fly fishing only. No Sunday fishing. Boats with or without motors available.
Loch Maree	Wester Ross	Salmon Sea Trout Brown Trout	May-Oct.	Loch Maree Hotel, Achnasheen IV22 2HL. Tel: (044 584) 288.	Several boats available.
				Kinlochewe Holiday Chalets, Kinlochewe. Tel: (044 584) 234/256.	2 boats available. Fly only - end June onwards.
Loch Meadie	Tongue	Brown Trout	Mar. to Sept.	Altnaharra Hotel, By Lairg IV27 4UE.	Average weight of fish caught: 8oz to 1lb. Popular flies: Pennel, Goats Toe, Zulu. 1 boat available.
Loch Meig	Strathconon	Brown Trout	1 Apr. to 30 Sept.	John MacMillan Newsagent, The Square, Strathpeffer. Tel: (0997) 421346.	Average weight of fish caught: 1lb. Strictly fly fishing only. 3 boats are available.
Melvich Hill Lochs	Melvich	Brown Trout	June to Sept.	Melvich Hotel, Melvich, by Thurso KW14 7YJ. Tel: (06413) 206.	Fly fishing only. A boat is available.
Loch Merkland	Overscaig	Brown Trout	30 Apr. to 30 Sept.	Overscaig Lochside Hotel, Loch Shin, by Lairg IV27 4NY. Tel: 054 983 203.	Boat available. Fly only. No Sunday fishing.
Loch Migdale	By Bonar Bridge	Brown Trout	May to 31 Oct.	Dunroamin Hotel, Bonar Bridge, Sutherland. Tel: (08632) 236.	1 boat available.
Loch More	N.W. Sutherland	Salmon Sea Trout Brown Trout	1 May to 15 Oct.	Scourie Hotel, Scourie IV27 4SX. Tel: (0971) 502396.	Fly fishing only. Boats available.
Loch Morie	Head of River Alness	Brown Trout	15 Mar. to 6 Oct.	Novar Estates, Estate Office, Evanton, Ross-shire. Tel: (0349) 830205.	Bank fishing only. Any legal method.
Loch na Dail (Polly Loch)	Nr. Achiltibuie	Brown/ Sea Trout	1 Apr. to 30 Sept.	Polly Estates Ltd,. Inverpolly, Ullapool IV26 2YB. Tel: 085 482 452.	Fly fishing only. No Sunday fishing. Boat available.
Loch nan Clar		Wild Brown Trout	1 Apr. to 15 Oct.	Garvault Hotel, by Kinbrace. Tel: Kinbrace 224.	Average weight of fish caught: 8oz. Popular flies: Loch Ordie, Black Spider, Black Pennel. Fly fishing only.
Loch Navar		Salmon Brown Trout	March to End Sept.	Altnaharra Hotel, By Lairg IV27 4UE.	Average weight of fish caught: Salmon - 8lbs, Brown Trout - 8oz. Popular flies: Trout - Pennel, Zulu, Peter Ross. Salmon - Invicta, Pennel. Other baits: toby and sprat. 3 boats available.
Loch Palm		Wild Brown Trout	1 Apr. to 15 Oct.	Garvault Hotel, by Kinbrace. Tel: Kinbrace 224.	Average weight of fish caught: 8oz. Popular flies: Loch Ordie, Black Spider, Black Pennel. Fly fishing only.
Loch Rangag	Latheron	Brown Trout	1 Apr. to 30 Sept.	John Anderson, Lochend Cottage, Latheron, Caithness. Tel: (05934) 230.	Average weight of fish caught: 12oz. Fly fishing only. Boats are available.

Water	Location	Species	Season	Permit available from	Other Information
Rhiconich (50 lochs)	Nr. Kinlochbervie	Salmon Sea Trout Brown Trout	15 Feb. to 15 Oct.	Rhiconich Hotel, Kinlochbervie.	Fly fishing only. 7 boats available.
Loch Rhifail		Wild Brown Trout	1 Apr. to 15 Oct.	Garvault Hotel, by Kinbrace. Tel: Kinbrace 224.	Average weight of fish caught: 8oz. Popular flies: Loch Ordie, Black Spider, Black Pennel. Fly fishing only.
Loch Rhimsdale		Wild Brown Trout	1 Apr. to 15 Oct.	Garvault Hotel, by Kinbrace. Tel: Kinbrace 224.	Average weight of fish caught: 8oz. Popular flies: Loch Ordie, Black Spider. Fly fishing only.
Loch Rhuard	Latheron	Brown Trout	1 Apr. to 30 Sept.	John Anderson, Lochend Cottage, Latheron, Caithness Tel: (05934) 230.	Average weight of fish caught: 12oz. Fly fishing only. Boats are available.
Loch Rossail		Wild Brown Trout	1 Apr. to 15 Oct.	Garvault Hotel, by Kinbrace. Tel: Kinbrace 224.	Average weight of fish caught: 8oz. Popular flies: Loch Ordie, Black Spider, Black Pennel. Fly fishing only.
Loch Ruith a Phuil	by Strathpeffer	Brown Trout Rainbow Trout	15 Mar.-6 Oct. All year	The Tarvie Lochs Trout Fishery, Tarvie, by Strathpeffer IV14 9EJ. Tel: (0997) 421250.Zulu,	Average weight of fish caught: Rainbow - 1lb 8oz, Brown - 12oz. Popular flies: Black Pennel, Invicta, Sedge. Any legal baits or methods permitted. Bank fishing only. Open all year, except Xmas.
Loch St. Johns	Caithness	Wild Brown Trout	7 Apr. to 31 Sept.	Hugo Ross Fishing Tackle, 16 Breadalbane Crescent, Wick. Tel/Fax: (0955) 4200.	Boats are available from above.
Scourie Lochs	N.W. Sutherland	Salmon Sea Trout Brown Trout	1 May to 15 Oct.	Scourie Hotel, Scourie IV27 4SX. Tel: (0971) 502396.	Fly fishing only. Boats available.
Loch Sgeirach		Wild Brown Trout	1 Apr. to 15 Oct.	Garvault Hotel, by Kinbrace. Tel: Kinbrace 224.	Average weight of fish caught: 8oz. Popular flies: Loch Ordie, Black Spider, Black Pennel. Fly fishing only.
Loch Shin	Overscaig	Brown Trout Ferox Trout	30 Apr. to 30 Sept.	Overscaig Lochside Hotel, Loch Shin, by Lairg IV27 4NY. Tel: 054 983 203.	Boats and outboards available.
	Lairg	Brown Trout Char	15 Apr. to 30 Sept.	Bank permits: R. Ross (Fishing Tackle), Main Street, Lairg IV27 4DB. Tel: (0549) 2239.	Average weight of fish caught: 7oz. Popular flies: Kate McLaren. Spinning & worm permitted, fly preferred. Boats and engines available from boathouse from 1 June.
Loch Sionascaig (& 9 other lochs)	Ullapool	Brown Trout	1 Apr. to 30 Sept.	Polly Estate Office, Inverpolly, Ullapool IV26 2YB. Tel: 085 482 452.	Boats & outboards available. No Sunday fishing. Fly fishing only, trawling for ferox permitted. Noted for large ferox.
Skyline Loch	Forsinard	Brown Trout	1 May to 30 Sept.	Forsinard Hotel, Forsinard. Tel: (06417) 221.	Popular flies: Black Zulu, Silver Butcher.

Water	Location	Species	Season	Permit available from	Other Information
Loch Sletill	Forsinard	Brown Trout	1 May to 30 Sept.	Forsinard Hotel, Forsinard, Sutherland. Tel: Halladale 221.	Fly fishing only. Bank & boat fishing.
Loch Stack	N.W. Sutherland	Salmon Sea Trout Brown Trout	1 May to 15 Oct.	Scourie Hotel, Scourie IV27 4SX. Tel: (0971) 502396.	Fly fishing only. Boats are available. Ghillie mandatory on loch.
Loch Staink	Tongue	Brown Trout	Mar. to Sept.	Altnaharra Hotel, By Lairg IV27 4UE.	Average weight of fish caught: 8oz to 1lb. Popular flies: Pennel, Goats Toe, Zulu. 1 Boat available.
Loch Stemster	Latheron	Brown Trout	1 Apr. to 30 Sept.	John Anderson, Lochend Cottage, Latheron, Caithness. Tel: (05934) 230.	Average weight of fish caught: 12oz. Fly fishing only. Boats are available.
Tarvie Lochs	By Contin	Brown/ Rainbow Trout (stocked)		Sports & Model Shop, Tulloch Street, Dingwall. Tel: (0349) 62346.	Main loch: Fly fishing only. Boat available. 'Troutmaster water.' Small loch only: coarse methods.
Loch Tarvie	by Strathpeffer	Brown/ Rainbow Trout	15 Mar.-6 Oct. All year	The Tarvie Lochs Trout Fishery, Tarvie, by Strathpeffer IV14 9EJ. Tel: (0997) 421250.	Average weight of fish caught: Rainbow - 2lbs 4oz, Brown - 1lb 12oz. Popular flies: Black Pennel, Zulu, Invicta, Sedge. Fly fishing only. Boat fishing only. Open all year, except Xmas.
Tongue Lochs (14)	Tongue	Brown Trout	15 Mar. to 6 Oct.	Ben Loyal Hotel, Tongue. Tel: Tongue 216. Post Office, Tongue. Tel: Tongue 201.	
Loch Uidh Tarraigean (Upper Polly Lochs)	by Achiltibuie	Brown Trout	1 Apr. to 30 Sept.	Polly Estates Ltd., Inverpolly, Ullapool IV26 2YB. Tel: 085 482 452.	Fly fishing only. No Sunday fishing.
Ulbster Estate Lochs (9 hill lochs)	Halkirk	Brown Trout	15 Mar. to 6 Oct.	Ulbster Arms Hotel, Halkirk, Caithness. Tel: (084783) 206.	No Sunday fishing. Fly fishing only. 1 boat on each of 5 lochs.
Loch Watenan	Ulbster	Brown Trout	1 May to 30 Sept.	Mr. J. Swanson, Aspen Bank, Banks Road, Watten. Tel: (095582) 326/208.	Fly fishing only. 1 boat available.
Loch Watten	Watten Village	Brown Trout	1 May to 31 Sept.	Hugo Ross Fishing Tackle, 16 Breadalbane Crescent, Wick. Tel/Fax: (0955) 4200.	Boats for hire from tackle shop. Fish min. size 10". No Sunday fishing. Fly only.
		Brown Trout	1 May to 1 Oct.	J.A. Barnetson, Lynegar Farm, Watten. Tel: (095582) 217.	Average weight of fish caught: 12oz. Popular flies: March Brown, Butcher, Peter Ross. Fly fishing only. 1 boat available.
	(A882) Between Wick & Thurso	Stocked Brown Trout	1 May to 30 Sept.	John F. Swanson, Aspen Bank, Banks Lodge, Watten. Tel: (095582) 326/208.	Average weight of fish caught: 12oz to 1lb. Fly fishing only. 4 boats are available.

Water	Location	Species	Season	Permit available from	Other Information
Loch Weaster	by Wick	Salmon Sea Trout Brown Trout	1 Mar. to 31 Oct.	Mrs. G. Dunnet, Auckhorn Lyth, by Wick KW1 4UD. Tel: (095583) 208.	Fly fishing only. Boats available: 1 July to 31 Oct.

NORTH SCOTLAND
Sea Angling

Gairloch
Gairloch Bay is very popular with sea anglers. There is good fishing in this lovely sea loch, especially around Longa Island which lies near the entrance to the Loch.

Poolewe and Aultbea
Situated amidst magnificent scenery, the sheltered waters of Loch Ewe offer the sea angler opportunities of fine catches. Suitable accommodation is available in surrounding villages and local advice is always available.
Types of fish: Shore – pollack, coalfish, dab, codling. Boat – haddock, cod, codling, gurnard, skate, whiting, mackerel, flatfish.
Boats: Several boats available locally.
Bait: Mussels, lugworm, cockles, etc. from shore.
Season for fishing: April- October incl.

Little Loch Broom
Ten miles north east Aultbea.

Ullapool & The Summer Isles
Loch Broom and the waters encircled by the Summer Isles offer excellent sea angling. The banks can be approached from Ullapool, which is an attractive holiday village sited on a peninsula projecting into Loch Broom. The numerous banks and islands offer superb fishing and beautiful scenery in sheltered waters. Many attractions on shore via local shops; hotels and sporting facilities available throughout the season. Achiltibuie, a small village, also gives access to fishing grounds.
Types of fish: Shore – codling, coalfish, conger, pollack, mackerel, dabs, thornbacks, dogfish, flounders and plaice. Boat – as above plus haddock, whiting, wrasse, ling, megrim, gurnard, spurdog and turbot.
Season for fishing: June- October inclusive. Big skate best in autumn.

Lochinver
Lochinver is one of the major fishing ports in the north of Scotland. With a population of some 300 inhabitants it has a safe all - tides harbour with excellent shore services, including good moderately - priced accommodation and two fishing tackle shops. Excellent sea fishing within a short distance from the port, specialising in jumbo haddock, cod, skate and conger. It is one of the few areas where large halibut are caught. Boats available. A large fleet of fishing vessels operates from the harbour and bait is readily available.
Types of fish: Cod, haddock, whiting, saithe, gurnard, ling, pollack, mackerel, wrasse, conger, skate. Coalfish, pollack, cod and mackerel from the shore.
Tackle: Tackle is available from Lochinver Fishselling Co., Culag Square, Lochinver. Tel: (05714) 228/258.
Season for fishing: April- October.

Drumbeg
Seven miles north of Lochinver.

Caithness
With the prolific fishing grounds of the Pentland Firth, the north of Caithness has built up a reputation as being one of the premier sea angling areas in Scotland. It is now recognised that the chance of taking a halibut on rod and line is better in Pentland waters than anywhere else; more halibut have been taken here than in any other part of the British Isles. The presence of Porbeagle shark in these waters has been proved by the capture of two specimens, with many more hooked and lost. Among the notable fish caught were European halibut records of 194 lbs. in 1974, 215 lbs. in 1975, 224 lbs. in 1978 and 234 lbs. in 1979. This fish represented a world record catch for the species. The Scottish shore record ling of 12lbs 4oz was caught in these waters. With countless numbers of rocky coves and sandy beaches there is much for the shore angler to discover along the whole of the north coast of Scotland. Accommodation is available to suit everyone, from first class hotels, private B. & B. to caravan and camping sites with full facilities. It is also possible to have a full sea angling package holiday with full board at a hotel and all boat charges included. The number of angling boats available increases each year, but it is still advisable to book boat places in advance.

Thurso and Scrabster
Thurso is the main town on the north side of Caithness and gives access through Scrabster to the waters of the Pentland Firth, where there are first class fishing grounds. Thurso Bay and the Dunnet Head area are sheltered from prevailing winds and it is reasonably easy for anglers to get afloat to the marks. Scrabster 1 1/4 miles from Thurso, is the main harbour in northern Caithness. Most of the angling boats are based here. There is also some excellent rock fishing, while conger may be caught from the harbour walls.
Types of fish: Cod, ling, haddock, conger, pollack, coalfish, dogfish, spurdog, plaice, wrasse, mackerel, dab, whiting, rays, halibut, porbeagle shark.
Tackle: Harper's Fishing Services, 57 High Street, Thurso KW14 8AZ. Tel: (0847) 63179.
Bait: Mussels, lugworm can be gathered at low water, mackerel and squid from fish shops and local fishermen. Most species take lures, feather and rubber eels, etc. and most fishing done with this type of artificial bait.
Season for fishing: April- November.
Further information from: Caithness Tourist Board, Whitechapel Road, Wick, Tel: (0955) 2596 Jan- Dec.

Dunnet
Dunnet is situated 8 miles east of Thurso at the end of the famous Dunnet Sands, which are over 2 1/2 miles long. Few anglers fish this beach, as there is excellent boat fishing nearby. There is plenty of lugworm and the beach is well worth trying.
Types of fish: As for Thurso.
Boats and Tackle: As for Thurso.
Bait: Mussels from the rocks at low tide and lugworm all along Dunnet Sands.
Season for fishing: Shore – July and August. Boat – April- November.

Keiss

Good shore fishing is to be had around Keiss, a small fishing village between John o'Groats and Wick. It might be difficult to get out in a boat. The shore fishing is from the rocks around Keiss, and from the beach at Sinclair's Bay to the south of the village. Here some very good plaice have been taken and also anglers have caught sea trout while spinning for mackerel.
Tackle: Tackle shops at Wick.
Bait: Mussels and lugworm can be obtained at low tide.

Sutherland and Easter Ross Brora

Brora is a village situated on the A9, 12 miles south of Helmsdale. There is a small harbour and a few boats are available to sea anglers. There are rail links to Brora from the south and ample hotel accommodation and caravan facilities.
Types of fish: Cod, coalfish, cod, ling, haddock, rays and conger from boats.
Boats: Some owners are willing to take visitors at nominal costs.
Bait: Can be dug locally.
Season for fishing: July-September.

Grannies Heilan' Hame, Embo

This is a caravan holiday centre with extensive amenities 2 miles north of Dornoch.
Types of fish: Spinning for sea trout from the beach up to the mouth of

Loch Fleet. Coalfish, mackerel and flatfish from the pier. The rocks provide good cod fishing. From boats, coalfish, mackerel, plaice, cod, haddock and whiting at times.
Bait: Lugworm can be dug at the ferry landing area and there are plenty of mussels and cockles near Loch Fleet.
Season for fishing: April-September.

Dornoch

Dornoch gives access to the fishing banks off the north coast of the Dornoch Firth. There is good shore fishing from the rocks at Embo, but to get afloat it is necessary to make arrangements in advance. Youngsters can enjoygood fishing from Embo Pier.
Types of fish: Sea trout from shore. Flat fish, haddock and cod from boats.
Boats: Boats are difficult to hire but there are one or two in Embo which is three miles from Dornoch.
Season for fishing: April-September.

Tain

Tain lies on the south side of the Dornoch Firth and gives access to excellent sea trout fishing, both shore and boat, in sheltered waters of the Firth.
Types of fish: Shore – wrasse, flatfish, pollack, mackerel. Boat –

haddock, cod, skate, mackerel.
Boats: Available in Balintore, 6 miles from Tain and Portmahomack.
Bait: Available from the shore.

Balintore

The village of Balintore, near Tain, has over the past 4 years increased in status and is now one of the recognised centres for big catches. Catches of up to 1,000lbs of cod and ling have been made (8 anglers) in a single morning's fishing.
Types of fish: Cod, ling, wrasse, pollack and mackerel.
Season from mid-April to beginning of November.

Portmahomack

This fishing village is well situated in a small bay on the southern shore of the Dornoch Firth, 9 miles east of Tain and 17 miles from Invergordon to the south. There is a well-protected harbour and a good, safe sandy beach.
Types of fish: Cod from the shore. Haddock and cod from boats.
Tackle: Available at Tain.
Season for fishing: Spring to Autumn.

North Kessock, Avoch and Fortrose

These villages lie along the north-west side of the Moray Firth north of Inverness. This sheltered sea loch provides good fishing.

Constituent Area Tourist Boards

Area Tourist Board
Western Isles Tourist Board,
Area Tourist Officer,
Western Isles Tourist Board,
4 South Beach Street,
Stornoway,
Isle of Lewis PA87 2XY.
Tel: Stornoway (0851) 703088.

RIVER PURIFICATION AUTHORITY
WESTERN ISLES ISLAND AREA
(No formal Board constituted)

LOCHS

Water	Location	Species	Season	Permit available from	Other Information
LEWIS **Beag-Na-** **Craoibhe**	Stornoway	Brown Trout	15 Mar. to 6 Oct.	Sportsworld, 1 Francis Street, Stornoway. Tel: (0851) 705464.	Bank fishing. 1 boat available.
Loch **Blackwater**	13m West of Stornoway	Salmon Sea Trout Brown Trout	1 Jul.-14 Oct. 15 Mar. to 30 Sept.	The Manager, Garynahine Estate Office, Isle of Lewis.	Fly fishing only. Boats are available.
Loch **Breivat**	Nr. Stornoway	Brown Trout Arctic Char	15 Mar. to 30 Sept.	Estate Office, Scaliscro, Timsgarry, Isle of Lewis. Tel: (0851) 75 325.	Popular flies: Brown Muddler, Invicta, Soldier Palmer. Boats are available.
Breugach	Stornoway	Brown Trout	15 Mar. to 6 Oct.	Sportsworld, 1 Francis Street, Stornoway. Tel: (0851) 705464.	Bank fishing. Two boats available.
Loch **Bruiche**	Nr. Stornoway	Brown Trout Arctic Char	15 Mar. to 30 Sept.	Estate Office, Scaliscro, Timsgarry, Isle of Lewis. Tel: (0851) 75 325.	Popular flies: Brown Muddler, Invicta, Soldier Palmer. Boats are available.
Loch **Coirigeroid**	Nr. Stornoway	Brown Trout Arctic Char	15 Mar. to 30 Sept.	Estate Office, Scaliscro, Timsgarry, Isle of Lewis. Tel: (0851) 75 325.	Popular flies: Brown Muddler, Invicta, Soldier Palmer. Boats are available.
Loch **Fhir Mhaoil**	Nr. Stornoway	Salmon Sea Trout Brown Trout	June to 15 Oct.	Estate Office, Scaliscro, Timsgarry, Isle of Lewis. Tel: (0851) 75 325.	Spinning and worm fishing permitted. Boats are available.
Keose **(and** **other lochs** **in Keose** **Glebe** **fishings**	10 mls South of Stornoway	Brown Trout	15 Mar. to 30 Sept.	M. Morrison, 'Handa', 18 Keose Glebe, Lochs, Isle of Lewis PA86 9JX. Tel: 085 183 334. Sportsworld, 1 Francis Street, Stornoway. Tel: (0851) 705464. Tourist Office, South Beach, Stornoway.	Two boats, rods, tackle, life jackets. No Sunday fishing.
Loch **Langavat**	Nr. Stornoway	Salmon Sea Trout Brown Trout Arctic Char	15 Mar. to 15 Oct.	Estate Office, Scaliscro, Timsgarry, Isle of Lewis. Tel: (0851) 75 325.	Spinning and worming permitted. Boats are available.

Water	Location	Species	Season	Permit available from	Other Information
Loch MacLeod	Nr. Stornoway	Salmon Sea Trout	1 June to 15 Oct.	Estate Office, Scaliscro, Timsgarry, Isle of Lewis. Tel: (0851) 75325.	Popular flies: Garry Dog, Blue Charm, Donegal Blue. Boats are available.
		Salmon Sea Trout Brown Trout	1 Jul.-14 Oct. 15 Mar. to 30 Sept.	The Manager, Garynahine Estate Office, Isle of Lewis.	All legal methods permitted. Boats are available.
Loch nan Culaidhean	Nr. Stornoway	Salmon Sea Trout Brown Trout	1 Jul.-14 Oct. 15 Mar. to 30 Sept.	The Manager, Garynahine Estate Office, Isle of Lewis.	Any legal method permitted. Boats available.
Lochs Sgibacleit, Shromois, Airigh Thormaid	Nr. Stornoway	Salmon Sea Trout Brown Trout	May to 30 Oct.	Estate Office, Scaliscro, Timsgarry, Isle of Lewis. Tel: (0851) 75 325.	Spinning & worm fishing permitted. Boats are available,
Loch Tarbart	Nr. Stornoway	Salmon Sea Trout	1 June to 15 Oct.	Estate Office, Scaliscro, Timsgarry, Isle of Lewis. Tel: (0851) 75325.	Popular flies: Garry Dog, Blue Charm, Donegal Blue. Boats are available.
		Salmon Sea Trout Brown Trout	1 Jul.-14 Oct. 15 Mar. to 30 Sept.	The Manager, Garynahine Estate Office, Isle of Lewis.	All legal methods permitted. Boats are available.
Loch Tungavat	Nr. Stornoway	Brown Trout	15 Mar. to 15 Oct.	Estate Office, Scaliscro, Timsgarry, Isle of Lewis. Tel: 0851 75 325.	Average weight of fish caught: 6 to 8oz Popular flies: Soldier Palmer, Butcher, Invicta. Boats are available.
Vatandip	Stornoway	Brown Trout	15 Mar. to 6 Oct.	Sportsworld, 1 Francis Street, Stornoway. Tel: (0851) 705464.	Bank fishing. 1 boat available.
BENBECULA					
Loch Eilean Iain	Benbecula	Brown Trout	Mar. to Sept.	Orasay Inn, Lochcarnan, South Uist PA81 5PD. Tel: (08704) 298.	Average weight of fish caught: 1 to 3lbs. Popular flies: Soldier Palmer, Black Pennel, Ke-He, Worm Fly. 1 boat available.
Loch Hermidale	Benbecula	Brown Trout		Orasay Inn, Lochcarnan, South Uist PA81 5PD. Tel: (08704) 298. Colin Campbell Sports, Benbecula. Tel: (0870) 2236. Bornish Stores, Bornish, South Uist.Ross, Invicta.	Average weight of fish caught: 12oz to 1lb. Popular flies: Black Spider, Blue Zulu, Peter 1 boat is available.
South Langavat (Heorovay - Olavat) and numerous other lochs	Benbecula	Brown Trout	15 Mar. to 30 Sept.	Bornish Stores, Tel: 08785-366. Colin Campbell Sports Ltd., Balivanich. Tel: (0870) 2236.	Fly only. Boats available.
Loch Olavat (West)	Benbecula	Brown/ Sea Trout		Orasay Inn, Lochcarnan, South Uist PA81 5PD. Tel: (08704) 298.	Popular flies: Black Pennel, Invicta, Peter Ross, Grouse & Claret. 2 boats are available.
SOUTH UIST					
Loch Druim an Lasgair	South Uist	Brown Trout	15 Mar. to 6 Oct.	Orasay Inn, Lochcarnan, South Uist PA81 5PD. Tel: (08704) 298.	Average weight of fish caught: 12oz to 1lb. Popular flies: Soldier Palmer, Butchers, Black Spider.

Water	Location	Species	Season	Permit available from	Other Information
East Loch Bee	South Uist	Brown Trout	Mar. to Sept.	Orasay Inn, Lochcarnan, South Uist PA81 5PD. Tel: (08704) 298. Colin Campbell Sports, Benbecula. Tel: (0870) 2236. Bornish Stores, Bornish, South Uist.	Average weight of fish caught: 12oz to 1lb 8oz. Popular flies: Black Pennel, Ke-He, Bloody Butcher. 2 boats are available.
All hill and Machair Lochs	South Uist	Salmon Sea Trout Brown Trout	Jul. to Oct. Apr.-End Sept.	Resident Manager, Lochboisdale Hotel, Lochboisdale, South Uist. Tel: Lochboisdale (08784) 332. Orasay Inn, Lochcarnan, South Uist PA81 5PD. Tel: (08704) 298.	Fourteen boats available on lochs. Fly fishing only.
Loch Naid	South Uist	Brown Trout		Orasay Inn, Lochcarnan, South Uist PA81 5PD. Tel: (08704) 298.	Average weight of fish caught: 12oz to 1lb. Popular flies: Grouse & Claret, Black Pennel, Black Spider, Butchers.
NORTH UIST Lochs & Sea Pools in North Uist		Salmon Sea Trout Brown Trout	25 Feb.-15 Oct. 15 Mar.-31 Oct. 15 Mar.-30 Sept.	Bill Quarm, Lochmaddy Hotel, North Uist. Tel: 087 63 331.	Average weight of fish caught: Salmon - 5lbs 5oz, Sea Trout - 2lbs 5oz, Brown Trout - 8oz. Fly fishing only. No Sunday fishing. Boats are available on some lochs.
ISLE OF HARRIS Laxdale System	Isle of Harris	Salmon Sea Trout Brown Trout	15 Mar. to 15 Oct.	Tony Scherr, Borve Lodge Estates, Isle of Harris. Tel: 085 985 202.	Fly fishing only. Permits cannot be reserved in advance.

WESTERN ISLES

Sea Angling

The Western Isles
The Western Isles form a north-south chain of islands off the west coast of Scotland. Separated from the mainland by the Minches, much of their rod and line fishing remains to be discovered, not only due to a lack of boats in the area, but also due to a lack of communications between and within the islands. Car ferries run from Oban and Ullapool on the mainland and Uig on Skye. Regular air services to Barra, Stornoway, Lewis and Harris and Benbecula for the Uists.

Isle of Harris (Tarbert)
The largest community on the southern part of the largest of the Hebridean islands, Tarbert stands on a very narrow neck of land where the Atlantic and the Minch are separated by only a few hundred yards of land.

It is the terminal for the car ferry from Uig on Skye and Lochmaddy on North Uist.

Types of fish: Boat – mackerel, ling, coalfish, cod, rays, pollack and conger. Shore – plaice, haddock and flounder.

Boats: Check with Tourist Information Centre, Tarbert (0859) 2011.

Bait: Mussels available on the shore, lugworm, cockles.

Season for fishing: May- October.

Further information from: Tourist Centre, Tarbert.

Isle of Lewis (Stornoway)
Stornoway, the only town in the Outer Hebrides, is easily accessible by air from Glasgow Airport (1 hour) and Inverness (25 mins.); there is also a drive-on car ferry service from Ullapool (3 1/2 hours crossing). Another car ferry service connects Uig (Skye) to Tarbert (Harris), which is only an hour's drive from Stornoway. Stornoway is now

recognised as a mecca for sea angling in Scotland. There is an enthusiastic sea angling club with club boats and licensed premises which overlook the harbour. Each August the club runs the Western Isles (Open) Sea Angling Championships. Many skate over the 'ton' have been caught, the heaviest so far being 192 lbs. The Scottish blueshark record of 85 1/2 lbs. was off Stornoway in August 1972. Visiting anglers may become temporary members of the Stornoway Club (one minute from the town hall) and can make arrangements for fishing trips with club members in the club boats. Accommodation can be arranged through the Wester Isles Tourist Board, Administration and Information Centre, 4 South Beach Street, Tel: Stornoway (0851) 3088.

Types of fish: Conger, cod, skate, rays, ling, pollack, whiting, dabs, bluemouth, flounder, dogfish, wrasse, haddock.

Bait: Mussels in harbour area; mackerel from local boats.

Constituent Area Tourist Boards

Orkney Tourist Board,
Information Centre,
6 Broad Street, Kirkwall,
Orkney KW15 1NX.
Tel: Kirkwall (0856) 2856.

Shetland Islands Tourism
Area Tourist Officer,
Shetland Islands Tourism,
Information Centre,
Market Cross, Lerwick,
Sheltand ZE1 0LU.
Tel: Lerwick (0595) 3434.

PURIFICATION AUTHORITY
ORKNEY ISLANDS AREA
SHETLAND ISLANDS AREA
(No formal Boards constituted)

LOCHS

Water	Location	Species	Season	Permit available from	Other Information
ORKNEY					
Boardhouse	Mainland	Brown Trout	15 Mar.-6 Oct.	None required	Boats available locally. All legal methods permitted. Anglers are recommended to join Orkney Trout Fishing Association, Kirkwall, who make facilities available to visitors.
Harray	Mainland	Brown Trout	15 Mar.-6 Oct.	Merkister Hotel. Loch Harray, Orkney. Tel: 085 677 366.	See Orkney for further information. *
Hundland	Mainland	Brown Trout	15 Mar.-6 Oct.	None required	See Orkney for further information.
Kirbister	Mainland	Brown Trout	15 Mar.-6 Oct.	None required	See Orkney for further information.
Stenness	Mainland	Sea Trout Brown Trout	25 Feb.-31 Oct. 15 Mar.-6 Oct.	None required.	See Orkney for further information.
Swannay	Mainland	Brown Trout	15 Mar.-6 Oct.	None required	See Orkney for further information.
SHETLAND					
1000 lochs & voes	Sheltand Islands	Sea Trout Grisle Brown Trout	25 Feb. to 31 Oct. 15 Mar.-6 Oct.	Shetland Anglers Association, A. Miller, Hon. Sec., 3 Gladstone Terrace, Lerwick. Shetland Tourist Info. Centre, Commercial Street, Lerwick. Anderson & Co., Market Cross, Lerwick.	Average weight of fish caught: Brown Trout - 1 to 1lb 8oz, Sea Trout & Grisle - 2 to 8lbs. Popular flies: all dark flies - Black Pennel, Grouse & Claret, Ke-He, Invicta, Blue Zulu (sizes 10 & 12). Other baits: spinning where permitted with mepps spoons and toby lures. Association boats available on 5 popular lochs: Spiggie, Benston, Tinewall, Clousta, Punds Water.
Various	Yell Island	Brown Trout	15 Mar. to 6 Oct.	No permit required,	Fishing free. Average weight of fish caught: 8oz to 8lbs+ Popular flies: Bibio, Silver Invicta. Spinning permitted. 1 boat on Littlestar Loch, Burravoe. Boat permit available from Old Haa Museum.

Water	Location	Species	Season	Permit available from	Other Information
Huxter Loch	Isle of Whalsay	Brown Trout	15 Mar. to 6 Oct.	Brian J. Poleson, Sheardaal, Huxter, Symbister, Whalsay.	Average weight of fish caught: 12oz. Fly fishing only. 1 boat available.
Ibister Loch	Isle of Whalsay	Brown Trout	15 Mar. to 6 Oct.	Brian J. Poleson, Sheardaal, Huxter, Symbister, Whalsay.	Average weight of fish caught: 10 to 12oz. Fly fishing only. 1 boat available.

NORTHERN ISLES

Orkney

The waters around Orkney attract many sea anglers each year as big skate, halibut and ling are there for the taking. Ling of 36 lbs. skate of 214 lbs. taken by Jan Olsson of Sweden and the former British record halibut (161½ lbs.) taken by ex-Provost Knight of Stromness provide the bait which attracts anglers to these waters. The Old Man of Hoy, Scapa Flow and Marwick Head are well-known names to sea anglers. The Brough of Birsay, Costa Head and the Eday and Stronsay Firths are equally well known as marks for big halibut and skate. Fishing from Kirkwall or Stromness, there is easy access to Scapa Flow where wrecks of the German Fleet of the First World War provide homes for large ling and conger. In the fish rich sea surrounding Orkney the angler will find some excellent shore fishing, nearly all of which remains to be discovered. Furthermore, skate of over 100 lbs. are still common while specimens of over 100 lbs. have been recorded. More halibut have been caught in the waters to the south separating Orkney from the mainland than elsewhere in the U.K. Shark have also been sighted and hooked but none so far have been landed. Around the islands, in bays and firths, there is excellent sport for the specimen fish hunter and the Orcadians are eager to help sea anglers share the sport they enjoy. There is a regular car ferry service from Scrabster (Thurso) to Orkney and daily air services from Edinburgh, Glasgow and other points of the U.K.

Types of fish: Sea trout, plaice, pollack and coalfish, mackerel, wrasse from the shore. Skate, halibut, ling, cod, pollack, haddock, coalfish, plaice and dogfish from the boats.

Tackle: available from Stromness and Kirkwall.

Bait: Available from most beaches and piers.

Season for fishing: June- October.

Shetland

Shetland offers the best skate fishing to be had in Europe; during the years 1970-74 more than 250 skate over 100 lbs. were caught. These included a European record of 226½ lbs., and 12 other skate over 190 lbs. During the same period, Shetland held nine British records, ten Scottish records and six European records, giving some indication that the general fishing is of no mean standard. Halibut and porbeagle of over 300 lbs. have been taken commercially in the Sumburgh area with porbeagle shark now being landed by anglers from this area. The Scottish record porbeagle shark of 450 lbs. has been landed here and bigger fish have been taken by commercial boat. Shore- fishing remains for the most part to be discovered.

Types of fish: Shore – coalfish, pollack, dogfish, mackerel, dabs, conger and cod. Boat – skate, halibut, ling, cod, tusk, haddock, whiting, coalfish, pollack, dogfish, porbeagle shark, Norway haddock, gurnard, mackerel, cuckoo and ballan wrasse.

Boats: Many boats available for hire throughout the islands. Boats can also be arranged through the Shetland Islands Tourism, Market Cross, Lerwick, Shetland.

Tackle: Available from J.A. Manson, 88 Commercial Street, Lerwick and Cee & Jays, 5 Commercial Road, Lerwick.

Bait: Fresh, frozen or salted fish bait available from fishmongers. Worm bait, crabs, etc. from beaches.

Season for fishing: Limited to May to October by weather conditions.

Haddock

MAPS

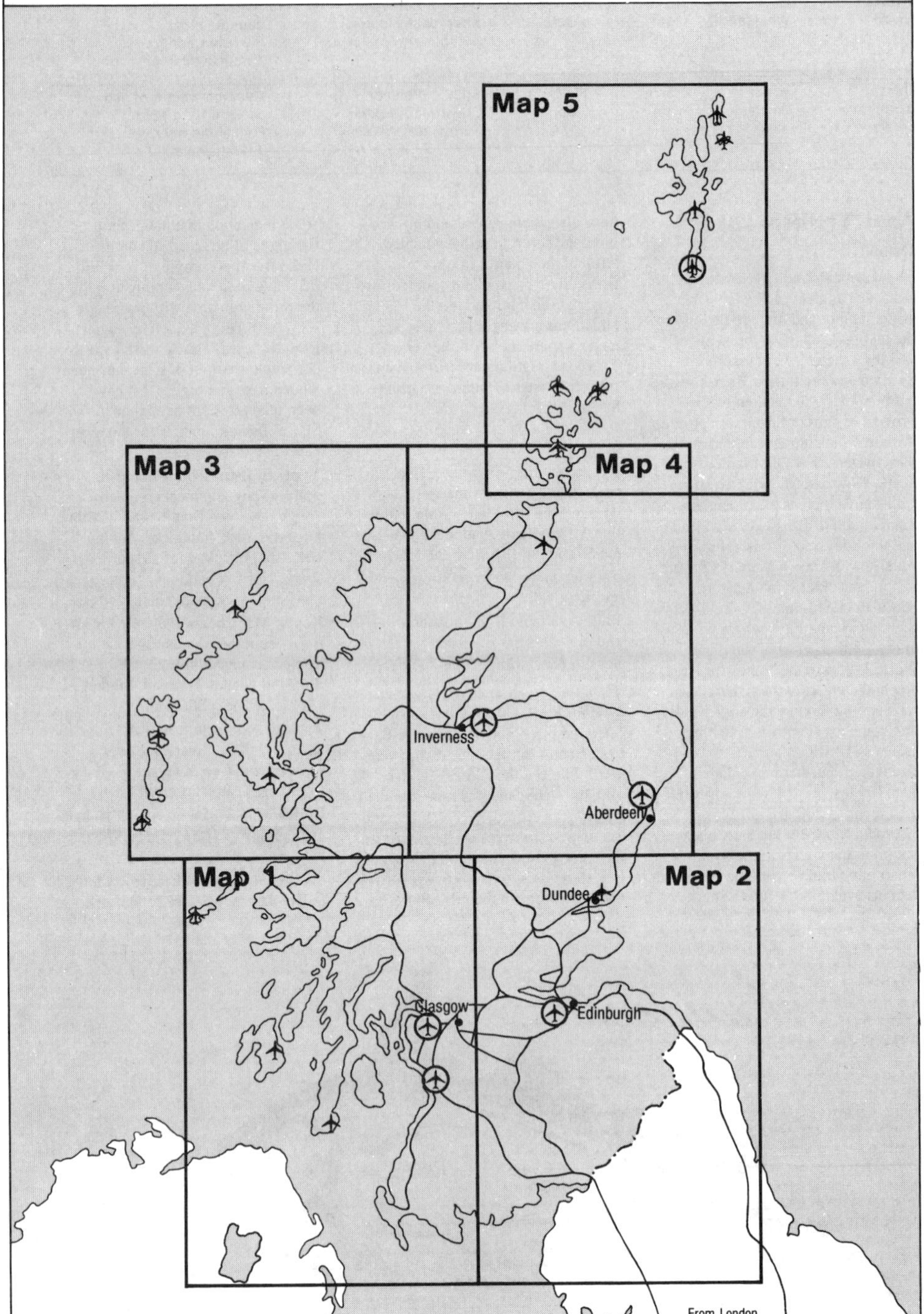

Map 5

Map 3

Map 4

Inverness

Aberdeen

Map 1

Dundee

Glasgow

Edinburgh

Map 2

From London

⊕ MAJOR AIRPORTS —— RAILWAY ROUTES © Baynefield Carto-Graphics Ltd 1991

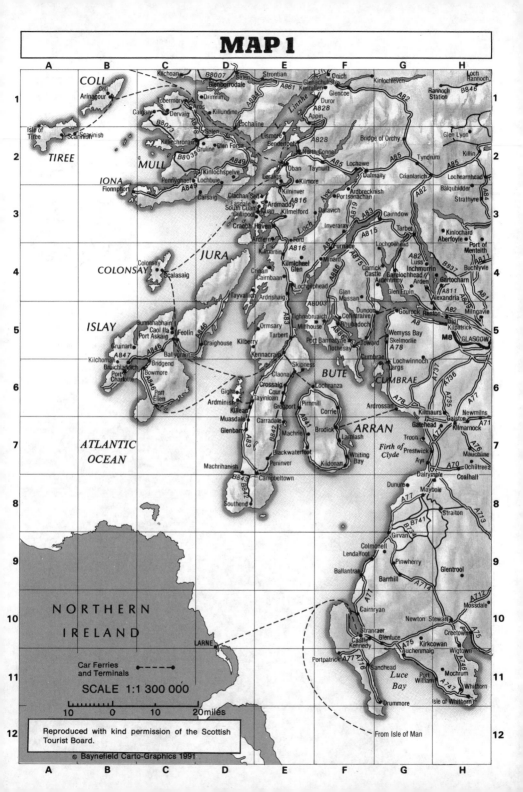

MAP 2

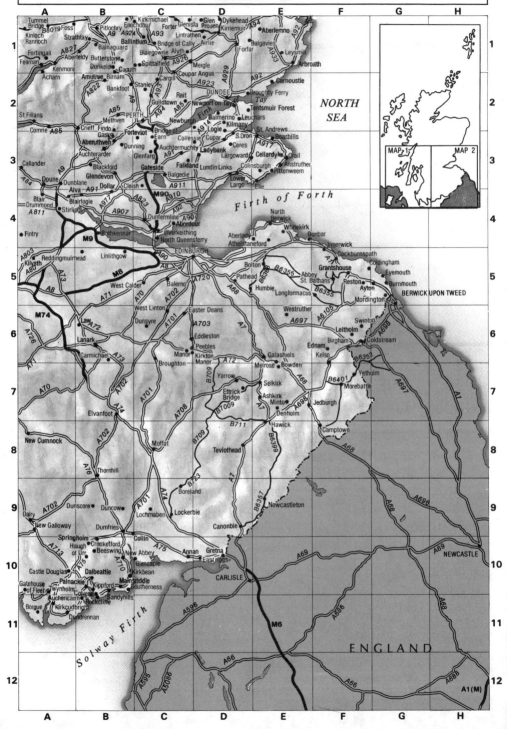

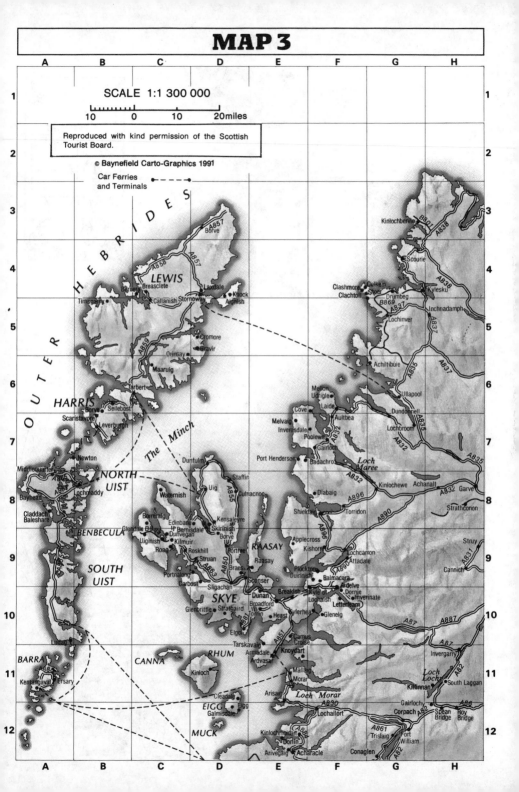

MAP 4

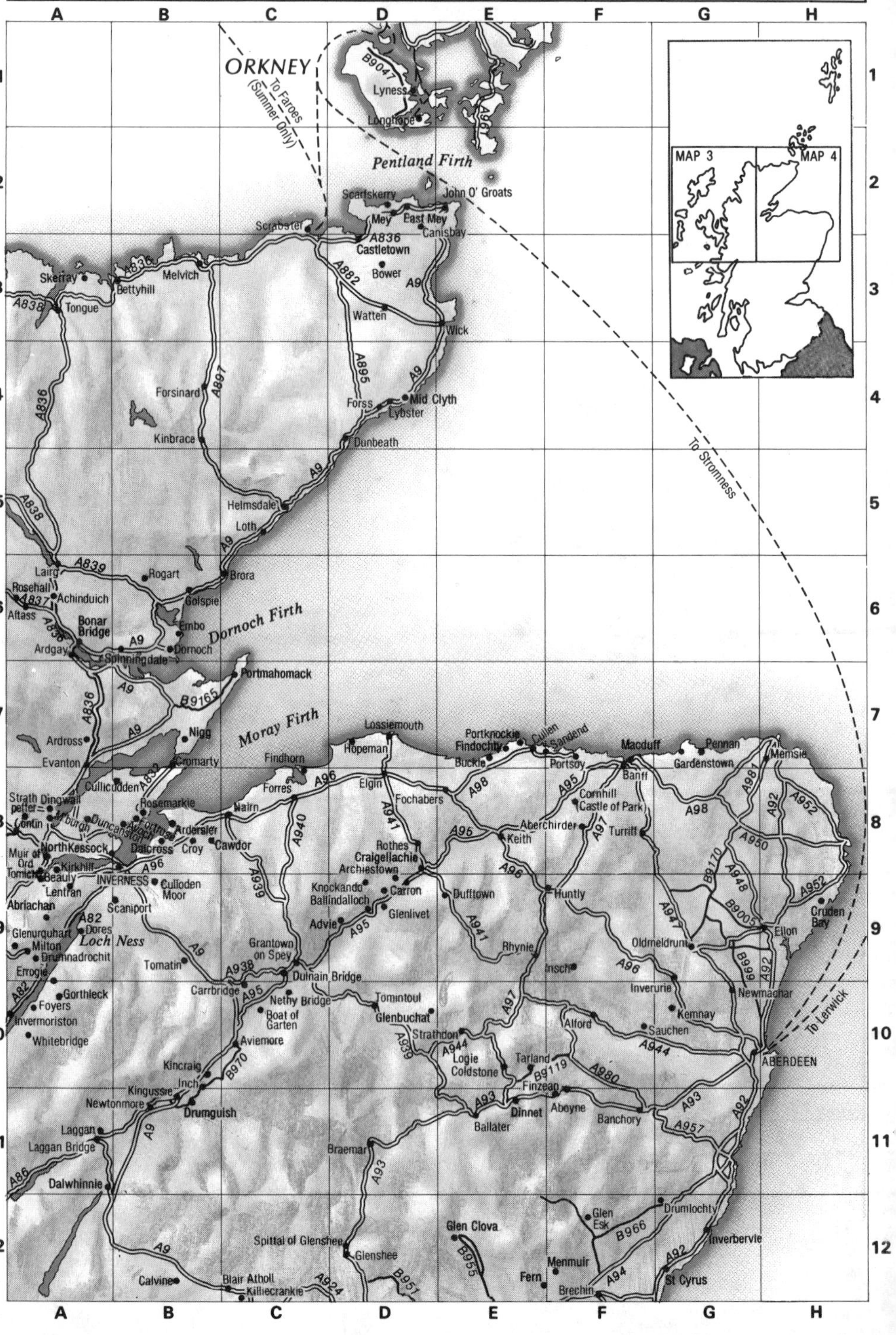

A map of northeastern Scotland including the Orkney area, with grid coordinates A–H horizontally and 1–12 vertically.

Labels (selected):

ORKNEY
To Faroes (Summer Only)
B9047
Lyness
Longhope
Pentland Firth
Scatskerry
John O' Groats
Scrabster
Mey
East Mey
Canisbay
A836
Castletown
Bower
A9
Watten
Wick
A882
Melvich
Bettyhill
Skerray
Tongue
A838
A836
Forsinard
A897
Forss
Mid Clyth
Lybster
Kinbrace
Dunbeath
A895
Helmsdale
Loth
A9
A836
Lairg
A839
Rogart
Brora
Rosehall
A837
Achinduich
Golspie
Altass
Bonar Bridge
Embo
Dornoch
Dornoch Firth
Ardgay
A9
Spinningdale
A836
B9165
Portmahomack
Ardross
Nigg
Moray Firth
Lossiemouth
Portknockie
Cullen
Sandend
Macduff
Pennan
Memsie
Evanton
Cromarty
Findhorn
Hopeman
Findochty
Portsoy
Gardenstown
Banff
Strath Dingwall
peffer
Forres
A96
Elgin
Fochabers
A98
Cornhill
Castle of Park
Contin
Rosemarkie
Nairn
A939
Fort
Aberchirder
Turriff
A97
A98
A92
A952
Muir of Ord
Beauly
Ardersier
Croy
Cawdor
A940
Rothes
Keith
A950
Kirkhill
North Kessock
Dalcross
A941
Craigellachie
Archiestown
B9170
A948
Tomich
Duncanston
INVERNESS
A96
Culloden Moor
Knockando
Ballindalloch
Carron
Dufftown
Huntly
A941
A96
Oldmeldrum
Ellon
Cruden Bay
Abriachan
A82
Dores
Scaniport
A9
Advie
A95
Glenlivet
Rhynie
B9999
Glenurquhart
Loch Ness
Grantown on Spey
Insch
Newmachar
Milton
Drumnadrochit
A938
Dulnain Bridge
Inverurie
Kemnay
Errogie
Carrbridge
A95
Nethy Bridge
Tomintoul
A97
Alford
Sauchen
A944
Gorthleck
Boat of Garten
Glenbuchat
A944
Foyers
Tomatin
Aviemore
Strathdon
A939
Invermoriston
Kincraig
A944
Logie Coldstone
Tarland
B9119
ABERDEEN
Whitebridge
Inch
B970
Finzean
A980
Kingussie
A93
Dinnet
Abeyne
Banchory
A957
Newtonmore
Drumguish
Ballater
Laggan
A9
Laggan Bridge
Braemar
A86
A93
Dalwhinnie
To Lerwick
Glen Clova
Glen Esk
Drumlochy
Inverbervie
A9
Spittal of Glenshee
Glenshee
B9955
Menmuir
A92
St Cyrus
Calvine
Blair Atholl
Killiecrankie
A924
B951
Fern
Brechin
A94
To Stromness
MAP 3
MAP 4

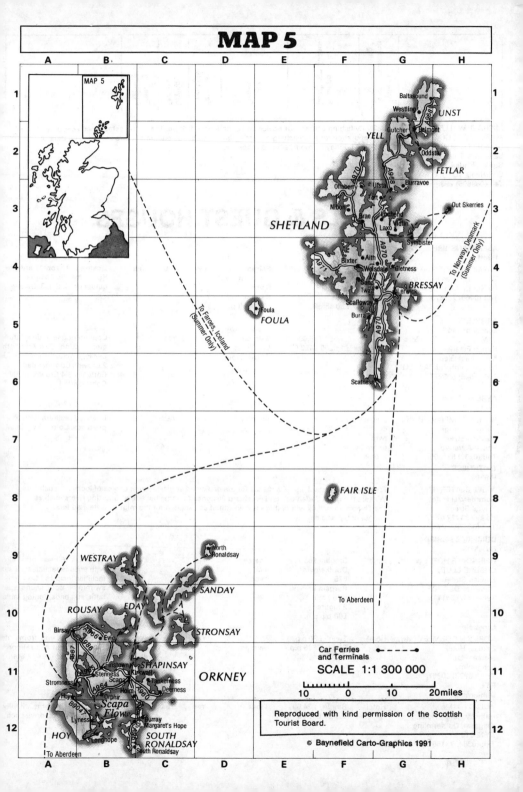

	Type of Accommodation + No. Sleeping	Price per unit. Low/High Season	Type of Fishing	Permits Available	Drying Facilities	Freezing Facilities	Special Feature
MICHAEL WALLER & MARGARET COCKBURN, School of Casting, Salmon & Trout Fishing, Station House, Clovenfords, Galashiels TD1 3LU. Tel: (089695) 293.	Weekly fly fishing courses for novice and experienced fishers. The oldest established school with a fine reputation for the teaching of casting and fishing. Full equipment hire including waders. A wonderful holiday by mountain and moorland						

HOTELS & GUEST HOUSES

ABERDEENSHIRE
Huntly

	Type of Accommodation + No. Sleeping	Price per unit. Low/High Season	Type of Fishing	Permits Available	Drying Facilities	Freezing Facilities	Special Feature
PATRICK CARTER (Mr.), The Old Manse of Marnoch, By Huntly AB54 5RS. Tel: (0466) 780873.	Country House Hotel	From £30 sharing double/ twin. £50 single.	Salmon and sea trout on River Deveron, sea fishing.	Yes	Yes	Yes	Licensed. All rooms ensuite. Recommended by major guidebooks. S.T.B. Deluxe.

ARGYLL
Lochgilphead

D.W. BRACEY (Mr. & Mrs.), Kirnan Estate, Kilmichael Glen, by Lochgilphead PA31 8QL. Tel: (0546) 605217.	House S/C Cotts	£13.50-£15.00 £140.00-£450.00	Salmon Sea Trout Brown Trout	Yes	Yes	Yes	Country house in delightful glen. Fishing River Add both banks, 4 miles. House - S.T.B 2 Crowns Commended. Cottages 3-4 Crowns Highly Commended.

AYRSHIRE
Patna

SHEILA CAMPBELL (Mrs.), Parson's Lodge, 15 Main Street, Patna, Ayrshire. Tel: (0292) 531306.	Single, double, twin or family rooms	£12.50 - min. £15.00 - max.	Salmon & trout	Yes	Yes	Yes	Licensed restaurant on premises. Colour TV's in all rooms.

CAITHNESS
Halkirk

NIGEL SLATER (Mr.), Commercial Hotel, Bridge Street, Halkirk KW12 6XY. Tel: (084783) 223.	Fresh and sea water fishing, a mecca for the dedicated angler. A huge choice of lochs i.e. Loch Watten, the great Badanloch and Forsinard Fisheries to name but a few! Sporting rivers such as the Thurso, to Halkirk where there is a wealth of sea angling for the mighty skate, haddock, conger eel, plaice etc.						

DUMFRIESS-SHIRE
Dumfries

CAIRNDALE HOTEL & LEISURE CLUB, English Street, Dumfries DG1 2DF. Tel: (0387) 54111.	Hotel	Single - £65 Double/twin - £75 Bargain breaks rate - min. 2 nights £60 p.p.p.n.	Coarse loch rivers	Yes	Yes	Yes	Hotel has 76 bedrooms, all with ensuite facilities. Leisure facilities include 14m swimming pool, sauna, spa bath, sun beds, toning table

Langholm

NORMAN GORMLEY (Mr), Eskdale Hotel, Market Place, Langholm. Tel: (03873) 80357.	Hotel	Twin - £20 p.p. Single - £25 p.p.	Trout Salmon	Yes	Yes	Yes	River Esk 100 yds. from hotel Excellent trout and salmon fishing. Hotel - A.A. 2 Star.

FIFE
Dunfermline

W. LLOYD (Mr.), Halfway House Hotel, Kingseat, Dunfermline KY12 0TJ. Tel: (0383) 731661.	Hotel	Single - £24.00 Twin - £37.50	Trout	Yes	Yes	Some	Hotel has 12 rooms, all fully ensuite. 2 mins. drive Loch Fitty.

	Type of Accommodation + No. Sleeping	Price per unit. Low/High Season	Type of Fishing	Permits Available	Drying Facilities	Freezing Facilities	Special Feature
Freuchie							
EVAN BEUSEKOM (Mr.), Lomond Hills Hotel, Freuchie. Tel: (0337) 57329/57498.	Hotel	10% on regular prices for 2 days or more. £41.50 - single, £58.00 - double.	Fly Rainbow Trout Brown Trout Salmon	Yes	Yes	Yes	Free use of leisure facilities including indoor pool.
INVERNESS-SHIRE **Beauly**							
F.J. MacARTHUR (Miss), The Arkton Guest House, Westend, Beauly. Tel: (0463) 782388.	Guest House	£15.00-£17.00	(Salmon only) Fly. Spinning on lower reaches. Trout fishing available.	Yes	Yes	Yes	The Guest House is licensed and 2 Crowns Approved. River Beauly, Loch Tarvie (other lochs available) permits available next door to hotel.
Inverness							
J.N. MANSON (Mr.), Glen Mhor Hotel & Restaurant, 9-12 Ness Bank, Inverness IV2 4SG. Tel: (0463) 234308.	Twin bedroom	£25.00-£35.00	Salmon or Brown Trout	Yes	Yes	Yes	Possibility of fishing several rivers and lochs. Activities for non-fishers.
ALASTAIR MacKAY (Mr.), Inchmore Hotel, Kirkhill, Inverness. Tel: (0463) 83296.	Hotel	Single: Low - £25.00 High - £30.00 Twin/double Low - £20.00 High - £22.50	Trout Salmon River Sea & loch	–	Yes	Yes	Very friendly and comfortable with excellent food and all amenities. S.T.B. 4 Crown Commended, A.A. 2 Star.
Kincraig							
RAINBOW (Mrs.), Ossian Hotel, Kincraig PH21 1NA. Tel: (05404) 651242.	Licensed Hotel	Feb/Mar/Nov: £14.00 High Season: £28.00	Trout & Salmon on Loch Insh and River Spey	Bank & Boat permits daily or weekly.	Yes + laundry	Yes	Family-run hotel, good food and wines, ensuite bedrooms.
Onich							
RONALD YOUNG (Mr.), Camus House Lochside Lodge, Onich PH33 6RY. Tel: (08553) 200.	Guest House	£18.50-£26.00	Trout Salmon Sea	Yes	Yes	Yes	–
Whitebridge							
IAN MILWARD (Mr.), Knockie Lodge, Whitebridge IV1 2UP. Tel: (045 63) 276.	Hotel	D. B. & B. from £60.	Brown Trout (Fly only)	N/A	Yes	Yes	Family-run hotel in magnificent setting on hills above Loch Ness.
PEEBLESHIRE **Peebles**							
NORMAN KERR (Dr.), Kingsmuir Hotel, Springhill Road, Peebles EH45 9EP. Tel: (0721) 20151.	Hotel	Single: £31.00-£37.00. Twin: £27.00-£31.00.	Trout (Spring) Salmon (Autumn)	Ask	Yes	Yes	Family run hotel, all rooms ensuite. Traditional Scottish cooking using fresh local produce. Personal attention by owners.
JIM DOONAN (Mr.), The Glentress Hotel, Kirnlaw, Peebles EH45 7NB. Tel: (0721) 20100.	Hotel	B. & B. per person: £19.50-£25.00	River/ Loch	Yes	No	No	Hotel with all rooms ensuite, is 5 mins. from River Tweed. All home cooked meals.

Please mention this Pastime Publications guide

	Type of Accommodation + No. Sleeping	Price per unit. Low/High Season	Type of Fishing	Permits Available	Drying Facilities	Freezing Facilities	Special Feature
PERTHSHIRE **Glenfarg**							
B. WHITING (Mrs.), The Glenfarg Hotel, Glenfarg PH2 9NU. Tel: (0577) 830241.	Hotel	£25.50	Salmon/ Trout	Yes	Yes	Yes	Hotel: AA (2 Star), S.T.B. 3 Crowns. Loch Leven, River Tay and offshore fishing all arranged for you.
Pitlochry							
J.C. WILSON (Mrs.), Craigower Hotel, 134 Atholl Road, Pitlochry. Tel: (0796) 472590.	Hotel	£20-£25 per person	Salmon Sea Trout Perch	Yes	Yes	Yes	Ghillie/boatman available. Boat hire. Bait purchased locally. Shooting. All bedrooms are ensuite.
DAVID PENKER (Mr.), Scotland's Hotel, 32-46 Bonnethill Road, Pitlochry PH16 5BT. Tel: (0796) 2292/472292.	Hotel	£36.00-£60.00	Salmon/ Trout	Yes	Yes	Yes	Secure car park. Indoor swimming pool and leisure club.
ROSS-SHIRE **Cromarty**							
STEWART & YVONNE MORRISON Royal Hotel, Cromarty IV11 8YN. Tel: (03817) 217.	Hotel	Low-Oct-May: £25.00. High-June-Sept: £28.50.	Sea	Free	Free	Free	Hotel has double/twin room with private facilities. Excellent fishing and the be of Highland hospitality. A wonderful combination.
Poolewe							
HARRISON (Mr.), Pool House Hotel, Poolewe IV22. Tel: (0445) 86272.	Hotel	B. & B. per person: £31.90-£37.40. B.B.E.M. £48.40-£52.80.	Trout	Yes	Yes	Yes	Family run, walking distance to Inverewe Gardens. Supe view over Loch Ewe and beyond. Personal attention by owners.
SUTHERLAND **Brora**							
MARY COOPER (Mrs.), Lynwood, Golf Road, Brora KW9 6QS. Tel: (0408) 621226.	House	£14-£19	Loch River Sea	Local fishing tackle shop	Yes	Yes	Ideally placed for fishing, golf. Overlooking Brora Harbour. House has 3 bedrooms. Home cooking.
Lairg							
D.A. WALKER, Sutherland Arms Hotel, Lairg. Tel: (0549) 2291.	Hotel	D. B. & B. Low: £45.00-£49.00 High: £47.00-£55.00	River-salmon Hill lochs-wild brown trout	Salmon-Yes weekly Brown Trout- daily lets.	Yes		Hotel - 3 Stars, 3 Crown S.T.B. Fully inclusive fly fishing holidays available. Pleased to supply details a brochures on request.
WIGTOWNSHIRE **Isle of Whithorn**							
JOHN RICHARD SCOLLAR (Mr.), Steam Packet Hotel, Harbour Row, Isle of Whithorn. Tel: (098 85) 334.	Hotel	£22.50	River Sea	No	Yes	Yes	Local sea angling centre wi good boat and shore fishin

SELF CATERING

	Type of Accommodation + No. Sleeping	Price per unit. Low/High Season	Type of Fishing	Permits Available	Drying Facilities	Freezing Facilities	Special Feature
Write to: PAM COPELAND (Mrs.), Bailey Mill, Bailey, Newcastleton Roxburghshire TD9 0TR. Tel: (06978) 617.	Houses Flats	£78-£398	Esk & Liddle waters. Salmon & trout fishing Lake fishing.	Yes	Laundry room	Yes	House and flats on farm complex, sleep from 2-10 x in Longtown, Cumbria. On site sauna, solarium, multi-gym, games room, Jacuzzi, horse riding. Bar.

	Type of Accommodation + No. Sleeping	Price per unit. Low/High Season	Type of Fishing	Permits Available	Drying Facilities	Freezing Facilities	Special Feature
BERDEENSHIRE **onymusk**							
M. UREN (Mr.), 'rite to: 'iory Farm, ppledore Road, enterden, Kent N30 7DD. el: (0322) 38 4646/ 5806) 4161.	Fishing Lodge	Accom- £188.00 p.w. Fishing- £188.00 p.w. Total = £376 p.w.	Salmon Sea trout Brown trout	2 miles single bank River Don £188 per week.	Yes	Yes	10 named pools on 2 miles River Don near Monymusk.
RGYLL **och Aweside**							
ONATHAN C. SOAR (Mr.), onachan House, ortsonachan, y Dalmally PA33 1BN. el: (08663) 240.	6 lux. flats (upto 8) 1 house (upto 7) 3 chalets (upto 6) 4 lochside c'vans (upto 6)	£150.00-£395.00 £185.00-£440.00 £155.00-£385.00 £115.00-£245.00	Brown Trout Rainbow Trout Pike, sea trout Perch, salmon Char	Yes	Yes	Yes	Lochside mansion house. Free shore fishing ⅓ mile. Boat hire. Permits.
alavich							
A. WATTS (Mrs.), Vrite to: he Old Rectory, lphamstone, Bures, uffolk CO8 5HH. el: (0787) 269340.	2 Houses	£95.00-£280.00 inc. Elec.	Fly - salmon, trout. Coarse - pike etc.	Yes	Yes	Ask	Houses sleep 6. Boat hire both Lochs. Avich (fly only), Awe (all kinds).
INVERNESS-SHIRE **viemore**							
MACKENZIE (Mrs.), alavoulin Executive ungalows, rampian Road, viemore PH22 1RL. el: (0479) 810672.	Luxury Bungalows	Low - £50 p.n. (s/c 4 persons). High - £60 p.n. (s/c 4 persons). B. & B. £4 extra p.p., if required.	–	–	Yes	Yes	Private sauna and gas barbecue. Central to all amenities of Aviemore. Superior standard brochure available. Also hotel accommodation available.
A. BUSWELL (Mrs.), '2/3 Nursery Cottages, vergarry PH35 4HL. el: (08093) 297.	Chalet	£85.00-£240.00	Salmon Trout	Loch Garry Loch Lundy River Garry	Yes	Yes	Chalet sleeps 4 in 2 bedrooms. S.T.B. Commended 2 crowns. Mini-bus available for transport.
OTHIAN **unbar**							
. MARRIAN (Mrs.), owerhouse, Dunbar -142 1RF. el: (0368) 62293.	Cottages sleep 4/8	£90.00-£280.00	Sea & Loch	Ask	Yes	Yes	New fishing loch with bar/restaurant. Sea fishing in Firth. Fully equipped accommodation.
OSS-SHIRE **orridon**							
WILSON (Mr. & Mrs.), nnat Lodge, Annat, orridon IV22 2EU. el: (0445) 791200.	4 Cotts 4 Res. C'vans	£125.00-£250.00 £ 90.00-£130.00	Salmon Sea trout Brown trout Sea Angling	2 rods and boat Loch Damph.	Yes	Yes	Converted Blackhouse. Both overlooking Loch Torridon. Hotel ¼ mile.

Please mention this Pastime Publications guide

NOTES

SCOTLAND FOR FISHING
A Pastime Publication

I/We have seen your advertisement and wish to know if you have the
following vacancy:

Name ....

Address ....

....

Dates from pm ....

Please give date and day of week in each case....................................

To am ....

Number in Party ....

Details of Children ....

(Please remember to include a stamped addressed envelope with your enquiry.)

SCOTLAND FOR FISHING
A Pastime Publication

I/We have seen your advertisement and wish to know if you have the
following vacancy:

Name ....

Address ....

....

Dates from pm ....

Please give date and day of week in each case ....

To am ....

Number in Party ....

Details of Children ....

(Please remember to include a stamped addressed envelope with your enquiry.)